UVELLE FRANCE, LE MEXIQUE ou NOUVELLE ESPAGNE, LE NOUVEAU MEXIQUE, LES ISLES DE TERRE NEUVE, DE CALIFORNIE,
BOIS, DANOIS, et PAR LES ESTATS GENERAUX DES PROVINCES VNIES ou HOLLANDOIS. Tiré des Relations de toutes ces Nations . Par le S.Sanson Geographe ordinaire du Roy. 167

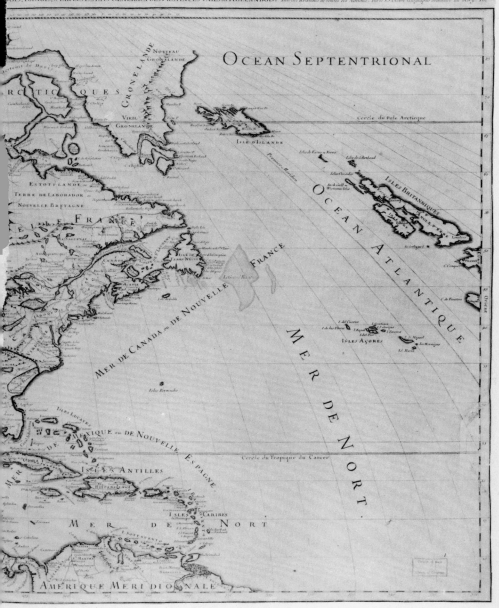

ERNA FERGUSSON

" One of that small and honorable group of travel writers who combine appreciative observation, human interest and study with a sensitive and active literary conscience, and thus produce work of genuine value." — *New York Times Book Review.*

has also written

DANCING GODS

" Tells you precisely what you would see if you lived among the Indians of the Southwest." — *New York Herald Tribune.*

FIESTA IN MEXICO

" Here is a delightful book. Do not miss it." — DOROTHY CANFIELD.

GUATEMALA

" A careful and convincing study of a country and its people. It is well observed, well thought out, well written." — *New York Times Book Review.*

VENEZUELA

" A fascinating mélange of travel, history, quick-flash interviews, and contrasting biographies of Bolívar the Liberator and Gómez the Tyrant."
—JOHN CHAMBERLAIN, *Harper's.*

THESE ARE BORZOI BOOKS, PUBLISHED BY ALFRED · A · KNOPF

OUR

SOUTHWEST

I was born in Old Albuquerque, New Mexico, of pioneer people. My German grandfather, Franz Huning, came across the plains, afoot with a wagon train, in 1848. He lived in Santa Fe until about 1851, when he decided that Albuquerque was going to be a bigger town, and moved there.

I grew up with Albuquerque. Then came private school, public schools, and the University of New Mexico. I took a master's degree at Columbia University and taught for a couple of years. As a representative of the Red Cross during the World War, I went into every county and almost every town of my state, and I discovered that I liked it. With a partner I established the Koshare Tours and was known as the first woman dude wrangler. Later that business was absorbed by the Harvey Company.

In 1930 I began to work on DANCING GODS,[1] into which I put what I had learned of Indians and their ceremonies in New Mexico and Arizona. After that I had an opportunity to go to Mexico, and that led to FIESTA IN MEXICO.[2] In 1936 I was invited by the Committee on Cultural Relations with Latin America to be a member of the faculty for their first seminar in Guatemala, which resulted in my writing GUATEMALA.[3] Subsequently my interest turned to Venezuela, and I completed a book on that country in 1939.[4] In OUR SOUTHWEST I have returned once again to the region in which I was born and grew up, that fabulous land in which modern American culture is superimposed on an earlier Spanish civilization, and both of them on a prehistoric Indian mode of life that still survives.

DESERT CACTUS

[*photo, Ruth Frank*]

OUR SOUTHWEST

BY

ERNA FERGUSSON

PHOTOGRAPHS BY RUTH FRANK AND OTHERS

ALFRED · A · KNOPF

New York & London

1940

Copyright 1940 by Alfred A. Knopf, Inc.

FIRST EDITION

Published simultaneously in Canada by The Ryerson Press

for

CLARA HUNING FERGUSSON

DAUGHTER OF PIONEERS

and a

REAL SOUTHWESTERNER

ACKNOWLEDGMENTS

I T IS IMPOSSIBLE to thank by name all the people who have helped me to write this book, because there are so many and because I have learned from them all my life in private talk and by watching them live.

It is impractical to name the specialists in many lines who have given me valuable assistance by lending me reports and manuscripts, by discussing them with me, and by reading and criticizing certain of my chapters. They have put me right on facts; my conclusions are my own. And as it frequently happens that my consultants in official or academic positions do not agree with me, or with each other, I should do them no service by naming them. So I limit myself to thanking them thus in anonymity.

I may and do with real gratitude mention Miss Wilma Shelton, Librarian of the University of New Mexico, and her assistants, who have been most patient and painstaking in meeting my trying requirements.

I also am deeply indebted to Dr. Dorothy Woodward, Assistant Professor of History at the University of New Mexico, who has generously given much time to reading my manuscript and checking it for historical errors.

CONTENTS

I: WHAT IS THE SOUTHWEST?   3

II: FORT WORTH IS WHERE CATTLE BEGIN   21

III: SAN ANTONIO IS SPAIN IN TEXAS   40

IV: THE BORDER AND BORDER PEOPLE   56

V: EL PASO, CROSSROADS OF THE SOUTHWEST   75

VI: TUCSON: DESERTS AND DUDES   94

VII: BROKEN POTS AND PREHISTORIC PEOPLE   113

VIII: UNCLE SAM'S SOUTHWEST   133

IX: PHOENIX AND THE DESERT RECLAIMED   154

X: PRESCOTT AND TWO WOMEN   172

XI: FRED HARVEY, CIVILIZER   190

XII: GALLUP AND THE NAVAJOS   208

XIII: ALBUQUERQUE, "HEART OF THE WELL COUNTRY"   227

CONTENTS

XIV: VILLAGES OF THE SAINTS   246

XV: SANTA FE IS ALWAYS SANTA FE   265

XVI: THE PEOPLE OF THE PUEBLOS   284

XVII: TAOS AND THE ARTISTS   303

XVIII: THE HIGH PLAINS ARE THE FORTY-NINTH
        STATE   321

XIX: DANCES, FIESTAS, FAIRS, AND RODEOS   340

XX: THE INTERPRETERS   357

INDEX   *follows page* 376

ILLUSTRATIONS

Desert Cactus   FRONTISPIECE

Cowboy with a herd of yearlings   26

Modern cattle are sleek and curly   26

The Mission of La Concepción at San Antonio   50

The San Antonio River meanders through the city   50

Santa Helena Canyon on the Big Bend of the Rio Grande   66

The Joshua Tree. Desert growth makes beauty out of its
struggle for water   98

Irrigation ditches can turn deserts into fertile fields   98

Montezuma's Castle, Arizona. Many prehistoric people
made homes in cliffs   114

The patient plodding burro has hauled water across the
desert   146

Boulder Dam, the most stupendous irrigation project   146

The greatest yellow pine forest in the United States
crosses New Mexico and Arizona   162

Who can describe the Grand Canyon?   194

The young Navajo tries to adapt to a changing world   210

A Navajo Family making camp before a dance   210

Kit Carson defeated the Navajos in Canyon de Chelly, Arizona   230

Santa Fe has developed a new architecture from the old-style adobe house   238

Simple living may be very pleasant in the New Mexico valleys   238

A Quick Storm over a mountain village   274

Stormy days and winter nights old people spin, weave, and tell tales   274

Taos, the northernmost pueblo, was there when the Spaniards came in 1540   290

Young men have short hair, but even a long-haired Indian can use a fountain-pen   354

Indians travel for miles to see the dances   354

The cross the Spaniards brought still dominates   370

MAPS

A CONTEMPORARY MAP OF
NORTH AMERICA IN 1674   *endpapers*

NORTHERN NEW SPAIN ABOUT 1700   *at front of book*

SOUTHWESTERN UNITED STATES
ABOUT 1870   *at front of book*

THE SOUTHWEST—
PAINTED BY MIGUEL COVARRUBIAS   *page 20*

OUR SOUTHWEST TODAY   *after the index*

OUR

SOUTHWEST

I

WHAT IS THE SOUTHWEST?

THE SOUTHWEST IS NOT, LIKE OTHER SECTIONS OF THE United States, exactly bounded. Dixie lies south of Mason and Dixon's line, and its eastern and southern boundaries are indisputably the Atlantic Ocean and the Gulf of Mexico. New England is beyond controversy, largely because New York would not permit of being linked with New England nor New England with New York. But lines west of the first settlements have always been variable. Time was when Ohio was West, Alabama and Tennessee Southwest. Some of us go east to Kansas City, noting on the trains that men have shrunk in height and width of shoulders and of hat. Chicago is altogether East, where travelers run to paunches, stiff manners, even derbies, and are distinctly short of stature.

Geographically Southwest should be where South and West have crossed. Take everything south of Mason and Dixon's line extended to the Pacific and west of the Mississippi, and what do you get? You get the southwestern part of the United States, certainly, but not the Southwest. The Southwest is a

3

crossing of South and West, but in the sense of breeding to produce offspring. It is neither South nor West, but a mestizo partaking of the characteristics of both parents, and like a child, baffling to both.

The region west of the Mississippi and south of the thirty-ninth parallel includes Louisiana and Arkansas, Southern states by every test. Then Kansas, Oklahoma, Colorado, Utah, and Nevada, which, though they are thoroughly Western, lack certain features distinctive of the Southwest. California has shared most of the history of the Southwest but it carries its past along only as tourist attractions in Spanish names and Spanish missions. Its living and its thinking have been modified by Middle Western invasions knowing nothing of pioneering. California has grown up, out, and away. Who would recognize its Gargantuan congeries of Iowa villages as Southwest? What has the movie capital in common with Marfa or Raton, with Flagstaff or Mesilla? Who living under a hedge of mammoth geraniums on a California farm, miscalled a ranch, knows anything of an arid Southwest? San Francisco is California too — zestful, with heady air and youth forever renewed. But San Francisco is of the West and of the Pacific Empire it recognized in its exposition. Most of California is separated from the Southwest by the Sierra Nevada range, which catches the clouds from the Pacific and pitches their spill down the seaward slope. Back of the Sierras lie the arid wastes, wonderland of colored rocks and writhing desert growth; the semi-arid grazing-lands, flecked with sparse green or silvery golden grass; and occasional upland valleys where irrigation will bring forth rippling fields of oats and maize, orchards and gardens. Such land produces people very different from those who find living easy. Only the deserts of California are indisputably Southwest.

A good deal of Texas likewise is not Southwest. A fault runs through Texas, a geographical fault. From the university tower at Austin one sees green lowlands rolling off eastward toward the Gulf of Mexico. All Texas rivers flow that way, carrying rich silt to make black lands worked by black people raising cotton. Live oaks droop with Spanish moss, hibiscus and oleanders grow. Westward one sees the grasslands of the great plains. Olive-green cedars, dusty gray cenizo, light and feathery mesquite, and cactus, gray and thorny. Between these types of country is Balcones Fault, as definite as a garden wall. In San Marcos the old Burleson house sits on a cedar-dotted hillside like many in New Mexico or Arizona. And two miles away eternal springs gush out of the rock and pour clear icy water from the Rockies over the lowlands. The Rio Grande Delta, though it saw the beginnings of the cattle business, is not Southwest either. Irrigated from the great river, its citrus groves are a second California, owned and operated by Middle Westerners who have found their paradise. So, west and east, the Southwest is bounded by the Sierra Nevadas and Balcones Fault.

One, trying to define the Southwest, said: " You know. When you get that first clear breath of high, dry air. That's the Southwest." Along about La Junta on the Santa Fe when the Kansas wheat-fields drop behind and the horizon becomes a blue and jagged glory; that is Colorado. Northern Colorado belongs to the West of Wyoming and Montana, which knows cattle but not the Mexican, which has more cold and less laziness than the Southwest, and was settled by Northerners; but southern Colorado is altogether of the Southwest. The valleys of the upper Rio Grande, the San Luis, and the Animas employ or leave unemployed thousands of sugar-beet pickers, sheep-shearers, and miners who prefer to deal in Spanish. And its Indian ruins in the Mesa Verde belong to the archæological region south of them.

Another said: " You can't leave out Oklahoma. Look at Will Rogers! "

A Texan whose ancestors fought for their lands countered: " Bosh, they think pioneering began in 1889 with free lands."

Still, there is Will Rogers. The most engaging of all Southwesterners, he was born in Oklahoma and lived in California. He said he never met a man he did not like, but he said it with his quizzical smile. He was unimpressed by wealth or position. He took his own importance with utter simplicity. He was honest and direct. He dressed like a cowboy, twirled a rope with the best of them, talked like folks, and chewed gum. He was the bright example of the best Southwesterner. I include Will Rogers.

One who knows the trails in northern Mexico said: " How can you leave out Sonora, Chihuahua, and Coahuila? They're more Southwestern than Oklahoma ever was."

One who visits Utah's parks every year and knows divorce dude ranches near Reno voted for Nevada too.

Clearly, whatever I elect to include in *Our Southwest*, somebody will question the decision, either for taking in too little or for leaving out too much. I had thought that both Texas and California, immensely rich and bursting with pride, would scorn to be included in a region. But I found both Texans and Californians claiming heatedly their right to be part of the Southwest. Perhaps the best way to get at it is from the inside out.

There is no argument about the twin states of New Mexico and Arizona. They are Southwest. For most of their history they were one; Arizona acquired a name and a separate standing in 1863. They entered the Union on the same piece of paper; most people cannot tell them apart yet. " Oh, you're from New Mexico," they say. " I had a cousin who spent the winter in Phoenix."

New Mexico and Arizona are two states lying side by side along a three-hundred-mile state line. They understand each other very well, for their problems are alike and their variations only add distinction and interest to their thousand miles from Texas to California. New Mexico's eastern counties look and act and talk like Texas. Arizona's western border is indistinguishable from desert California and Nevada across the Colorado River. What are the special features of these states that may be used as a guide to the whole Southwest?

They are mountain states with plains dropping off on either side of the sierra. The arid plains are even more significant than the mountains, for what has most marked Southwestern life and thought, philosophy and religion, humor and despair, is aridity. In contrast with the ancestral homes of our race with heavy timber and abundant rainfall, most of this land must struggle along on between ten and twenty inches of annual precipitation. The worst of it, the California and Arizona deserts, can count on much less than that; many weary, burning years that get none at all.

The people who pray best for rain are the Indians who have practiced it for æons. Every state in the Union has Indians, but in these Southwest states more than elsewhere have they made its history, and they still do. Over eighty-two thousand Indians live in New Mexico and Arizona, most of them self-supporting. And while they do not exercise their constitutional privilege of the vote, preferring to live tax-free, their wealth and their woes play a large though indirect part in politics. And how they do add character and attract business in the way of tourists!

The Southwest has also a strong Spanish infusion. Much of our blood base, much of our language, even our English, most of our place names, and three-quarters of our history lead directly back to Spain. Nothing can be understood of these states without understanding Spain in America. There are few Spanish-Americans as the terms German-Americans and Polish-Americans are used. For centuries few people have arrived from Spain to become hyphenated Americans. With us, Spanish-American means people who came up from Mexico, whether with Coronado's conquering army in 1540 or with later explorers or settlers. For many years after they became citizens of the United States people of Spanish descent were called Mexicans, and they still are in Texas, in California, and in Arizona. But within the last twenty-five years Spanish-American has become the correct designation in New Mexico. They number half of New Mexico's four hundred and fifty thousand people, a smaller proportion of Arizona's population, and they all speak Spanish as well as English.

Maury Maverick, in *A Maverick American*, says: " This Texas of mine is historically the beginning of the South-west. . . . Now the Southwest includes — in addition to Texas — Oklahoma, New Mexico, Arizona, and parts of Colo-rado, Utah, and California."

Mr. Maverick, with admirable state pride, overlooks the fact that the Spaniards crossing part of his Southwest in 1540 named it *Nuevo Mexico,* referring to the region from the Mississippi to the Pacific and on north indefinitely. In 1598 they established a capital at the confluence of the Chama and the Rio Grande, and in 1610 at Santa Fe. From then until the

American invasion the region was known not only to the Spanish, but to other European geographers as well, as *Nuevo Mexico*. The name Texas, at that time spelled Tejas, was applied to a tribe of Indians who wandered about half naked in the swamps. Only as part of *Nuevo Mexico* was Texas historically where the Southwest began. But from the point of view of the United States, Mr. Maverick is right. People from the Southern states pushed west into Texas. Slave-owners took up lands along the rivers, built their houses and lived there as they had in the Old South. Their descendants still considered themselves Southern. Later-comers were owners of slaves too, but only a few. Ten or twelve maybe instead of a hundred. They were looking for chances to better themselves and they pushed a little farther west, taking up land along the creeks, still afraid of the great plains. They had a few cattle, farmed, built houses such as they had left back in Tennessee or Kentucky.

This forest-dwelling frontiersman did not develop into the Southwesterner until he had pushed beyond trees, beyond dependable rainfall and streams that ran water all the time; that is, as Walter Webb so convincingly establishes in *The Great Plains*, beyond the ninety-eighth meridian. There he struck conditions such as he and his forebears had not met since they left semi-arid stretches of Asia Minor and migrated into the European forests. He found a country which was, and still is, endlessly perplexing to a simple man. Everything about the Southwest is untrue about some other part or phase of it, except that it is dry. True, one of its greatest hazards is sudden flood; but one must have some certainty in an unstable world. The Southwest is arid, or at least semi-arid.

In altitude, it rises from Death Valley — two hundred and seventy-five feet below sea level — to Pike's Peak, fourteen thousand feet above it. In Texas, dude ranches advertise fresh mountain breezes at two thousand feet altitude, and Santa Fe, the capital of New Mexico, seven thousand feet above the sea and parallel with the Carolinas, is delightful outdoors in midwinter and too cool for comfort on summer evenings.

Between its depth and its peaks the Southwest has every kind of climate and all the flora and fauna from subarctic to subtropical. In Death Valley date palms rear their topknots above deserts where men have died of thirst and the swiftest motor cannot overtake the mirages. In certain untouched pockets along the Mexican border, mountain sheep still defy the hunter from barren crags, and *javelina* (peccary) root for acorns among scrub oak and cactus. And the peaks, San Francisco in Arizona, Wheeler in New Mexico, and Pike's in Colorado, are arctic islands where snowshoe rabbits, marmots, and ptarmigan feed on scanty subarctic growth. The Southwest also runs a long gamut through the ages. The Colorado River in digging the Grand Canyon has uncovered rocks down to the primeval granites of the Archean age, the basal earth stuff of the oldest period geologists know. In its walls all succeeding ages are represented, even to the cement walks on top. In the Carlsbad Caverns stalagmites and stalactites have been building toward each other, drop by drop, for six million years. In both canyon and cavern, color and form and immensity have baffled human descriptive powers as long as man has known them. No words can describe them, for they engage all the senses and something beyond. One does not see the Grand Canyon or the Carlsbad Caverns; they are experienced, and one is never the same again.

Traces of man in the Southwest are very recent compared with its geological exposures. Folsom man, known by arti-

10

facts found in 1925 near Folsom, New Mexico, is our oldest inhabitant, perhaps the oldest American, and he belongs to the glacial era: a mere ten or twelve thousand years ago. At that time he was cutting fine stone-flaked javelin points for hunting the dinosaur and the prehistoric bison, but of his other habits he has left no record. His descendants or later-comers did better for us, and the entire Southwest is dotted with remains of their homes, their implements and utensils, and with legible records of their moves.

This ancient country has been made and is being changed daily by violence. Snowfall on the peaks begins early in September, and in May ten-foot banks of feathery white begin to melt into torrents of muddy water which roar down the mountainsides, loosening boulders, converting dry canyons into foaming rivers. Walls of water eight or ten feet high roll down the arroyos and leave them dry again within a few hours. Motorists are struck by signs beside sandy stretches: " Don't try to cross here when water is running." And many a driver who did not heed has been capsized and drowned in what we call a dry wash in Arizona, an arroyo in New Mexico, and an Act of God in the insurance policies. Native sons and daughters treat their dry creeks with respect. The first car to dare a crossing generally carries a foreign license. Floods have destroyed so many bridges that we often have cement aprons now instead, further confusing the motorist who ar-rives in a wet season and complains because large streams are not bridged. Too many arroyos on the rampage at one time carry away bridges, swamp dams, and pour such tons of wasted water into the Pecos, the Colorado, and the Rio Grande that towns are swept away and international relations strained. For the Rio Grande never has stayed put and probably never will. You may find yourself a resident of Mexico one day and of the United States the next at almost any point along that boundary stream.

For variability, rivers have nothing on climate. From San Antonio to Palm Springs the deserts attract visitors who, along with acres of epidermis, display touching confidence in their own pulchritude and in the final taming of the old-time gunman who shot first and inquired later. In December and in January tourists frivol in the minimum, ride all day in cotton shirts, and broil their steaks and sing their songs on balmy nights perfumed with cactus flowers. But in none of those centers of tourist and dude trade must one mention summer temperatures. Nor spring winds, nor sudden northers.

The Southwest does not get the worst of the terrific storms that scourge the rest of the country. They pass to the north of us. We read of blizzards in Minnesota, then in Chicago, finally in Pittsburgh, and next week we get its tail, but that tail lashes out. A Texas youth, asked if it always blew like that, replied: " Oh, no. Sometimes it takes a notion and blows the other way a spell." And sometimes it takes a notion and blows a norther. The sunniest winter day in the warmest tourist refuge may be cut across by a mean and nasty wind that roils the air with northern fog, heavily laced with sand. Debris whirls through the streets, confusion enters the soul, and whatever you wear — winter coat or summer dress — turns out to be all wrong by noon. And in the Panhandle, where wind never rests, a norther is an icy blast from frozen seas. They say that between the Panhandle and the North Pole " there ain't nothin' but a bobwire fence, and that blew down in the last norther."

West of the Panhandle northers do not blow, but a Southwestern sandstorm anywhere is an experience, and no place is exempt. Electricity fills the air. Walk across a carpet and touch metal with the friendliest intention and it snaps back with fire and pain. For days everybody's nerves tighten with increasing tension. The dry sky clangs back peevishly at the dry earth, and nothing happens. Then trees begin, impersonally, to roar. They bend, saluting the wind which whips every loose thing until it leaps. Corrugated iron rises and flies away. Garbage pails roll clattering down the streets. Brittle old trees snap and fall. Tumbleweeds do witches' dances. And sand, stinging, acrid, golden sand sweeps across counties and states in billows that relent and renew their wailing assault, it seems interminably. For hours it may rage so, even for days. We used to say that the wind went down with the sun, when it didn't blow all night. Trains have been stopped by sand on the tracks. Motorists are halted by impenetrable blankets of sand before the windshield. And then the wind drops, the air is as fresh as though washed by a gentle rain, the pale blue sky looks down with mild reproof on a littered earth, and women again remark on what happens after you clean house.

That is March, or April, or even May. In June, or July, or maybe August, or maybe not at all, comes the rainy season. In May cumulus clouds begin to erect enormous masses in the blue sky. From mid-morning on they stand as stately and immobile as sculptured marble, dead white against the blue until the sunset turns them every tone of red, rose, and rose gold. At night they disappear, to repeat their false promises next day. Occasionally they turn purple at the edges, let down a gauzy curtain of rain, and rattle their thunders far away. June clouds never seem to drop their showers where anybody needs water. Hoses play all day, creeks are emptied of their snow waters, even the Rio Grande shrivels to a wet streak in a dusty bed. Then, perhaps in July, perhaps not until many

13

Indians have danced their prayers, the rains come. Afternoon showers pound up puffs of dust and then pound it down and make mud and running rills, and streams and rivers. Sometimes the clouds burst and rain falls not in drops, but in sluices and sheets which work more havoc than all the drought and all the winds together.

These are, of course, the thorns on the climate, which, like the cactus, offers its glowing loveliness as well. That the sky is bluer, the sun more prevalent, the air fresher, the stars nearer, the moon clearer, and the days lazier, longer, and happier than anywhere else in the world is set forth in every chamber of commerce bulletin. They fail to note the beauty of starkness, of strength, of incalculable and invincible Nature, jealously guarding a beloved land that shall not be tamed into a kitchen garden. This is what the pioneers saw, what their seed still loves, resenting the effort to make it over into the image of an Eastern meadow, ready always to speed the parting guest who longs for gentler, greener pastures.

Such a country, inscrutable, unconquerable, and like nothing his kind had ever seen before, naturally affected the man who dared to face it. It made, in fact, a new type of man who may renew himself in other challenging conditions or who may prove to be only a passing phase due to submerge in the babbittry which has come in with trains. But whatever happens to the true Southwesterner, he has left his trail broad and easy to read in his trenchant sayings and in his efforts to remold the mountains and the deserts into something he could use.

To the firstcomers and even to newcomers today, the Southwest is never what it seems. Water, they say, runs uphill, for so it looks as you approach a mountain. All of us have doubted the trusty car as it labored on an easy stretch until a

14

backward glance proved that it was gallantly pulling in high a grade steep enough for second or even low. Tenderfeet used to set out from Albuquerque for a stroll to the mountains and believe they were ten miles away only when a three hours' walk brought them no nearer. One traveler was so convinced at last that clear air made distance seem shorter that he was caught pulling off his clothes to swim an irrigation ditch.

Even the fauna, as seen by men who were not zoologists, seemed to be what they were not. Buffalo are bison, jack rabbits not rabbits but hares, the prairie chicken is a grouse, and the prairie dog is a marmot whose flesh, under a name unassociated with man's best friend, might have made him a favorite dish with whites as he was with redskins. Our pronghorn antelope is not related to any real antelope, but is a unique species which certainly deserved a name of its own.

The transplanted Easterner got so used to believing impossible things that his imagination awoke and he grew into the tallest taleteller of all time. Exaggeration was his meat, and his method a guileless plausibility growing imperceptibly into such magnificent and large-scale lying that only the wariest were not taken in. And now, altogether too clever, the wary one probably refuses to believe simple truth.

Who, hearing it for the first time, would believe that a bird could frighten a snake, that good firewood is underground, and that one may drink from a cactus? Yet all these statements are simple gospel truth. A chaparral bird can scare a rattler stiff and peck it to death. Mesquite roots make a fine, hot bed of coals, and many a man would have died of thirst if he had not known how to get water from a cactus.

The newcomer, trying to keep his balance among the impossibilities, spoke many pungent phrases which still salt our speech.

" This is the damnedest country you ever saw. You dig for wood, climb for water, spell hickory with a *j*, and call a pretty girl a bone-eater." The Spanish *j* is pronounced *h*, and *bonita* means " pretty " in the feminine sense.

" Out there they've got more creeks and less water, more cows and less milk, you can look farther and see less than anywhere in the world."

" Don't tell me to go to hell. I'm in Texas already, ain't I? "

The Southwesterner's tales are tall, but they describe no paradise. They describe the horrors he faced, and the boasting is implicit. It was a hell of a country, and it took a hell of a fellow to stand it. Place names are indicative. Many a Devil's Gulch, Alkali Flat, Skeleton Crossing, and Dead Man's Peak has been rechristened with a prettier name by a tenderer generation.

The old-timer did not weep nor weaken. He faced it, defied it, and in his irritation secreted a kind of humor which infected the whole nation and made American jokes equally incomprehensible and offensive to our European cousins and our Latin-American neighbors. It began with skepticism, not only of facts but of people. Conditions demanded certain things of a man. If he could handle a horse and a gun, take care of himself, and pull his own weight, it was immaterial how many earls he could count in his pedigree or how many crimes stained his own record. What his name had been back home was of even less moment. Frontier horseplay was designed to strip the tenderfoot of all his extraneous supports and get down to the essential man. If there was an essential man all else was forgiven, like earls, and omitted from the record, like crimes.

Along with humor, the Southwest developed tolerance and

friendliness. Differences not only of religion but of moral standard were accepted without criticism, without even that more insulting effort to convert. The New Englander, coming from a society which denied heaven to the unconventional, and the Southerner, so sure of his lady and his gentleman, merged into people who forgot their sectional differences and lived as helpful neighbors with folk of race and color, religion and moral codes different from their own. Every house was open to every wayfarer and he was welcome to the best there was in the way of food. No man refused to go to the aid of another. Fighting Indians, riding in posses against the occasional intolerable malefactor, and building towns, they learned a very fine sort of co-operation. They had to. On a lonely ranch or in a little community miles from the next one few things mattered, but they mattered very much. You could kill a man without being a murderer, live with a woman without being immoral, brand a calf without stealing. But men had to trust each other, help each other for their common safety, often for their very lives. The democratic friendliness of the Southwest has deep roots in its history.

Besides being sturdy, humorous, friendly, and tolerant, the Southwesterner came to count on the unexpected. Nothing he undertook ever panned out as planned. His failures were colossal, but almost never his fault. His successes were not the result of steady thrift and the homely virtues, but of unpredictable caprices of nature. In the old days he struck gold just in time, or the railroad boomed his town and he made a fortune by cutting the calf pasture up into building lots. Artesian water gushed out to turn a dry valley into a garden spot. Oil spouted black gold over the poorest towns. He either made enormous wealth overnight or went broke working faithfully to raise beans without water. In either case, many people moved away. Like every other part of the country, but in greater degree, the Southwest is a land of moving men. Here as elsewhere the brighter and more aggressive drift to the great cities. New York's literary, theatrical, editorial, and business worlds have their share. Great universities boast of Southwesterners as particular stars of their faculties. A baseball idol, a metropolitan mayor, the best of the G-men are proud of having been born in some dusty Southwestern town. Literally most erstwhile Southwesterners have gone to California, which is one reason California is not of the Southwest. They went in search of dependability. I know more Albuquerque people in California now than in Albuquerque. That town, which is typical, changes almost entirely every twenty years. The people who made it and most of their children have left in disappointment. Los Angeles was the city of their dreams. When they found they could not turn the desert into continuous oases they realistically went where the oases were. They called the Southwest the country God forgot. God's country was California.

The arid Southwest has always been too strong, too indomitable for most people. Those who can stand it have had to learn that man does not modify this country; it transforms him, deeply. Perhaps our generation will come to appreciate it as the country God remembered and saved for man's delight when he could mature enough to understand it. God armored it, as the migrating Easterner learned in his anguish, with thorns on the trees, stings and horns on the bugs and beasts. He fortified it with mountain ranges and trackless deserts. He filled it with such hazards as no legendary hero ever had to surmount. The Southwest can never be remade into a landscape that produces bread and butter. But it is infinitely productive of the imponderables so much needed by a world weary of getting and spending. It is wilderness where a man may get back to the essentials of being a man. It is magnificence forever rewarding to a man courageous enough to seek to renew his soul.

The Southwest

is too big and diverse to be adequately presented in one book, or by one person in any number of books. One can only touch certain spots, high for one reason or another, and from them try to suggest its vast sweep of desert, plain, and mountain, and the equally varied human types who have made its history.

The traveler who would explore our Southwest for the first time must know that it is divided very neatly into winter and summer country. The desert and near-desert country from San Antonio, Texas, to Los Angeles, California, is delightful in winter; much of it is too hot for vacationing in summer. The northern half of New Mexico and Arizona and certain southward-reaching spurs of the Rockies are lofty enough to offer a fine summer climate; much of it is cold in winter. This book follows these lines, going westward along the routes best suited for winter travel and returning by the highways most comfortable in summer. And, this being the erratic and contradictory Southwest, the plan will not be followed with any consistency.

II

FORT WORTH IS WHERE
CATTLE BEGIN

T WAS MY GOOD FORTUNE TO REACH FORT WORTH WHEN the " Southwestern Exposition and Fat Stock Show " was on. I had been in Dallas. Dallas is east of the ninety-eighth meridian and looks north and east rather than toward the Old South, though with a strong clerical tincture reminiscent of the South rather than of the North. The largest bookstore west of Chicago belongs to the Methodist Church and supports many superannuated Methodist preachers and Southern Methodist University, which dominates the city's cultural life. Dallas, made first by the railroads and then by oil, has always been a traders' town and the business center of an extensive territory. It claims the best women's dress shop west of Gotham, and a gathering of rich women could pose for *Vogue* at any moment. Air in Dallas may be fresh; certainly it is washed and conditioned to the perfect temperature, but it breathes as though enclosed in plethoric banks and hotels, proper art galleries and stores as artistically correct, and perfectly appointed homes. Its people seem encased in correct clothes, right ideas, sense of class. Dallas represents something the United States has made with money. But it is not Southwest, nor (with the exception of the editor of the *Southwest Review*) does it wish to be.

Thirty miles west of Dallas is Fort Worth and there, as they advertise, " The West Begins." There you get that first deep breath of clear dry air, largely because so much of the city still reveals the regardless extravagance with which the first cattle barons threw their money around. Their sons, the oil magnates, outbuilt their fathers by tons of stone, miles of wrought iron, acres of conservatories, and indoor swimming-pools. Fort Worth boasts of the biggest high school, the most extensive park, the best race track, the largest and liveliest grain and stock market in the West and the most open-handed and generous citizen in the United States.

Amon Carter, editor of Texas' most flamboyant newspaper, the *Star Telegram*, wears hats of the greatest liquid content, gives away more sombreros, entertains more important people at more lavish parties, and presents more turkeys — smoked or on the hoof — to the White House than anybody. His only ungenerous aspect is his hatred of Dallas. He loathes that town as a rattler loathes a chaparral. When the Texas legislature chose Dallas for its Centennial Exposition in 1936, Mr. Carter instigated and put through Fort Worth's more glittering and girly Fort Worth Frontier Centennial. They say that when he goes to Dallas on business, he takes his lunch, not to spend a cent in the hated rival city.

So into Fort Worth and the stock show, which was rightly entitled " fat." The only old-time Texas longhorns were shown as museum exhibits. The admired stock were fat, curled and curried, slothful Angus Aberdeens, Herefords, and Shorthorns, heavy with beef; and the curious humped and short-haired Brahma cattle which have been introduced because they are less subject to ticks than the hairier breeds. In the ring all the old cowboy stunts were performed by men presented by the announcer as " positively not professionals," though their names much resembled those on every rodeo program from San Antonio to Cheyenne. For nights they had imported Paul Whiteman.

The hotels were filled with women whose loyalty to Amon Carter's town had clearly not deterred them from sneaking off to Nieman Marcus in Dallas for their clothes — and men who still hold out against all that as Will Rogers used to do in the movies. For every sleek and super-finished woman there was a long and loose-jointed man whose clothes looked so comfortable you could forget them as he did. All down the ages no more becoming costume has ever been invented for a man. The *ersatz* cowboy gives himself away at once as his softness bulges over his belt and his pale neck denies the usefulness of his neckerchief. But for a real man inured to the saddle, tight trousers to encase long legs and end in ornate boots, soft shirt to flutter against lean ribs, belt low on hard hips, and broad hat to emphasize his height and the width of his shoulders, make the supreme masculine costume. Women may change all they like; the Western man knows when he looks well and he'll stay like that, " thank you, ma'am." Nor has his speech changed. For every woman speaking in clipped imported accents which could not conceal the flat Southern *a* and the hard Western *r*, there was a chuckling cowman rolling out the lazy Texas drawl, softened with " sho' nuff," and " how come."

I heard one of them, a fairly old man to be sure, say to another: " Sally? She jus' wen' high-tailin' by here. . . .

23

The' she is now." And Sally, who would have died if she'd heard him, turned out to be one of the most elegantly got-up ladies in the lobby. Such ladies, I was told, suffer other harassments than crude-talking menfolks, for where the West begins, the servant problem ends, in that there are no more servants. The ease of East Texas with its subservient Negroes, and South Texas where Mexicans like to serve, ends abruptly at Balcones Fault. West Texas folk don't mind hiring out to help in a crisis, but they never serve.

Fort Worth, first an outpost on the remotest frontier, grew into a settlement when veterans of the Confederate Army came straggling west. It has shared all the latest wealth-making doings of Texas, but it most relishes exploiting its heyday as a cowtown. That was the short period of driving cattle from the brush country in South Texas to the railhead in Kansas. When Forth Worth was only " a whistling-post on the desert " San Antonio was the capital of the cattle business, for there the herds were gathered, men hired, and provisions laid in for the months on the trail. The cattle business, along with the rest of San Antonio's heritage, came from Spain via Mexico.

In 1519 Cortez entered Mexico with sixteen horses, which Bernal Díaz, in his account of the conquest, described more lovingly and individually than he did any of the soldiers. And two years later Gregorio de Villalobos joined him with " a number of calves." When Coronado in 1540 went north in search of the golden cities of Cíbola, he took along five hundred cows, besides sheep, goats, and pigs, to supply his army with food. William MacLeod Raine and Will C. Barnes in their *Cattle* suggest that we owe a good deal to Coronado's poor herding. For, lured along by the golden image of the Gran Quivira, he lost stock as far as the plains of eastern

Kansas, and from his strays sprang the wild horses of the West and the longhorns, which ran free from Sinaloa to the Gulf of Mexico. Lean, quick, and vicious, the longhorn was fleet as a deer and a game animal worthy of anybody's mettle. Many a newcomer got his first taste of Texas hunting cattle along the Brazos and the Nueces.

Under Spain there were great cattle ranches along the Gulf and also along the Pacific from below San Diego to San Francisco. The original barons were *hacendados* (ranchers) whose methods, dress, and vocabulary Texans were to carry wherever cattle went. In California the salubrious climate and the Latin temperament produced a sort of ranching that left no mark on the United States, except in certain California traditions and fiestas. It was the romance of the cattle business and it ended in 1849 when the pushing and aggressive gringos began to acquire the great ranches and cut them up into farms. In Texas a harsher life developed a sturdier man, an epic rather than a romantic hero, who was to become our national ideal.

The frontiersman was above all adaptable — a trait supremely illustrated by his quick adjustment to the life of the range and his development of the cattle industry. Everything about it was new to his experience, beginning with the longhorn. Cattle, as his forebears had known them, were cows driven slowly to market by smocked drovers or gently milked by red-cheeked dairymaids. This sharp-horned, long-legged, short-tempered beast, quick as an antelope and mean as a rattlesnake, demanded a new treatment. No man on foot could manage him, so the cowboy adopted the vaquero's method of herding on horseback, and modified that word into buckaroo. He tamed the *mesteño*, that short, wiry, hard little descendant of the Arab steed, which he called a mustang.

Mounted in the Mexican high-cantled saddle with heavy horn and long stirrups, he swung a wide loop and dropped his lariat as neatly as vaquero ever swung and dropped the original *la reata*. The Indian, who was his constant harrying enemy, had captured wild horses long before and the Texan had to learn many Indian tricks to meet him fairly. He could swing along his horse's flank, shoot under his neck, load as his pony ran, and kick his feet out of the stirrups to fall free if his horse stumbled or was killed. He became a horseman fit to rank with any legendary rider. And when a Connecticut Yankee named Samuel Colt invented a pistol with a revolving chamber, the buckaroo became a dead shot and a single-handed fighter who has never been excelled. The cowboy was ready for his historic role.

During that time he gathered up the wild cattle, branded them, and drove them north to the railroad, fighting off Indians the while. Many made fortunes, but the most important thing the cowboy made was himself. Not since knighthood had the Nordic had such a chance to apotheosize himself. All his virtues rose to heights; his shortcomings did not matter. Self-reliant, brave, and resourceful, he was completely independent and recognized no master. Eugene Manlove Rhodes said: " If Genghis Khan, Alexander, Napoleon, and a cowboy were out together, there would be just four men in camp."

A cowboy had to be young, vigorous, and physically able to work sixteen or eighteen hours a day on short hours of broken sleep, and to thrive on irregular meals and alkali water or water thick with mud. He had to be keen of eyesight and hearing and able to trail an Indian, a rustler, or strayed stock. He needed an unfailing sense of direction, a " feel " for water, and a knowledge of " cow-critters " and their requirements. He must have proved himself trustworthy when un-

COWBOY WITH A HERD OF YEARLINGS

[*photo, Ruth Frank*]

MODERN CATTLE ARE SLEEK AND CURLY

[*photo, Ruth Frank*]

watched for months on the trail and responsible for a fortune on the hoof or for saddlebags heavy with gold. He was always alert, even in his sleep, quick of decision, and dependable in a crisis, even at the risk of his own life. For he was threatened by constant danger of Indian attack, prairie fire, sand- or snow-storm, rivers high with flood or treacherous with quick-sand, cattle-thieves, or the stampede which might be precipitated by any of the others. And for all this he might have been paid as high as thirty dollars a month.

Every trick that today thrills rodeo audiences from here to London was the cowboy's daily task. He had to be able to ride anything with four legs because he had little choice in the way of a mount. To brand he had to be able to rope in heavy brush or in a moving herd, to catch a steer by the tail and throw him or by the horns and force him to his knees. Time was essential to get the job done, and not to win the purse.

All that life has been so widely celebrated that everybody knows its fiction and its fancy. For its facts, nothing is better than Emerson Hough's *The Story of the Cowboy*, which pictures the man at work and shows how all his habits, dress, and gear grew out of his needs. His Stetson (and the cowboy's hat was never as big as the Mexican's sombrero) bent readily to shade his eyes, and not only was rainproof but would hold water to drink. His neckerchief kept sun off the back of his neck, dust out of his mouth and nose, and was useful as towel or napkin. He tucked his trousers into his boots to keep them from tearing on thorns, and his boots' high heels kept his foot in the stirrup. His chaps, *chaparrejos*, were much-needed protection against chaparral or brush.

In *On a Mexican Mustang through Texas* Sweet and Knox describe him: " The cowboy is a man attached to a gigantic pair of spurs. He inhabits the plains of Texas . . . is in season the year round, and is generally found on the back of a small pony. . . . This fact has given rise to a widely diffused belief that the cowboy cannot walk. . . . Some scientists, however, dispute this, as several specimens have been seen — under the influence of excitement and while suffering from intense thirst — to detach themselves from their mustangs and disappear into business houses where their wants were attended to by a man wearing a diamond breastpin and a white apron."

Away from his job, the cowboy's virtues were knightly. Many were church members, for most of their mothers were of the old-fashioned evangelical persuasion, and religion was always respected and preachers deferred to. He was for law if he made it, for order if he enforced it, and he felt no compunction about changing a law which no longer fitted the case. If there is an " American way," is not this it? Everybody believed in fair play and saw that everybody else got it — except perhaps Indians. Texans boasted that they never left an Indian alive, but an imagination wide enough to include an alien and enemy race was not a cowboy virtue. Like the knight of old, the cowboy was polite to the ladies and prompt in their defense. A good woman was treated with reverence; even a prostitute could count on rough protection.

Like knighthood, cowboy life had its music, generally ballads written to old tunes and relating how the cowpuncher left his girl or she left him, or how he chased a wild steer or rode a bucking bronco. N. Howard Thorpe, whom we know better as Jack Thorpe, published the first collection as *Songs of the Cowboys* in 1908. He says these verses are merely samples, for every song had hundreds of stanzas made up around the campfires and such pungency that much of his job was to

make them printable. Most hands, Mr. Thorpe insists, could not sing; " they just whistled or hummed on night herd, and all the fancy didoes, the yodels and yip-yippies are drug-store cowboy stuff."

And like the knight, the cowboy had his coat of arms, though it appeared on the animal instead of on the man's armor. Brands had been used in Mexico since 1545, and the de Baca family of New Mexico still registers the cow's head brand it has used for over two hundred years. It was important to have a mark that could not easily be altered into another; and the burned-in brand on the animal's hip or shoulder was often augmented by a cut on the ear, such as John Chisum's famous " jingle bob." The descriptions run to lazy W's, flying V's, diamonds, crosses, bars, and circles. By the brand an owner's cattle could be identified in the roundup and headed toward the home range. Calves were branded with the mark on the mother, and if a calf had left her, it was a maverick and anyone might brand it. The name came from Samuel Maverick, who a century or so ago took over some cattle on a loan and left them in charge of a Negro family who let the calves run unbranded. So all unbranded calves came to be called mavericks. In the days when " Texas was lousy with cattle," branding mavericks was no crime, and any man with rope and running iron could gather himself a respectable bunch of cattle in no time. W. S. James in his *Cowboy Life in Texas* says flatly that the men who grew rich were best at branding mavericks. But having grown rich, they disapproved the practice, and the many cattle and stockmen's associations fought rustling by all the means at their command, even in time by law.

The vices and villains of the cowboy's world were an evil growth from the same root that produced his virtues. The malefactor, like the hero, was nervy and cool, quick on the draw, hardy, a good horseman, and a good — far too good — judge of cattle. That he was the villain rather than the hero was often due to circumstances. An election might turn a desperado into a sheriff, outlaw a former officer. Only a horse-thief was forever beyond the pale, because to leave a man afoot in such a country was to take an unfair advantage. As long as a man had a fighting chance, anything was considered fair. The cowboy's villain was so like himself in kind and caliber that their clash has given our literature and our screen drama a well-balanced conflict with greater box-office appeal than any other. The issue is clearly drawn, but for us as for his contemporaries it is sometimes difficult to choose between Billy the Kid and Pat Garrett, who shot him in the dark, or between Joaquin Murrieta, who became an outlaw in defense of his sister's honor, and the sheriff who trapped and killed him. They were all young, gallant, and justified in their own eyes.

There was, of course, a villain not so appealing. For many years the Southwest was the dumping-ground for evil-doers from states where law and order had been established. That there was no law west of the Pecos was not quite true. There was no statute law and few citizens missed it. But there was the law that every man packed on his hip and the order that was enforced by men who wanted homes and women, children and schools, towns and churches. The few bad men, " wild and woolly and full of fleas, never been curried above the knees," were so obstreperous that they have cast a lurid light over the whole period; but none of the rip-roaring towns roared for very long. Fort Worth, Dodge City, Wichita, and Newton one by one wearied of promiscuous shooting and relieved all comers of their guns as soon as they hit town. Las

Vegas, New Mexico, when it had suffered enough from the riffraff that followed the railroad, posted this notice where all could see it:

Las Vegas, New Mexico
April 8, 1880

A Timely Warning to

MURDERERS, CONFIDENCE MEN, AND THIEVES

The citizens of Las Vegas have tired of robbery, murder, and other crimes that have made this town a by-word in every civilized community. They have resolved to put a stop to crime, even if in attaining that end they have to forget the law and resort to a speedier justice than it will afford. All such characters are therefore notified that they must either leave this town or conform themselves to the requirements of law or they will be summarily dealt with.

The flow of blood MUST and SHALL be stopped in this community, and the good citizens of both the Old and the New towns have determined to stop it if they have to HANG by the strong arm of FORCE every violator of the law in this country.

THE VIGILANTES

It meant exactly what it said, as its signers proved more than once.

The best sheriffs were cowboys who made their rules as they went and who were held in such esteem as no desperado ever won. The Southwest, once its youthful exuberance had blown off, civilized itself within one generation.

Cowboys were reckless and disorderly as college boys are. Youngsters, generally under twenty years of age, they liked to skylark and show off. But the kid grew up — in time —

31

into the cattleman who was the hero of a later time. As a rule he started as a "hand" and a trail driver. With more than average foresight and business acumen, he bought cattle in South Texas and sold them in Kansas. As conditions changed he changed with them, moving his herds westward and then north until the Long Trail had been pounded into the prairies and the Texas longhorn and the Texas cowboy were common sights as far away as Wyoming and Montana.

Texas cattle began to move north in '68. Herds were thrown together at every hamlet or military post and branded for the trail. A trail boss was appointed; he rode ahead to locate water and bed grounds and to watch for Indian signs. Experienced men rode "at point" to direct the lead steers and to set the pace. If a herd went too fast it would not reach the market in good shape, but it could browse along at between ten and fifteen miles a day and put on weight, for in the early days buffalo and mesquite grass grew knee-high and good watering-places were not too far apart. Other men rode "at swing" where the herd widened out, and a couple urged "the drags" along. Unskilled boys wrangled the horseherd, called the "caviya" from the Spanish *caballada*. The cook brought up the rear, or made short cuts from bed ground to bed ground, driving the chuck wagon loaded with supplies and bedrolls. Nobody was more important, or more cantankerous, than the cook. A brave man might sass the boss, but not even the boss dared sass the cook. The average trail herd was about twenty-five hundred or three thousand head, driven by sixteen or eighteen men with a caviya of fifty or sixty ponies.

The first trail was named for Jesse Chisolm, a half-breed Cherokee trader, related to Sam Houston's Indian wife and to Senator Owen of Oklahoma. The Chisolm Trail started at San Antonio, crossed the Colorado River three miles below

Austin, left Fort Worth on the right (it was still a whistling-post), crossed the Red River and the Little Washita, and then went straight across the Indian Territory and to the railroad at Abilene, Kansas. 'Sixty-nine was the big year on that trail. Raine and Barnes estimate that three hundred and fifty thousand steers were shipped from Abilene in that year. Within three years that figure rose to a million and prices reached thirty and forty dollars for a good animal in the Chicago stockyards. Business men began to note the possibilities, banks were opened, and cattle were bought and sold on paper instead of with gold in the saddlebags. Then the depression of '73 broke the market. Texans, suddenly cattle-poor, began to spread over onto the free grass in West Texas where herds could be held when there was no ready sale. In the seventies the prairies from Mexico to Canada would support one hundred head of cattle per square mile. The same country today will not support forty.

This was the period of open range, free grass and water. Nobody owned anything except his herds; nobody wanted to own land. Only buffalo and Indians disputed the white man's advance. A hundred tales of sacked and burned ranch houses, women violated and killed, babies' brains dashed out against rocks, children carried off into slavery, account for the frontier dictum that the only good Indian was a dead Indian. But there were also white women who lived contentedly with Indians, and captured children who refused to return to their own people. Texas boasts that she never had a squaw man, presumably classing Sam Houston as a Tennesseean in that connection.

These owners beat another trail into the prairie which was known as the Western or Dodge Trail. Starting also at the Gulf, it swung west at San Antonio, left Texas at Doan's Crossing, and made a straight line through the Indian territory to Dodge City.

The third great trail, the Goodnight-Loving Trail, was laid out by those two men and by John Chisum, the first to dare the " dry drive " across the plains of Texas. In 1858 *Charles Goodnight,* whose history has been recounted by J. Evetts Haley under that title, drove a herd through the Pecos River at Horsehead Crossing and up to Fort Sumner in New Mexico, where the government was buying beef for captive Indians. It was a desperate business, for sometimes the stock had to make ninety miles without water. Many died of thirst. Many died of overdrinking at the river, or were killed in their crazy rush to reach the water.

Cattle that Goodnight could not sell at Fort Sumner he drove on into Colorado, where the grama grass was fine. At Raton Pass, Uncle Dick Wootton charged ten cents a head at his toll gate, and Goodnight found a crossing farther east by way of the Cimarron Seco, the South Trinchera, and so northwest to Picketwire, and on to the high plains of Wyoming. The longhorn put on weight on the tall buffalo grass and sweet water, and herds were regularly driven north for the summer's fattening and south again for the winter and breeding. Drives of two thousand miles were not rare, and Owen Wister could write *The Virginian* about the cowboy who was at home all over the West.

John Chisum, when he migrated from Texas in '67, drove six thousand head of cattle across the flats of Texas and settled in the lovely Bosque Grande where Roswell is now. He lost count when his herds numbered about seventy-five thousand, but he is said to have owned the largest one-man herd in the world.

During the seventies the great ranches began to develop.

A real ranch ran from two thousand to fifty thousand acres; anything less was just a home place. Prospects of big money attracted foreign capital, and the cattle business became one of the greatest in the country.

Momentous changes were inevitable. The longhorn, a fine animal on the trail, could stand anything and rough through any winter, but only the strong-toothed could eat the beef he made. The market demanded tender steaks; Herefords and Shorthorns were introduced, and the longhorn's day was done. So was the reckless roper's, for these expensive beasts required care and could not be " busted " just for fun.

Then another Yankee invented barbed wire, and the railroads which had made a market for cattle began bringing thousands of settlers who wanted fenced-in farms. Cattlemen complained, and still do, that the government has always favored the farmer, that the country was natural range and unsuited to farming. How they hated " bob-wa'ar "! Cattle and horses got cut on it, fences obstructed the trails and cut up the range. The cowman, who had been such a stickler for law against the rustlers, began to cut fences — even when his herds overran and ruined crops — and the whole country was torn by miniature but deadly wars between cattlemen and " squatters " or " nesters." Then the cattleman began to fence. He generally enclosed only the waterholes or the streams, for who controlled water controlled the West. But one outfit was accused of having a hundred and thirty miles of illegal fences.

Texas, eager to get its West settled up, encouraged such practices by its Eight Section Act, which allowed a man eight sections of land, which need not be in one piece. By paying filing fees for his cowboys, employing them while they " proved up," and taking over the homestead for the debt, many men acquired vast holdings. One such citizen was quoted as saying that he did not want all the land; just what adjoined his.

After fences came windmills, and the mechanic was quite as important a person on the ranch as the bronco-buster or the cook. Cowboys began to ride fences with pockets full of wire staples, and to carry a can of grease for the screeching windmill. Trails grew shorter as railroads linked the Western towns and ranches, and finally the cowboy drove a Ford and was a motor mechanic as well as a windmill man. The limitless reaches of the plains were cut up a thousand ways and overgrazing began to make the Dust Bowl, though few men could foresee that desolate end. Charles Goodnight said in his old age that West Texas did not then have one-third of the living water he had known there fifty years before. He, like many men, had lived to see the complete transformation of the Southwest.

The cattle business as those men knew it is as dead and gone now as knighthood. Its survivors meet in the Old Trails Drivers Association to reminisce and to dispute every foot of the trails they used to ride. They smile wryly at rodeos in city auditoriums and riding and roping as commercialized stunts. The modern cowboy rides fences in a car and drives into town to the movie. The rich owner breeds stock experimentally, throws an occasional big party at his tiled Spanish mansion on the ranch, and lives in town. Many little fellows are still just barely making a living out of cattle, but even they motor into town for a weekly luncheon.

Southwestern history is so closely telescoped that at the Fat Stock Show in Forth Worth all these phases of its life were represented. An old gentleman from El Paso who had driven steers up Jesse Chisolm's trail sat in a box, and I noted

the men who came to greet him — men who certainly knew
Colonel Goodnight, who might have similar records of their
own. Slow-moving now, but still erect and robust, they wore
business suits, as a rule with heeled boots, always with wide
hats. And their sons came too, very like Eastern city men
except for the size the Southwest produces and its unmistak-
able but indefinable manner. In fundamentals, it seemed to
me, they are of a piece with their grandfathers. Machines
have changed their outer lives, but their mental habits have
not altered much.

The old-time cowman was a man of action, adaptable to
new conditions, not scared by the unknown. But among the
manifold dangers he met and overcame were few ideas. He
was shy of thought and uncritical. He was for religion and
education, but he was, as one said, a brother-in-law of the
church; his wife belonged. He was always generous with
his family, dressed his wife well, sent her traveling, bought
her grand pianos and plush curtains in Dodge City or New
Orleans; and he accepted her taste in all things.

His grandson is quite as ready to provide art galleries,
streamlined motors, and training in the arts. He supports
the churches liberally and dozens of denominational colleges.
The State University is one of the wealthiest in the world,
but the legislature, trying to prevent graft, has decreed that
its vast oil revenues shall be used only for buildings — a neat
reversal of the conception of a university as Mark Hopkins
on one end of a log and a student on the other. Himself a
graduate of one of these colleges, the typical Texan pursues
culture no farther, to judge by the paucity of bookstores in
his towns and their offering. He leaves all that to his wife
and her advisers, generally women. Grandfather's limitations
seem to persist.

Will the modern Southwesterner carry the old man's virtues over into modern life? The old-time cowboy was an individualist in that he could face hardships and make decisions alone and rely on himself in emergencies. But he had a fine spirit of co-operation too. Unawed by extraneous or meretricious greatness, he judged a man as a man, dealt with him as a neighbor. He belonged to the honorable line of Anglo-Saxon stalwarts who go back to Magna Carta and who take Magna Carta wherever they go. They had the Nordic ability to accept as final the expressed will of the majority, and the democratic belief that the poor and simple man is worth as much as the rich and clever. Can his grandson hold on to these basic conceptions in a fast-changing world? Has he got the imagination to realize a neighbor he has never seen, whom he has scarcely heard of, and to deal fairly with him as man to man? Who can say?

Between Fort Worth

and San Antonio one drops from stimulating air with electricity in it, and often sand, to the laxer atmosphere of softer,
greener lands. Fort Worth looks westward across the great
plains. San Antonio, for all its Spanish background, looks
backward, homesick for the Old South.

About half-way between them is Austin, the capital and
home of the State University. Like its namesake, Texas' first
great gentleman who tried to deal honorably and honestly
with both the Spanish government and the colonists he
brought from the States, Austin tries to reconcile many di-
vergent points of view. As the university has been built,
faster and faster, trying to catch up with its oil revenues,
changing tastes have given it every architectural style. It
culminates in the library, whose central stack runs up twenty-
seven stories with a Spanish patio half-way up and a Greek
temple on top. Frank Dobie, scornful of aping foreign ways
and glorifying alien backgrounds instead of those of Texas,
said: " That tower would be all right if they'd just lay it down
and run a gallery round it."

III

SAN ANTONIO IS SPAIN
IN TEXAS

AN ANTONIO IS SPAIN IN TEXAS, AND PROUD OF IT.
That is, it is proud of it lately. Texas spent nearly a century
apologizing for its Spanish background, even for its Spanish-
speaking people, and trying to be as much like a city of the
Old South as possible. The preponderant group goes on replacing fine old buildings with skyscrapers and filling-stations.
But within the last twenty years the historically minded have
saved a few storied houses before their adobe walls sank into
the earth and their carved beams were chopped up for kin-
dling. This labor of love has been aided by the tourists' taste
for the quaint. Business men understand dollars, even if they
clink for old mud houses, street singers, and chile joints. San
Antonio likes to be compared with Quebec and New Orleans,
and it calls attention to its antiquities in hundreds of bronze
plaques and highly colored leaflets. But San Antonio is more
than picturesque. The only considerable town the Spanish
built in what is now Texas, it has been the center of every

phase of Texas life from then till now. Often almost extinguished by war or massacre, plague or poverty, San Antonio has repeatedly come back to a position of importance, and it has now real beauty and personality.

The little San Antonio River saves the town from conformity to the usual American city plan. For fifteen miles it meanders along in irregular bends, actually looping back on itself in the busiest downtown section, and deflecting the streets from the straight everywhere. Many streets run for only a few blocks, and the main avenues are apt to change their names in mid-course and without warning. But these names recall every period of San Antonio's history, and it would be a shame to alter them; above all, the Spanish ones, though these are difficult for the English tongue to say and practically impossible for one who knows Spanish to understand as Texans pronounce them. But even if you have missed a street, it is a recurring joy to come upon that rippling stream below the sidewalks, surprisingly clear and free from litter, with grassy banks and occasional trees and shrubs. It soothes the most feverish annoyance and makes certain that one takes San Antonio in the only way to savor its Spanish spice: leisurely.

The Spaniards settled, of course, along the river. That story and much else has been told by the Federal Writers' Project in its *San Antonio, An Authoritative Guide*. Intelligently compiled, well written, beautifully printed, with good maps and pictures, it is comprehensive and useful. It repeats San Antonio's claim that Alvar Núñez Cabeza de Vaca saw this spot in 1534 on his footsore journey from Florida to Mexico, saving his own life by healing sick Indians, daily performing miracles no more phenomenal than his survival to tell the tale.

41

Historians have long disagreed about that lost Spaniard's wanderings, but the most recent book on the subject, Cleve Hallenbeck's *Alvar Núñez Cabeza de Vaca,* leaves no doubt that the site of San Antonio was on his way. This is San Antonio's only claim to antiquity as Spain in Texas, for Cabeza de Vaca only passed by, leaving no trace. Texas had no interest for Spain until the eighteenth century when she needed outposts against France, pushing westward from Louisiana. Adaes was the first capital; the first building on the San Antonio River was the mission of San Antonio de Valero, built in 1718, which has come to fame and long remembrance as " the Alamo." The *presidio,* fort, was called Bexar, which Texans mispronounce as Bear with bruin himself for its symbol. San Fernando, now a part of the city, was settled by Canary Islanders whom the King ennobled for their daring and who could consequently feel very snobbish toward the simple soldiers' families in the *villita* (little town).

From San Antonio de Valero the Franciscan missionaries paddled their canoes down the river to establish other missions. Four churches still stand and enough of other walls and *acequias* to suggest the thriving missions of the eighteenth century with their farms, vineyards, and orchards, granaries and mills; the church and school where docile Indians learned the *doctrina* along with agriculture, crafts, and civilized living. The churches are magnificent. Towers and cloisters, carved stone and frescoed walls, soft-toned bells, convent gardens, and tonsured Franciscans re-create the old pious life. And walls too thick for an arrow to penetrate, loop-holes, watchtowers, and walled courtyards where hundreds of people could take refuge recall the savage Apaches and Comanches whom Spain never conquered.

Besides her fort and missions, Spain set up a civil government on Military Plaza, where the " Governor's Palace " still stands. It is a pleasant old adobe house, restored and furnished to show how it used to be, a more pleasing effect than is given by the ill-assorted archæological and historical museum in the Governor's Palace of Santa Fe. Spanish governors lived there during the last half of the eighteenth century, and Lieutenant Zebulon Montgomery Pike was entertained there in 1807. That gay and lone invader of Mexico had been picked up above Santa Fe with papers issued by that Wilkinson who was Aaron Burr's associate. Lieutenant Pike said he thought he was on the headwaters of the Red River. If so, there was something wrong with the geography they taught at West Point.

The Spanish authorities treated him courteously, but they confiscated his papers and sent him to Chihuahua for examination, and then returned him to the United States by way of Coahuila and San Antonio. Lieutenant Pike was an engaging roamer, and surely no suspected spy was ever so lavishly entertained. He described San Antonio's palace as candle-lit, hung with brocades, and redolent of the banquet prepared for him. The ladies were, as ever in this young man's adventures, most kind.

After that the old mansion went into a pitiful decline, as second-hand store, restaurant, and saloon, " The Hole in the Wall." In 1929 the city, harried into it by the San Antonio Conservation Society, bought the ruin for fifty-five thousand dollars. Little remained but the front wall with the Habsburg coat of arms over the door's heavy walnut lintel. But Harvey P. Smith, the architect, with painstaking research and good feeling, brought the old rooms back. The original *vigas* probably were squared and carved; gentlemen's houses did not use rough-hewn round poles; but most of it gives a feeling of rightness. The patio is paved with colored pebbles around beds of flowers that might have bloomed there in the eighteenth century, and freshened by a fountain. There is also a well into which you drop a penny to make sure you will return to San Antonio.

Pike was only the first hint of what was to be. After the United States had acquired Louisiana, others besides Aaron Burr could look west and think thoughts long enough to touch the Pacific. Tall men with long guns began to emerge from the Mississippi Valley, hungry for land, ready to fight. When Mexico declared its independence of Spain in 1811, Texas revolted too. Its first efforts were put down hideously with the leader's head displayed on a pike, prisoners' throats cut in violation of paroles, and hundreds of surrendered men allowed to suffocate in an air-tight granary while their women wailed, as Dolorosa Street testifies. Many place names, both English and Spanish, honor the republicans of that time, but the town was almost destroyed. What the Spanish left, Comanche and Apache raiders stole. Almost every family had lost stock and stores of food, and in the first decade of the century over two hundred women and children were carried away. The new Republic of Mexico, too weak and disorganized to protect its frontier outposts, rejoiced when responsible citizens of the republic to the north asked permission to enter.

The first of them was Moses Austin of Missouri, who rode into San Antonio on his only horse followed by his only slave on a mule. In 1820 Mr. Austin petitioned the Spanish Governor for permission to settle three hundred families on the Brazos and Colorado rivers. He agreed to bring in only Catholic colonists, former Spanish subjects from Louisiana, who would become loyal citizens of Mexico and who would never countenance slavery. But destiny was to prove stronger than any gentleman's agreement, and Texas was fated to become a state of the Union, Protestant, and devoted to slavery, which it fought for in the Civil War. Moses Austin and his son Stephen kept their agreement as long as they could. Their colonists were well behaved, and at intervals Catholic priests came along to perform nuptial mass for couples who had contracted the habit of matrimony so long since that they often presented several candidates for baptism on their wedding day. But the scrupulous Austins were followed inevitably by gentlemen less scrupulous.

About ten years behind Moses Austin, Sam Houston appeared in San Antonio. Born in Virginia, he had been Governor of Tennessee, United States Congressman, a Cherokee by adoption, and the husband of a beauty of that tribe. His flamboyant taste in blankets, feathered headdresses, and oratory was contradicted by a truly noble refusal to discuss his divorce from a Tennessee girl who had been his wife for less than a week. In a time when any divorce was a scandal, his flared into the wildest gossip and threatened duels. But Sam Houston was never goaded into a word, nor would he hear one on the subject. To this day, nobody knows what really happened. Houston went to live with the Indians and proved to be one of the few Americans who understood that people and might have lived peaceably with them. He might even have taken their lands without bloodshed. But his largest contribution to history was in the taking of Texas.

Marquis James, Houston's biographer under his Cherokee name, *The Raven,* quotes a letter from Sam Houston to President Jackson which is highly suggestive:

" I am in possession of some information that . . . may

be calculated to forward your views, if you should entertain any, touching the acquisition of Texas by the United States."

The letter goes on with an accurate prognostication of what was to occur: the revolt of Texas from Mexico, its ultimate admission to the Union. But not in a minute, not without provocation.

Santa Anna, President of Mexico, forced a break when he proclaimed a new constitution abrogating the rights of individual states. Texas, even then for state rights, boiled with rancor, and when an order went out to disarm, men faced with savage Indians declared their independence of a government that was giving them no protection.

Houston was a conspicuous figure in Texas from the day he arrived, and by 1836 he had been made commander-in-chief of the Texas Regulars. He had no authority over volunteers, but he knew that a small detachment which was trying to hold San Antonio was outnumbered and doomed, and he tried to get them to retreat. William Travis of South Carolina was in command, with Davie Crockett and James Bowie, of the bowie knife, as his right-hand men. They refused to surrender. Instead, they barricaded themselves in the old Mission of San Antonio de Valero, which had come to be called the Alamo because of the cottonwoods that shaded it. They were a hundred and fifty men, a few women and children. It was a forlorn hope, misguided and foolhardy, but surely one of the world's most exciting examples of sheer courage. Santa Anna, arriving with a couple of thousand dragoons and plenty of provisions, laid siege to the mission on February 23. On the 24th Travis smuggled out his letter, said to be the most heroic document in American history. It is preserved now in the state capitol at Austin, where the four women who guard it opened the vault and put it into my hands.

It is handled as reverently as the Ark of the Covenant, for Texas independence is a religion in Texas, and the defenders of the Alamo its archangels. Here is the letter:

Commandancy of the Alamo
Bejar, February 24, 1836

To the People of Texas and
All Americans in the *world*

Fellow citizens and compatriots, I am besieged, by a thousand or more of the Mexicans under Santa Anna. I have sustained a continual Bombardment and cannonade for twenty-four hours and have not lost a man. The enemy has demanded a surrender at discretion, otherwise the garrison are to be put to the sword if the fort is taken. I have answered the demand with a cannon shot, and our flag still waves proudly from the walls. *I shall never surrender or retreat.* Then, I call on you in the name of Liberty, of patriotism and everything dear to the American character, to come to our aid, with all dispatch. The enemy is receiving reinforcements daily and will no doubt increase to three or four thousand in four or five days. If this call is neglected, I am determined to sustain myself as long as possible and die like a soldier who never forgets what is due to his own honor and that of his country.

Victory or Death
William Barret Travis
Lt. Col. Comdt.

P.S. The Lord is on our side. When the enemy appeared in sight we had not three bushels of corn. We have since found in deserted houses eighty or ninety bushels and got into the walls twenty or thirty head of beeves.

Travis

As everybody knows, help did not reach them. On March 6 Santa Anna ordered a final attack, with no quarter, and every fighting Texan fell dead before the Alamo was taken. Their bodies were burned, an insult, but later certain bones were identified and given military burial in the Cathedral of San Fernando. But Santa Anna's day was done. Texas had her deathless tradition of heroism, and her battle-cry. On April 21 Sam Houston's army, inspired to invincibility by " Remember the Alamo! " defeated Santa Anna and routed his force at San Jacinto. Texas was free, a republic under the Lone Star flag.

It is a heroic tradition. Surely nobody could read the story and Travis's letter without the thrill that brings tears for men's courage.

Unhappily, it has been used, and still is, to make bad feeling against Mexicans. A district judge recounted that he had, as a child, heard an old man tell the story of the Alamo, where he was trapped with his mother. " I never see a Mexican without thinking of that," said the judge. An advanced student of history at the University of Texas said: " I hate Mexicans because I know how my people fought to win Texas."

So Texas history, as taught in Texas, makes every pitiful peon pay, a hundred years later, for Santa Anna's cruelty. They forget that Mexicans signed the declaration of Texas' independence, that Mexicans died in the Alamo. Some day a great Texan will turn the page and read how, during the Mexican War, cadets in Mexico's Military Academy at Chapultepec died rather than surrender to our invading army. They were defending their country against invaders, whereas the brave defenders of the Alamo were trying to hold land they had invaded. The Mexican cadets, like the heroes of the Alamo, died to the last staunch defender. Mexico has raised a statue to her *Niños Heroes,* Boy Heroes, in front of Chapultepec Castle. When Texans can thrill to that monument of unselfish courage as they do at the Alamo, we shall have taken one more step toward civilization.

Texas was a republic for ten years, and on February 16, 1846 it entered the United States, the Lone Star flag came down, and Texans fought in the Mexican War.

San Antonio grew, but with violence and jerkily. The river, though often choked with dead animals, was a better artery of communication than the streets, knee-deep in mud or dust. There were more saloons than stores, and men went out of town only in armed bands. Mexicans raided across the border, and Americans chased them back or made raids of their own. Bad men from both countries made San Antonio their headquarters, and peaceful citizens in vigilante committees made certain trees historic. Mrs. Mary A. Maverick, a young wife there in 1838, relates in her delightful *Memoirs* that young women went berrying only under armed escort. Her husband, a " minute man," kept his war-horse saddled, ready to set out after Indians on a moment's notice. She recounts how Comanche chiefs who had come in for parley violated their parole with hideous war-whoops, and precipitated a battle which raged at her front door and in her back garden. That brush ended when an Indian woman promised to return to her tribe and effect an exchange of prisoners. But, Mrs. Maverick writes: " All the Comanches howled and cut themselves with knives and killed horses for several days, and they took all the American captives, thirteen in number, and roasted and butchered them to death with horrible outcries." Such episodes — and the history of the frontier is full of them — blinded white men to the fact that they were the aggressors taking Indian lands.

But nothing halted the westward push. Volunteer fighters and scattered settlers were followed by fleets of prairie schooners, by pony express and stage-lines. And San Antonio, from being a terminus, became a way station and an outfitting post on the southern route to the plains of California.

During these years Germans came, escaping military conscription in the fatherland. Colonies under noblemen like Counts Braunfels and Castro (an Alsatian) settled towns which keep their European character to this day. Many migrated as individuals — professional men and professors or farmers and artisans who spread all over the Southwest. Mrs. Maverick describes the effect His Highness Prince Charles Solm Solm, son of the Grand Duke of Braunfels, had on General Somerville, who " was a noted laugher. He saw the Prince's two attendants dress His Highness, that is lift him into his pants, and General Somerville was so overcome by the sight that he broke into one of his famous fits of laughter and was heard all over the Point. The Prince and suite were all very courteous and polite to us. They wore cock feathers in their hats, and did not appear quite fitted to frontier life."

These Germans built the solid cut limestone houses which add such dignity to San Antonio and other Texas towns, and their names appear today on business blocks, banks and breweries, hotels and restaurants, schools and parks. German love of food and drink, of good music and hearty fun, went along well with Mexican fandangos and pioneer barbecues. And they were sturdy liberals of a breed that Germany may be needing today.

In 1936 New Braunfels celebrated her centennial. A German town, with a German press, German customs, and a deep love of old Germany, it invited the German consul in New Orleans to attend. That official could not accept, but his repre-

THE MISSION OF LA CONCEPCIÓN AT SAN ANTONIO

[photo, Harvey Patterson]

THE SAN ANTONIO RIVER MEANDERS THROUGH
THE CITY

[photo, Ewing Galloway]

sentative approved the program and admired the band-stand hung with United States and Texas flags. But he noticed an omission. Where, he wanted to know, was the Swastika? The committee explained that they were Germans, but not Nazis. They would not display the Nazi flag. Hitler's minion could not speak unless he saw his country's emblem. The committee was regretful, but firm. They mentioned the first train back to New Orleans, the Nazi departed, and New Braunfels celebrated its centennial and honored its German background with no recognition of Germany's present rulers.

Such men as these German pioneers steadied the Southwest through its adolescent growing-pains, for they did not share the racial, international, and later sectional hatreds that produced such violence. I have noted that the German, or the Jew (for many of these German pioneers were Jews), is the person to seek for an unbiased, realistic, and humorous account of a controversial episode.

Between the Mexican and the Civil Wars, everything brought money to San Antonio, which traded in cotton and fodder, manufactured goods from the States, and cattle from Mexico. Texas between the Nueces and the Rio Grande and the Gulf of Mexico was filled with longhorns which had strayed or been urged across the border. Texans were mounted on Mexican mustangs, and San Antonio became a rip-roaring cow-town, as well as a frontier post. It was erecting stone and brick houses, Protestant churches, and Catholic convents. Many of them remain, such as the Vance house, where Robert E. Lee used to visit, and the Menger Hotel where he fought the silent and terrific battle between his allegiance as an officer of the United States Army and his loyalty to Virginia.

The Menger Hotel is one of the many fine buildings in the

Southwest that someone with money and imagination ought to save. Its lofty lobby and two patios with palms and one of the original alamos are stately and cool, and its oldest Negro servants remember " rooming " Theodore Roosevelt when he came with the Rough Riders, General Wood on his way to Cuba, General Funston when he went after Villa in Mexico, Presidents Harrison and Taft. Surely its chambers are spacious enough to accommodate modern bathrooms, and taste and enterprise could re-create an atmosphere that San Antonio's wealthiest visitors would gladly pay for. The Menger is to be torn down for a filling-station. Then the Alamo Plaza will be entirely surrounded by tall buildings. Even the little Alamo, shrine of Texas liberty, is dwarfed by a museum on one side, and on the other government money is erecting a replica of the Alamo itself — sharper on the edges, fresher of plaster, a bit larger — to house a patriotic society.

Lately San Antonio vies with Florida and southern California as the mecca of the great winter motor migration. Quiet couples escaping blizzards up north occupy tourist-camp cabins for months or rock on the porches of rooming-houses and small hotels. And tourist-conscious San Antonio has discovered that they like Mexico in the United States. So guide books play up the Mexican quarter, where one might live a lifetime without a word of English, and many do. Markets and open booths along the streets offer not only food and raiment, but love potions, rhymed prayers and newsy ballads, Mexican spices, and Spanish books. One may read in a library presented by a Mexican president, see movies, join clubs, attend church or school, and all in Spanish. One may celebrate all the Mexican holidays, saints' days, and any private festival of his own among people who know how to enjoy feast days. And any night he may hear street singers who know all the Mexican ballads and the newest popular songs.

There is a sad side to " Mexican town " which no visitors and few San Antonians know. Too many people live there, huddled eight or ten to a room in pitiful tenements. Nor does the city seem aware of the danger of blocks of frame shacks, tinder for a major holocaust some day. Owners of textile factories and pecan orchards have protested heatedly against the minimum-wage law, and Maury Maverick, who concerns himself with such things, says the factory workers are pitifully undernourished and hopeless. Only a few of the younger and more intelligent are trying to organize to help themselves. The entire weight of public opinion is against them, though pay is low even among white-collar workers.

A thoughtful merchant told me that San Antonio, though a city of two hundred and fifty thousand, has few buyers of books or magazines, concert or lecture tickets. Salaries are so low that they permit only the cheapest diversions. The rich, and there are many, buy elsewhere and spend most of their time in travel. To them, even to his own family, Maury Maverick is a dangerous radical, an agitator, a traitor to his class. For democratic Texas, republic of the pioneer tradition, is chock-full of class feeling, as even a glimpse of its society shows.

San Antonio society is cosmopolitan. Germans and Old Mexican families have intermarried and lost their sharp distinction, but Mexican refugees from recent disturbances bring Spanish into the drawing-room. Soldiers — afoot, ahorseback, and in the air — put snap into the parties, go in for polo and racing, and have made San Antonio one of the Army's most frequent mothers-in-law. And the city is full of Northerners — investors in business, sojourners in the expensive hotels or in their own winter homes, oil- and cattle-men, writers and painters. But the tone of San Antonio society, more Southern than Western, is set by its organized Daughters. All our national and sectional Daughters are there and active, and even more patriotic Daughters of Texas' founders, fighters, signers, or early arrivals. In Texas, being descended from one who was present at an early date or on a historic occasion is equal to a patent of nobility elsewhere. One wrote down as her proudest distinction: " Native Born Texan." It is interesting to meet these gentle and charming Daughters in their flower-scented houses, filled with furniture from the Old South, to hear their talk of family and their complaints of the annoying lower classes, and to read between parties the firsthand accounts of their grandfathers.

One dainty lady, hearing Sam Houston described as a rough fellow in a coonskin cap, protested: " He never wore a coonskin cap. Sam Houston was a gentleman. Why, he was an ancestor of mine! " And another, discussing a float in the San Jacinto Day parade, was indignant that the girls were to be dressed as French, Dutch, and Belgian peasants. " What honor would it be to Texas," said she, " to be recognized by peasants? " So the Republic of Texas was doubtless recognized by Louis Philippe, the dull-witted King of France, and lecherous Leopold of Belgium. What they did about Holland, whose queens delight to wear the dress of their people, I did not learn. Perhaps Texas should suppress grandfather's account in the interest of his fastidious descendants! He was of a roughness and a toughness these ladies shudder away from, but to a wilder Westerner he seems to make up for what he lacked as an aristocratic ancestor in the uncompromising manliness that made him a great Southwesterner.

Driving westward

from San Antonio is like driving through a garden. Along the streams are oak groves and mesquite thickets with ever taller trees in closer growth, and now and then a lone huisache sprays scent from its wide and lacy tent of bloom. Spanish bayonets march like an army with flowering lances, and bluebonnets spread away to the horizon in solid fields of sky color. All along the roads native trees and shrubs have been planted with such good taste that the state's entire highway system composes a botanical display. Even in the dryest regions desert plants beside the roadway show how beautiful are their form and color, and how wide their variety when they are spaced to set each other off.

West of San Antonio one feels Mexico close at hand. The Rio Grande, more impressive on a map than in actuality, does a very lackadaisical and slovenly job of keeping two nations apart. It has, in fact, never done so. For a hundred years the two peoples have met in war and in amity, in trade, and in both understanding and misunderstanding. There is no understanding the Southwest without knowing something of that rich field for misunderstanding.

IV

THE BORDER
AND BORDER PEOPLE

Once in Mexico, a Texas lady, wishing to be kind, tried to account to a Mexican gentleman for the attitude of her people toward his.

"We should really all come to southern Mexico," she said generously. "The trouble is that we Texans judge all Mexicans by the border people."

The Mexican, bowing with the aplomb of generations of gentle breeding, said so suavely that the impact of his words was long delayed: "That madam, is a mistake we Mexicans never make. We never judge by the border people."

A Mexican living in Los Angeles sent his children to the public schools. He is, as it happens, a pure blond and, as is true of many Mexicans, a graduate of a European university. When his children brought home registration cards, he wrote in the proper spaces: Mexican, white, Catholic, the address, and so on. The next day the cards came back. The teacher had said a Mexican could not be white, and it must be done again. This man was amused. With the revolution, Mexicans are outgrowing the snobbishness Spain gave them (*puro blanco es caballero;* all white is a gentleman) and are beginning to take pride in their Indian heritage. Even those who are of pure Spanish descent appreciate that much of their country's culture is Indian and proudly claim a share of it. As is always true, snobbishness flourishes most among those who know least of cultural backgrounds and of how wavering and uncertain any line of descent really is. Only a very ignorant dictator could make " race " a basis for right, and only very ignorant or very fearful folk could accept his standard. But simple people and children are hurt by such stupidity, and the entire Southwest is tinctured by its effects.

José Vasconcelos, the Mexican educator and philosopher, tells in his *Ulysses Criollo* of his schooling in Eagle Pass, Texas. He came from a cultivated home of books and music, where several languages were spoken and taste prevailed. His schoolmates came mostly from homes with no pretensions whatever to cultivation, with little more than common school education. Yet little José had to fight with his fists to prove that a Mexican was not inferior. His superiority came out finally in the philosophy on which modern Mexico's school system is founded, and in most stimulating discussions of the flexibility, educability, and artistic aptitudes of mixed peoples.

The sort of young ruffian who baited little José and got his nose properly punched may grow up into such a writer as Owen P. White, who boasts that he knows Mexico because he was born in El Paso. In *Them Was the Days* Mr. White describes an amusing set of drunks and illiterates in a border town as proof that Mexico is unfit for self-government. It would be too easy to be sporting to match Mr. White's feckless

Mexican with an equally comical assortment of illiterates in the United States; or to introduce Mr. White to a group of Mexicans whose broad culture, linguistic gifts, and humane tolerance would never judge by the border people.

The border people have done neither nation justice. Both frontiers were originally far from centers where educated men understood that Greek and Roman culture, modified by the Latins or the Nordics, expressed in Spanish or English, was culture still. The Spanish colonial, cut off by thousands of miles and many years from Spain, inevitably accepted the shaggy mountain man who behaved so boorishly in his plazas as a fair representative of a crude and heretical people. What could he know of the gentlefolk of Boston or of Charleston? The mountain man did not know them either. Ignorant, often illiterate, and coming from a section where a white skin was a mark of superiority, he found all brown-skinned people inferior and a language he could not understand mere gibberish. What could he know of Mexico, the city of palaces, with its university a century older than Harvard? To his limited Protestantism a " Romanist " was not a Christian, as to the ignorant Catholic a Protestant was a heretic. A Protestant missionary, recounting his evangelical labors in New Mexico in the eighties, wrote kindly of a young Mexican: " He was a Catholic, but clean and honest."

It is not surprising that such people, unaware of each other's background, ignorant of each other's speech, disrespectful of each other's faith, should have made bad feeling along the border. The wonder is that there has been, and is, as much good feeling as exists among the best people of both heritages. The history of the border is a long and tragic tale of the efforts of good men and women to restrain their bad neighbors.

The border has moved along with invasion and conquest.

Once on the Mississippi, it is now on the Rio Grande. Once fought over by murderous savages, it now keeps its hands off its gun and its bowie knife, though it still has its savages. They fight for land still, but in the courts. They fight for water. And they fight for place in politics and in social snobbery.

Every Spanish explorer, beginning with Fray Marcos de Niza in 1539, claimed the land from where he stood to the farthest point he had ever heard of. So Nuevo Mexico, as a map of 1670 shows, extended from the Mississippi to the Pacific, and its northern limits faded off into the arctic mists.

Spaniards were unexcelled as explorers, conquerors, and administrators. Courageous and curious, they went everywhere and intelligently noted what they saw. They conquered against such odds as few men have faced, for they overcame not only savage tribes, but terrifyingly difficult country from the Rockies to the Andes, deserts as well as jungles, tropical heat as well as mountain cold. But they never cut the umbilical cord that bound them to the mother country. They went in armies, fully panoplied, under orders, and bearing with them both church and state. And they governed, down to life's pettiest detail, hordes of subject peoples and held them in one of the vastest empires the world has ever seen, and the longest-lived. These conquerors were not pioneers. No Spaniard wanted to take a gun and an ax and set off alone to carve himself a home out of the wilderness. He didn't want to chop or dig. Indefatigable as a soldier, he sought always a subject population to hew his wood and draw his water. Where he found that, preferably with gold and silver thrown in, he settled. Where he did not, as on the Texan plains, he passed by. Consequently the Spanish domain in what is now the

United States was limited to the arable valleys, especially where sedentary Indians dwelt.

That was the situation when the Nordic arrived, advancing into Mexico by two routes — from Louisiana into Texas and from St. Louis along the Santa Fe Trail to the capital of the province of Nuevo Mexico. Though Mexico was apprehensive about her neighbor's intentions and jailed members of the first expeditions, nothing could stem that westward tide. Mexicans welcomed the traders, and the Santa Fe Trail became a valuable trade route. Mexico assessed high duties and made all sorts of vexatious requirements. A man might have to pay at every state line, and he was always at the mercy of collectors whose palms invited a lot of greasing. Every account complains of such abuses while relating how they were evaded. Furs were smuggled through; wagons, which were assessed five hundred dollars apiece, were halted just outside Santa Fe and several cargoes piled onto one. Nevertheless trade grew, and traders and merchants made friends and marriages in all the Mexican villages.

The situation in Texas was quite different. The Lone Star State had fought for her own freedom from Mexico, and she entered the United States as a state and with privileges no other state has ever had. Her history exemplifies the triumph of individual enterprise, love of personal freedom, of personal courage, and of the hardness and intolerance that are so apt to go with those qualities. Mexico had been the enemy; Mexicans, even after they became citizens of the United States, were consistently treated with the sort of disrespect which breeds resentment and its consequent evils.

Among the evils were border bandits and the methods of suppressing them. Walter Prescott Webb, in *The Texas Rangers,* relates how that body of men pursued Mexicans into

Mexico, invading a foreign country without a shadow of right, and tried to pull the United States in after them. Sam Houston even evolved a plan for the complete conquest of Mexico, and chose one Colonel Robert E. Lee of Virginia as the future " Protector of Mexico." Texans could not get it out of their heads that their manifest destiny was to kill Mexicans and take over Mexico. But Texas was defending herself without much help from Washington; her Rangers were men of their times and they must be so judged. That reservation made, their integrity, devotion to duty, courage, and impudent dash must thrill any imagination not altogether atrophied. Their heyday is done now, but the modern Ranger clearly shows the marks of his outfit.

Asked what the service's requirements were, a Ranger captain did not mention bravery or resourcefulness, honesty or stamina. Too obvious, probably. He quoted the adored Captain McNelly as saying: " Don't shoot until you're right sure you're liable to hit the man you shoot at." And: " Be polite. Don't get into trouble if you can help it, but if you do, make it serious."

As early as 1826 Austin's colony had decided to keep thirty or forty rangers on constant duty. A ranger was a man on a horse who ranged around. After the battle of San Jacinto, President Houston held together a troop of six hundred to defend the border. Their appearance was described by Noah Smithwick in *The Evolution of a State:* buckskin breeches, shrunk out of shape and stiff with grease and dirt; home-made shoes or moccasins, nondescript shirts; " here a broad-brimmed sombrero overshadowed the military cap at its side, there a tall beegum rode familiarly beside a coonskin cap with the tail hanging down behind as all well-regulated tails should do." Equipment was quite as casual — quilts, store blankets, or buffalo robes; and mounts ranged from nimble Spanish ponies to big American horses, from half-broke mustangs to sober, methodical mules.

To this day, the Texas Rangers have no uniform, no drill, no distinctions between officers and men; and their officers are men who can command by force of personality and without the need of external props. Their policy is to be always ready, always quick, to take always the advantage of surprise; and to build up a reputation for asking and giving no quarter.

Between Texas independence and the War with Mexico, the Rangers were fully occupied with Indians and desperadoes. Lone men on the frontier killed Indians as they killed wild beasts, emulating the Indian's way of taking no prisoners, lifting scalps, killing women and children. The result was that they ran the Indians out of Texas; they even pursued them into other states and fought them there.

The Rangers who rode with General Taylor into Mexico were invaluable as scouts, but they gave him almost as much trouble as the Mexicans did. In the capital they rode so arrogantly through the streets that they were dubbed " *los diablos Tejanos*," a title which still persists. Texas boasts that Mexicans believe they could conquer the United States if Texas would stand aside. The retort is: " If we weren't so fond of Mexico, we'd fight her and make her take Texas back."

By the Treaty of Guadalupe Hidalgo, which ended the Mexican War in 1848, the United States acquired all Mexico's holdings north of a line which followed the Rio Grande from the Gulf of Mexico to the southern boundary of New Mexico — " north of the town called Paso " — thence across the desert to the Rio Gila, down that stream to the Rio Colorado, and along the line between Upper and Lower California to the Pacific Ocean. This gave the northern republic the enormous terra incognita of *la Pimería Alta,* which the Pima Indians called " Arizonac." Spain had never conquered it. She had scarcely maintained three perilous presidios at Tucson, Tubac, and Yuma. Mexico had abandoned even those. It was the land of the Apache, and the two republics would have to stand together against that wily and elusive warrior before he was subdued.

Meanwhile, the border had to be surveyed. An International Boundary Commission was appointed, consisting of a commissioner and a surveyor from each nation. General Pedro García Conde served Mexico throughout. The United States Commission, after several changes, was headed by John Russell Bartlett, whose *Personal Narrative* reflects a most engaging gentleman. Mr. Bartlett, who traveled with a retinue of a hundred carpenters, blacksmiths, stone-masons, saddlers, bootmakers, and tailors, besides botanists, geologists, and surveyors, was a social success from San Diego to El Paso. He even rescued a lovely Mexican maid named Inez from a gang of ruffians.

All went well from the Pacific to the Rio Grande. Then it developed that the first surveyor had erred by about a degree of latitude. This put the town of Mesilla on the Rio Grande into Mexico. Mr. Bartlett writes:

" Immediately preceding and after the war with Mexico, the Mexican population . . . were greatly annoyed by the encroachments of the Americans and by their determined efforts to despoil them of their landed property. This was done by the latter either settling among them or in some instances forcibly occupying their dwellings and cultivated spots. . . .

63

The [Mexicans] to avoid litigation and sometimes in fear of their lives, abandoned their homes, and sought refuge on the Mexican side of the river. . . ."

When it became known that the survey put Mesilla in Mexico, "their fears were removed, and a day set aside for public rejoicing." But Mesilla rejoiced too soon. The United States honorably ended the discussion by the Gadsden Purchase, which gave us 45,535 square miles of territory for ten million dollars and the cancellation of certain Mexican debts. Mesilla, El Paso, and Tucson belonged to the United States, and an all-weather route to California was assured.

At first it seemed that the Confederacy would get the benefit, for the whole region from Texas to California was declared the Confederate Territory of Arizona, with Mesilla as its capital. But General Carleton in 1862 marched in with his California column and brought it back under the Stars and Stripes.

With the settling of the border line the work of the Boundary Commission was by no means done, and it was continued as a permanent organization.

The erratic habits of the Rio Grande and the Colorado, which are always cutting *bancos* off one country and delivering them to the other, necessitate constant adjustments. As late as 1933 the channel of the Rio Grande below El Paso was straightened and five thousand acres of uninhabited land in the United States traded for its equivalent in Mexico. The commission also makes sanitary and other surveys and supervises flood control and irrigation projects. The Treaty of Guadalupe Hidalgo had carefully guarded the navigation rights of both rivers; irrigation was unthought of then as a major international difficulty. Yet it is the main concern of the Boundary Commission now.

The Colorado River, which rises in the state of the same name, drains also parts of New Mexico, Utah, Nevada, Arizona, and California before it gets to Mexico. Who owns its waters? The states involved discuss that question interminably and have for years. With the building of Boulder Dam, California has turned a good deal of it into the Los Angeles city mains. The other states still rage against California, though all agree that waters belong to the nation wherein they rise. Mexico's claim has always seemed unimpressive.

In the case of the Rio Grande it looks different. Its headwaters too are under the Colorado peaks; New Mexico and Texas dispute about its division below Elephant Butte Dam. But below El Paso, Mexico, by its Conchos, Salado, and San Juan rivers, supplies seventy per cent of the water which irrigates the Texas citrus-fruit region in the Delta.

Texas has going concerns, and in irrigated regions priority of beneficial use is generally recognized as giving a right to water. But Mexico is planning irrigation projects of her own. It is a nice international problem, happily safely in the hands of engineers who, with good feeling and mutual respect, are honestly trying for a fair adjustment. One proposal is a series of dams which could impound enough water to irrigate twice as much land in the United States and as much again in Mexico.

More entertaining, perhaps, are the doings of the immigration and border-patrol officers who guard our frontier. Immigration problems are like those everywhere. The Border Patrol has special difficulties because of the river's shallowness. Every night citizens of both countries wade across looking for better jobs, evading the law, or sneaking " wet cattle " over. Border men watch also for youngsters who swim the river for a day's diversion in the United States. In towns like

El Paso and Douglas, rounding them up and shooing them home again is a regular evening chore. Sometimes an urchin, swimming and splashing on the Mexican side, may land all naked in Texas or Arizona with a pellet of dope under the tongue or in the armpit. Serious offenders find it harder and harder to avoid our border officers, as they have been equipped with modern means of lengthening the eye, the ear, and the shooting arm.

National good feeling is manifested in two international parks. Texas led off in 1939 with a bill to set aside a million acres for a state park in the Big Bend of the Rio Grande, its area to be matched by Mexico for an International Peace Park. It is Texas' wonderland, made of tumbled rocks and steep cliffs whose angularities are pointed up by prickly pear and spiny maguey or by the ocotillo's snaky wands. Draws are softened by the round fluffiness of mesquite, and along the Rio Grande are thickets of cottonwood where Pancho Villa hid his horses, or anybody's horses. The Chisos Mountains, at the Big Bend's farthest tip, are a biological island, whose varied flora runs from lower Sonoran cactus and leafless shrubs to Upper Canadian yellow pine, fir, and spruce. Between are fourteen species of oaks and lesser growth in amazing variety. From their highest point, Mount Emory's seventy-eight-hundred-foot peak, one can look a hundred miles into Chihuahua. From there a seven-thousand-foot drop would land the investigator in the Canyon de Santa Helena, half as deep as the Grand Canyon and ruggedly impressive. Roads have been built, trails are in contemplation, the whole region is to be a great play-place for two nations.

Another project is the Coronado International Monument on the line between Arizona and Sonora. In 1539 Fray Marcos de Niza crossed that line, and a year later Coronado fol-

ANTA HELENA CANYON ON THE BIG BEND OF THE
RIO GRANDE

[photo, National Park Service, Santa Fe]

lowed him — the forerunners of white settlement in the United States. Where they crossed our present frontier is a question that has been vigorously contested. Did they come up the Santa Cruz or the San Pedro? May Nogales claim the honor, or does Douglas deserve it? Historians have finally agreed on the San Pedro, but the National Park Service has chosen a spot near a highway and suitable for a museum, if not precisely the soil Fray Marcos set foot upon, where two nations may erect a monument to the explorers who made their common history.

So Mexico and the United States dramatize their first hundred years as neighbors. In spite of one war and various threats of war, their dealings have been generally marked by fair and gentlemanly behavior. Bad feeling has been personal; danger has lain and still lies in the greed which will risk international bad feeling for the sake of personal gain. But for the Southwest, and for the United States too, the most important and most delicate border problem is that between its Spanish- and its English-speaking citizens. Before the United States acquired New Mexico its geographical frontier was away up in southern Colorado. Its psychological boundary still is. The whole picture of the Southwest is colored by the efforts of people of different languages, traditions, and customs to live together amicably and to profit by each other's gifts.

This is not a unique situation. The United States has undertaken the world's first experiment in making a nation of diverse people without the supremacy of one group over all the others. Obviously it has not yet succeeded. In every state minorities are put upon by narrow and intolerant people sure their blend of bloods is the only one truly American. But in the Southwest this minority consists of the first inhabitants from Europe. Because they could not compete in the new language and under alien laws, many descendants of the Spanish conquerors and colonizers have become the under-privileged group, often subjected to discrimination, naturally responding with resentment and hurt feelings. The problem is livelier and perhaps more hopeful of solution in New Mexico because only in New Mexico is the balance fairly even. In 1939 the records of the National Youth Administration list fifty-three per cent of the state's population as " Spanish-American." No truer Americans exist. With a longer American history than the rest of us, they have proved their loyalty in both peace and war. The handicaps under which they labor are not of their own making, but the result of their history.

The " Occupation of New Mexico " was no conquest of a people fighting the invader. In 1846 the Republic of Mexico had been free of Spain for only twenty-five troublous years. Weak and rent by internal struggles, she could not protect her uttermost settlements. To most of them the bluecoats came as a welcome sword and shield; the war ended with a couple of skirmishes almost before it began. The United States, having no tradition of conquest, wished to treat her new citizens with complete fairness, so by the treaty she granted the entire population full rights as citizens and guaranteed the property rights of both whites and Indians. Now, a hundred years later, it is easy to see that our great failure was in not teaching English to these new citizens. Without the language they were the immediate prey of crooks and sharpers against whom the best of laws could not protect them. And they were the victims, too, of their inability to adapt themselves to the ways of a democratic state. Their tradition was that of a feudal society; they had no town-meeting background.

New Mexico, at the time of the American occupation, had

a class society. *Los ricos,* the rich, also called *gente de razón,* the right people, were very few, of pure Spanish blood, and wealthy in an easy, uncalculating way. No man really knew how large his holdings were, how many cattle grazed there, how numerous the flocks his herders drove to market, or how many gold pieces his *mayordomos* brought back in leather trunks. These people, a handful of families, lived in feudal style, driving all over the province to parties that lasted days or even weeks, intermarrrying even unto first cousins. Their children were sent to Mexico or to Europe, later to the States, to school. Some of the boys brought back degrees in law or in medicine. Many, as one of them said, were " too busy racing horses on every course from Denver to Mexico to bother with education."

Between master and man existed a kindly intimacy based on the Spanish gift, forever incomprehensible to us, of maintaining personal dignity and individual freedom under a rigid system. Don and peon rode, slept, and ate together, and used the familiar *tu;* the relationship, being well understood, required no outer props. Often the peon had Indian blood. Every family of *ricos* had Indian slaves. In 1866 a special Indian agent reported that " the pernicious system of slavery exists to an alarming extent." He estimated that about two thousand Indian captives were held as slaves in New Mexico, and he cited the case of a girl who sold for four hundred dollars. Their treatment varied from harshness to consideration as almost members of the family, and their children were not considered slaves.

If such domestic arrangements did not result in mixed blood, our Spanish forebears were the most restrained males known to history. Church records, many of which go back to the early eighteenth century, give the status of bride and groom as Spanish, Indian, or mixed. No more concealment was practiced than in Virginia, where descent from Pocahontas is aristocratic, or in Oklahoma, where an eighth, sixteenth, or even thirty-second part of Indian blood is matter for pride. In Mexico the noblest conquerors married Indian girls, and their descendants still boast of it. Only the people in the United States along the border are ashamed of any hint of the heritage of the brave and vigorous races whose people mingled with theirs for four hundred years.

Los ricos accepted the incoming Anglos as friends, as wives or husbands. They were dons, *" de origen noble,"* whose whiteness and superiority could not be questioned. For a couple of generations they maintained their old dominance. Their people had always turned to them for work, for advice, and for help. With citizenship, the poor man voted as his patron told him to; he could not imagine doing anything else. Dons, of course, used their power for good or evil according to their dispositions; but political machines were founded on trust and affection. I remember these old gentlemen well; a few still live, delightfully reminding us of more genial times. But the day of the dons is done; with general education and understanding of democracy, a new class has emerged.

Bright boys became newly aware that anybody could now aspire to political leadership, to place and power and wealth. They put themselves through school, or self-sacrificing families did, built up their flocks, made money, and sought such position as they had envied their old patrons. One said to me: " It wasn't until I'd been to France and come home that I realized I didn't have to vote as Don Jesús told me to. I was as good as he was. I could vote as I pleased! " That was in 1918; his fathers had had the right to vote since 1848.

The new class carries on, as is inevitable, the traditions of the old. As the old don was the ruler, the new leader turns to law and politics rather than to medicine or engineering. As a politician he does not, like the Nordic, campaign as a son of the soil; he prefers to be, like the old don, a descendant of the conquerors. And, by a natural reaction to a very real discrimination, he is inclined to demand the " rights " of his people. Unfortunately he too often means their full share of appointive positions and nominations.

About the time of the World War these aspirations were crystalized in the phrase " Spanish-American." The old dons knew no such word, nor felt its need. They were Mexicans, their people had come from Mexico. But the new leaders saw a chance to capitalize on misunderstandings; and making the most of a richly vituperative tongue, they stirred their people into furies of resentment.

Anglo politicians joined the new game, and both parties built political machines on hatred instead of on friendship, as the old dons had done. Such men had an easy field in which to work. The Territory of New Mexico did not establish its public schools until 1891. Many of the teachers did not speak English; many still have a Spanish accent. Only now are our children coming out of school familiar with the language they must use. In the largest towns of the Southwest many people are still limited to the few English phrases required by their jobs.

These difficulties can be overcome, I believe, only by a courageous facing of the truth. And that is beginning. We still have the Spanish-speaking politician who inflames his people with false appeals to " racial " pride. We meet the " Anglo " who, generally through ignorance, practices a silly discrimination. But they are being met and will soon be out-moded by the intelligent and tolerant of both heritages who speak the same language, whatever tongue they use. The best of these are the young men and women of Spanish lineage who are facing facts. I know a college professor, a government engineer, a labor leader, a farmer who is organizing his people, many teachers, an iron-worker, a trained nurse, who care not at all whether they are addressed as Spanish-Americans or as Mexicans. They are Americans, and they believe it is bad for any young man to be told he is entitled to position because of his birth.

I find this attitude well expressed by Juan García in a letter to a newspaper.

" How tell a Spanish-American from any other kind of an American? Surely not by his name. Judge Otero's mother was a blue-blood New Englander, his grandmother was a St. Louis socialite with not a trace of Spanish blood. Tradition has it that the first Otero in Spain was an Irishman named O'Terry. . . . How many thousands of people with Indian blood have Spanish surnames? Why shouldn't people with Spanish names have eighty or ninety per cent of the political jobs instead of only fifty per cent? Why not distribute all political pie on a hyphenated basis? Such and such per cent to Greek-Americans, to Masonic-Americans, to women-Americans? . . . Let's go to Spain. . . . Isn't there as much difference between the Andalusian and the Basque as there is between the McCormicks of Chicago and the Morgenthaus of New York? Yet they are both good American names. . . . Anyone who raises the race question is an enemy of the very same people he seeks to protect. We are all Americans or we do not belong here at all."

I am grateful to Mr. García, whom I know only through this letter, for expressing so effectively what many of us feel and try to live.

Freed of shibboleths, such men and women are studying the actual situation of our people and trying to ameliorate such conditions as exist among underprivileged groups everywhere. It is they who will lead us out of the sticky morass of resentments, snobberies, and hatreds wherein many of us are still mired. Perhaps our border people will achieve the American ideal of a democracy which does not discriminate against people because of blood or background.

West Texas

*contains a lot of country, mostly flat. Perhaps a tuck might
with advantage be run down through it. That would give a
few peaks, a bit of variety. Plains people gloat over city-
bound folk by boasting that they can see twenty miles from
the top of a windmill. But one used to blue mountains cutting
the skyline a hundred miles away feels the Texas horizon
as constricting as a string around the neck. The roads are
smooth runways, where the motor purrs along at even speed
for hours, while the black surface spins out behind and shows
up ahead with hypnotic changelessness. The only breaks are
the towns, all alike, and the roadside picnic places. Even at
the Pecos, the highway hairpins so easily down, it is hard to
realize this is the stream there was no law west of. It set
worlds apart. Even the buffalo did not cross the Pecos.*

*But even "transpecos" is so well-mannered now that a
moronic child of eight could cross it without mishap. Towns
offer a choice of "business route" or "by-pass." Intersec-
tions are blazoned forth in accurate detail. Nursery rhymes
assist your manners.*

A thoughtful driver dims his light
When he meets a car at night.

*Appeals to your better nature — "We love our children"
— alternate with tougher adjurations: "This is God's country.
Don't drive through it like hell." Filling-station lads, preter-
naturally polite everywhere, are especially soft-spoken in their
Texas drawl. "I sho' do thank you. Hurry on ba-ack."*

74

V

EL PASO,
CROSSROADS OF THE SOUTHWEST

HE RIO GRANDE, MEANDERING SOUTHWARD THROUGH the flattening country where the Rockies break down, cut for itself a pass between the Franklin Mountains and the Juárez, one of the northernmost ranges of the Mexican Sierra Madre. Who can say that prehistoric beasts did not pass through there on their dinosaurian way to the rocks in northern Arizona and New Mexico, whereon their tracks have recently been discovered? If all the Americas were populated, as the best anthropologists claim, by a gradual southward migration, certainly many prehistoric men knew this pass.

The first white man to see it was Alvar Núñez Cabeza de Vaca. He certainly crossed the Rio Grande, and it seems not unlikely that the village he found there occupied the site of modern El Paso. He describes a deep river which " ran between some ridges," and habitations which " were the first seen having the appearance and structure of houses." Cabeza de Vaca went on to Mexico, and his trail was not crossed until

1581, when three missionary monks with an escort of soldiers, went up the Rio Grande, blazing a new trail to the pueblos Coronado had found in 1540. All three missionaries were killed — the first martyrs. A year later Don Antonio de Espejo went north to try to find them. He was too late; but on his return he found a new river — the " River of Cows," which we call the Pecos. And he first used the name " New Mexico."

These men left no mark; that remained for Don Juan de Oñate, the first colonizer whose settlement endured. Castaño de Sosa had tried it; but lacking proper government endorsement, he was arrested and taken back to Mexico a prisoner. Spain was jealous of her " New Mexico." Oñate wisely complied with all the exactions, even though it delayed him a couple of years. He had agreed to enlist two hundred men, but he got off finally with only a hundred and twenty. They drove seven thousand head of stock: horses and cattle, sheep for mutton and wool, goats, and females of every species to assure the future. Eighty wagons were loaded with flour and jerked meat, tools and medicines, as well as guns and powder and lead. The caballeros, of course, had provided themselves with fine linen shirts, silk and satin doublets and hose, velvet cloaks, and hats with gold lace and floating plumes. This to impress the savages; and beads, mirrors, and other gewgaws to offer them as gifts. Monks were included in the roster as usual, but Oñate had recruited also families.

All this is recounted by Gaspar Pérez de Villagrá, one of Oñate's most devoted officers, in his *Historia de Nueva Mexico*.

Villagrá, who went ahead with a scouting party, writes: " For fifty days we marched, enduring hardships. . . . Our provisions gave out, and we were obliged to subsist on such edible weeds and roots as we found. The horses suffered most, poor dumb brutes; they were almost frantic with thirst, and their eyes nearly bulged from their sockets. After four days of travel without water, they were well-nigh blind, and could scarcely see where they were going, stumbling against the rocks and trees along their path. . . . Our faith was finally rewarded. . . . On the morning of the fifth [day] we joyfully viewed in the distance the long-sought waters of the Rio del Norte.

" The gaunt horses approached the rolling stream and plunged headlong into it. Two of them drank so much that they burst their sides and died. Two others, blinded by their raving thirst, plunged so far into the stream that they were caught in its swift current and drowned.

" Our men, consumed by the burning thirst, their tongues swollen, and their throats parched, threw themselves into the water and drank as though the entire river did not carry enough to quench their terrible thirst. Then satisfied, they threw themselves upon the cool sands, like foul wretches, stretched upon some tavern floor in a drunken orgy, deformed and swollen and more like toads than men."

Oñate overtook them there with the main body. " It was," crows Villagrá, " a happy meeting. We built a great bonfire and roasted the meat and fish, and then all sat down to a repast the like of which we had never enjoyed before."

This exultant barbecue probably occurred about fifteen miles below the pass, and there the Governor decided to rest while his men looked for a ford. And he improved the days of rest by taking possession of " New Mexico, and of its kingdoms and provinces, as well as those in its vicinity and contiguous thereto." A claim surely generous enough to justify quite a fiesta!

" The Governor then ordered a large chapel built under a

grove of shady trees. Here the priests celebrated a solemn high mass. Then some of the soldiers enacted a drama written by Captain Farfán.

" After this was over, the entire army began celebrating with great joy and mirth. The horsemen gathered in their most gala attire with splendid accouterments and glistening arms. . . ."

The Governor made an address, setting forth the spiritual and temporal reasons for conquering the Indians — naturally, for their own good — and friendly Indians, who had been fed and clothed and loaded with gifts, pointed out the shallow pass — El Paso el Norte.

So Oñate went on to conquer the pueblos up the river and to establish the first capital on the soil of the United States. He recorded his exploits on the face of Inscription Rock in western New Mexico. Many later travelers, Spanish and English, important and merely annoying, have carved their names on that magnificent autograph book; Oñate's, in 1605, is the first.

Many others followed Oñate's route up the *Río del Norte* or *Río Bravo*, fierce river; a name it justifies in flood seasons. In 1659 Fathers García de San Francisco and Juan de Salazar settled ten families of Christianized Indians at the mission of Nuestra Señora de Guadalupe del Paso. It was the first Christian establishment in Texas and the mother of the other Texas missions. The Brown Virgin, Mexico's holy patroness, is still venerated in the original church, though the name of the town was changed to Juárez after that liberator freed Mexico of the French, during our Civil War. Three hamlets grew up along the river, and by the end of the century they counted a couple of hundred villagers. Life must have been very pleasant, for the priests, along with the breviary and the hyssop, had brought the peach tree and the vine and the art of making wine and brandy. They planted grain too, and raised excellent crops, though the average rainfall of less than ten inches made the Rio Grande a very welcome farmer's aid.

From May until November there are infrequent frosts thereabouts, but the climatic curse is wind — ceaseless, nerve-racking wind, laden with stinging alkaline sand. The long growing-season is hot, with occasional rains, often amounting to cloud-bursts. But the erratic climate produces fruits and vegetables of extraordinary flavor, and three and sometimes four times a year the dark-green alfalfa-fields ripple with their purple blossoms and are ready for cutting.

El Paso's first real accretion of population came with tragedy. In 1680 the Indians of the whole province of New Mexico rose against the Spanish and killed hundreds of them. Nobody was spared, and only a few pitiful and terrified survivors rallied round their Governor in Santa Fe and got away to the south. The news reached the missions at El Paso del Norte when the first refugees staggered in, weak and exhausted from the terrible Jornada del Muerto. Governor Otermín found that he had escaped with fifteen hundred and seventy-six whites, with whom he set up camp at El Paso, two months after the Indians had fallen on them in their villages.

For twelve years the Spaniards at the pass were Spain's northern outpost. Then, in 1692, General Don Diego de Vargas Luján Ponce de León rested there on his way to reconquer the lost provinces of the north, " at his own expense." He carried with him, enshrined on her own *carreta,* an image of the Virgin, *La Conquistadora,* to whom he prayed for success. But Spain was not again paramount north of the Rio Bravo until 1698, a hundred years after Oñate's glittering ceremony of taking possession.

During the eighteenth century traffic increased prodigiously. In those days galleons from Spain anchored at Vera Cruz with cargoes of fine carved furniture, brass candelabra, crested, hand-wrought silver plates and goblets, gold-framed mirrors, tapestries and brocades for palaces in New Spain; for the churches, religious paintings by the greatest masters, statues of the saints, jewel-set gold vessels for the altars, priestly vestments, and bronze bells. They brought lace mantillas and tortoise-shell combs for the ladies of the Western courts, satin and velvet gowns, and exquisite laces and embroideries made by nuns in Spain for baptismal gowns and altar cloths. The hidalgo demanded no less elegance, and with his fine Toledo armor and sword, his cannons and arquebuses, were shipped silk-slashed doublets, fine leather goods, watches set with jewels, and gold and silver lace. From Vera Cruz such cargoes went to Mexico on muleback, or loaded on men with thick-muscled legs. There they competed with cargoes landed at Acapulco from China and the Philippines: embroidered shawls, Oriental pearls, spices, carved screens, and painted chests to hold the bridal array. They got rice from the Orient, too, and sugar and chocolate from Mexico. Nothing was too expensive for the masters of Mexico's fabulous silver mines, or too bulky to be carried to the farthest adobe house trying to maintain the formalities of home among the savages.

Even in remotest New Mexico, some men were rich enough to buy such luxuries, which were hauled from Mexico or Zacatecas by mule-trains, or even on carts with solid wooden wheels, screeching and smoking until water was doused to cool them. In the autumn the colonials journeyed south to Chihuahua or even to Mexico in caravans of as many as five hundred men, masters and slaves. The usual trip from Santa

Fe to Chihuahua and back took five months. The New Mexicans offered Indian slaves, buffalo hides, skins of otter, beaver, and muskrat, buckskin dressed soft as satin, blankets woven from their soft-dyed wool, piñon nuts, and salt. They also carried turquoise from the mines near Cerrillos, giving the trail the name of the Turquoise Trail. By 1788, exports from New Mexico were estimated as worth thirty thousand dollars. All of that went for luxuries, because the provinces produced what they ate and ordinarily wore. Much of their imported furniture, paintings, personal finery, and horse trappings may still be found — more of it, alas, in museums than among the families whose ancestors brought it in.

By 1800, El Paso del Norte, our modern Juárez, was a thriving little town where two thousand valley folk did business. It boasted a merchant prince, a ranchman who pastured twenty thousand sheep and a thousand cows, a school, and no vagrants or beggars. Early in the century it was discovered by men from the States, whose increasing numbers and overbearing manners itched the authorities like the light rash before a virulent pox. But traders brought money; Mexico decided to tax them heavily and bear with them. Of the first, we have no record, but the first notable was that ubiquitous Zebulon Montgomery Pike, on his way to Mexico under guard. Kit Carson went through, running away from the saddler to whom he had been apprenticed in Missouri, but that was of no consequence; he went everywhere. In 1839 Josiah Gregg took six wagons through El Paso as part of a caravan of fourteen.

In *Commerce of the Prairies* Gregg describes the town as " the northernmost settlement in the department of Chihuahua. Here our cargo had to be examined by a stern, surly officer, who, it was feared, would lay an embargo on our goods upon the slightest appearance of irregularity in our papers, but notwithstanding our gloomy forebodings, we passed the ordeal without any difficulty.

" The valley of El Paso is supposed to contain a population of about four thousand inhabitants. . . . These settlements are so thickly interspersed with vineyards, orchards, and corn-fields as to present more the appearance of a series of planta-tions than of a town. Here we were regaled with the finest fruits of the season: the grapes especially were of the most exquisite flavor. From these the inhabitants manufacture a very pleasant wine, somewhat resembling Malaga. A species of *aguardiente*, brandy, is also distilled from the same fruit, which, although weak, is of very agreeable flavor."

None of these northerners was more portentous than James Wiley Magoffin. Having paved (or paid) the way for General Kearny's pacific entrance into Santa Fe in '46, Mr. Magoffin set out for Chihuahua, hoping to do as much for General Woll. But at El Paso he was arrested and held prisoner until the war ended. Our government never admitted any official connec-tion with Mr. Magoffin, but Congress later appropriated thirty thousand dollars to reimburse him for his " expenses and losses," though without explaining why a private trader's af-fairs concerned the nation. By that time Mr. Magoffin had established himself on the United States side of the river and given the name of Magoffinsville to the post office, which was later known as Franklin.

There he entertained Mr. W. W. H. Davis, who writes in *El Gringo:* " We stopped there to pay our respects to Mr. M., the proprietor, whom I found living in nabob style in a large Spanish-built house that reminded me somewhat of the feudal ages." That house, with its big rooms, thick walls, three patios, and ditch-watered gardens, still occupies an entire block on Magoffin Avenue, and is lovingly cared for by Mrs. W. J. Glasgow, Mr. Magoffin's granddaughter.

El Paso was merely brushed by the Mexican War. Colonel Alexander W. Doniphan and his Missouri Volunteers, striking south after the capitulation of Santa Fe, met a Mexican troop at Brazito. But the Mexicans, in spite of their blue pantaloons, green coats, scarlet caps, and horsehair plumes, broke at the first fire and fled. Doniphan's men, heralded as infidels, heretics, and barbarians, won general popularity when the colonel ordered them to pay for everything they took. The Mexican troops had paid for nothing. So the Missourians settled down contentedly to eat fruit, drink mescal, pulque, beer, and wine, to gamble in the streets, and to dance at the fandangos.

All that was less important to the growing town than its development as a crossroads. As early as 1825 mail went by pony express from Santa Fe to Chihuahua, and an answer might be expected within three months. In 1854 the United States mail service between San Antonio and Santa Fe began to operate on a twenty-five-day schedule. Stage-lines also carried passengers for a hundred dollars " and found." Travelers were not required to do guard duty, though they were expected to push and to take a gun against Indians if need arose. In '58 the first " transcontinental " line was opened to carry mail and passengers from San Antonio, Texas, to San Diego, California. Its route was disputed by the fiercest tribes of Apaches, but nothing stopped the westward push and the little town of Franklin became a bustling transportation center. El Paso was still the other town on the Mexican side.

The forty-niners and later gold-seekers gave the town its greatest impetus toward growth and wealth. Hundreds of emigrants camped along the river and spent money to repair their wagons and harness, to buy fresh horses and supplies, and to partake of the delights of town. One Cox, in his diary as quoted in the *Southwestern Historical Quarterly,* reported that the " Mexican ladies were kind, warm-hearted, and generous — even to a fault." The men, jealous creatures, resented not only the foreigners' way with women, but their unceremonious manner of moving into their houses and of taking along what stock they needed when they moved out. But every evil-doer was gone before he could be brought to justice, and another had come and any money was good.

In the fifties four little settlements snuggled at the foot of Mount Franklin, and then the Rio Grande, making one of its lazy and muddy shifts, delivered three Mexican villages into the United States and Texas. As this occurred between the signing of the Treaty of Guadalupe Hidalgo and the establishment of the boundary line, it is easy to believe that a malicious imp lurked under the Rio's muddy waves. The river guessed right; the collection of gringo hamlets was to make the city. But that shift created an inordinate amount of confusion in the meantime. Nobody knew what country he lived in, and both governments, to be on the safe side, collected taxes.

During the decade before the Civil War many men laid the foundations of sizable fortunes. Mines were being discovered and lost in the fantastic ways Frank Dobie has set forth in *Coronado's Children* and *Apache Gold and Yaqui Silver.* Free and easy money made for turbulence. Freighters and prospectors, Indian fighters, Mexican-hating gringos, and gringo-hating Mexicans do not create a peaceful atmosphere. Grace Long, whose unpublished thesis " The Anglo-American Occupation of the El Paso District " has given me many facts, says guardedly: " The records do not prove the existence of an effective local government either in Texas or in New Mexico." So much for training in making only thoroughly verifiable statements. El Paso was, as a matter of fact, if not of record, a hot hell of gamblers, gunmen, prostitutes, and law-breakers, escaping from Mexico into the States, and of Americans illegally invading Mexico to retaliate for some Mexican's misdeeds. On neither side of the line could local governments restrain their malefactors.

In the Civil War, El Paso went Confederate with Texas, though with some doubt. The issue of slavery was unimportant; the only slaves were house or body servants in officers' families. The Northern troops evacuated Fort Bliss and Mr. Magoffin hoisted a Confederate flag over it, and Lieutenant-Colonel John R. Baylor arrived from Austin to take command. Confusion was added by the arrival of the defeated Texas force which had tried to hold Santa Fe. The thriving little town of Franklin, which had so richly fed and wined so many passers-by, went down into a miserable huddle of four or five hundred scared people.

Then word came of the advance of the California Column across Arizona. California had decided to stay with the Union, and General Carleton was marching east to hold the territory acquired from Mexico. The Confederates abandoned Fort Bliss, not in the best order; ostensible peace was established and the Overland Mail ran again. Actually only one more hate had been added to the older ones. Politics would for many years be embittered by sectional feeling. Democrats were resentful Confederates; Republicans, scornful Yankees.

But Northerner or Southerner, the gringo became the dominant force, held the offices, and controlled the elections in ways more comical than admirable. Rounding up batches of

Mexicans across the border, holding them overnight in high-walled corrals, and voting them at two bits a head was an accepted electioneering method. Laws, interpreted by Anglos who knew little Spanish, less Spanish law, and had little respect for either, were apt to favor the newcomer. Inevitably El Paso had its " war."

A hundred miles north of the town lay a great salt lake where people had for centuries dug salt for themselves and their animals. Then Charles Howard, with a Northerner's eye for business, filed on the land and ordered the Mexican salt-takers off. The Mexican could not understand that a new government admitted new rights, that one single individual might legally own those open lakes. He continued to drive his burro out there and dig salt.

Luis Cardis, an Italian who saw a chance to build a useful political machine, inflamed the Mexicans against the gringo heretic. He found two helpful allies in Chico Barela, a Mexican, and Father Borajo, the priest at the mission of Guadalupe, who is alleged to have sent word: " Kill all the gringos and I will absolve you." Whether he did or not, many armed Mexicans crossed the border. Howard killed Cardis, his bondsmen were killed, fighting was general, the commanding officer at Fort Bliss proved too slow to be useful, and the Rangers were called for. As always in these ructions, the best men of both heritages stood together. But bitter hatreds were sown. Both Howard and Cardis were to blame, and, most of all, the priest who added religious intolerance to the misunderstandings of language and custom.

Business continued to flourish. Vegetables, fruit, and grain found a market at Fort Bliss and were shipped out along all the trails. The legitimate cattle business competed with the sneaking of " wet " herds across the Rio Grande; but in spite of smuggling, duty was paid on almost half a million dollars' worth of imports in 1882. By that year El Paso had a street car and many frame houses which, though less comfortable, were thought more elegant than adobe. Saloons grew bigger and more ornate, and houses of prostitution, from tiny *jacales* (huts) up back streets, became drawing-rooms, furnished in the best Kansas City style. El Paso boasted of being the wickedest town between Kansas City and San Francisco, and young *elegantes* from New Mexico who could not quite afford the trip to Mexico City found ample opportunity to lose their sheep money and to mortgage their land grants right in El Paso. In those days towns advertised their iniquities as a business asset. Creede, Colorado, boasted: " It's day all day in the daytime, and we have no night at all."

The town's location kept on making its fate. Railroads found the same pass that had been known by Indians, conquerors, traders, gold-seekers, and armies. Six hundred miles from San Antonio, eight hundred and fifty from Denver and from Los Angeles, twelve hundred from Mexico, El Paso was bound to grow. In 1878 four trunk lines began to overlay the old trails with iron rails and to replace the old six-mule teams with iron engines. The Atchison, Topeka, & Santa Fe came down the Chihuahua Trail, the Southern Pacific found a less mountainous route down the Pecos Valley. The Texas Pacific and the Harrisburg & San Antonio more or less paralleled the old Butterfield Trail. In time they would be met at the pass by the Mexico Central coming up from Chihuahua. O. H. Bassett and H. L. Newman made El Paso's first big money when they cleared seventy-five thousand dollars on a contract to grade a hundred and fifty miles of right of way for the Texas & Pacific. But everybody got a cut. El Paso was the crossroads town. In 1878 the old mission towns of Ysleta, San

Elizario, and Socorro were paying eighty per cent of the county taxes; three years later the balance was the other way, and the gringos were the dominant group.

El Paso, like other towns, was finding business more lucrative than vice. A lot which had been traded for a wagonload of wood and a muzzle-loading shotgun, sold for ten thousand dollars. Men less improvident than the real pioneer began cautiously to pile up money and to establish families who could forever bask in the consciousness of superiority. Crude boasting of luck gave way to more gentlemanly gloating over thrift and enterprise.

In the days of Porfirio Díaz, the widely admired Mexican dictator, who kept the peace with his rurales and who favored United States investors above all Mexicans, El Paso was a mecca for wealthy Mexicans.

Terrazas, who owned most of the state of Chihuahua, and who ran four million head of cattle on seventeen haciendas, made frequent regal visits. He was wont to arrive with a band and a retinue of a hundred relatives and hangers-on. They would engage a whole hotel or several houses, and the ladies not seldom spent five or ten thousand dollars a day in the shops. This makes it easier to understand why starving peons, once they had the power, expropriated the Terrazas lands.

Few people could imagine the end of such grandeur; peons were like that — submissive, and fond of living on a handful of beans and a growing debt. That peons could ever revolt and make a revolution stick was inconceivable. But El Paso was to see one of the last acts of the old days, when our President Taft met Mexico's President Díaz on the international bridge. Each country tried to outdo the other in splendor and elegance. El Paso blazed with colored electric lights, fluttered with bunting and flags. The Army policed the town. Our

88

President was unquestionably bigger, probably the biggest President ever seen, but he was quite outshone by the Mexican's magnificence. In Juárez the old stone customs building was hung with priceless tapestries from Mexico's palaces, the banquet was served on gold plates bearing the Emperor Maximilian's crest, and carloads of jasmines and gardenias, orchids and lilies decked the tables. President Díaz, in a plumed chapeau, rode to meet his guest in a gold-lacquered carriage, driven by prancing thoroughbreds in gold-plated harness.

Then came the Revolution, and El Paso had a box-seat for almost every act in it. The town was full of newspaper men and rumors, and often business was suspended so everybody could watch the shelling of Juárez from the roofs and upstairs windows. Successive generals and presidents knew El Paso: Francisco Madero, tiny, dapper, and visionary; Carranza, the Constitutional Chief, with his bushy beard and his blue goggles; and Villa and his butcher, Rodolfo Fierro.

Villa was known by hundreds of people. Years later when the motion picture *Pancho Villa* was presented, the balconies were packed with ex-Villistas who went to sneer, but stayed to cheer. Wallace Beery did not look the part, but he had so caught the spirit of Pancho, his dash and bravado, that as the film unrolled, the audience rose whooping and yelling; and the picture played ten days to packed houses.

Victoriano Huerta, during his ascendancy, used to drive into El Paso in a big blue auto to eat strange gringo food. An El Pasoan who knew him well describes him as " saddle-colored, with high cheek-bones, aquiline nose, square-shouldered, and baldish. He was always immaculately groomed, with puttees over his soft Mexican shoes, and a silver-corded military cap." Once when he had come north after Orozco, a group of men gave him a dinner at the Sheldon Hotel. Huerta was unpopular with the revolutionary element along the border, and as he entered the hotel a crowd yelled threateningly. The general, pretending their shouts were approving, bowed right and left and walked unhurriedly through. After his fall he lived in Europe, but, trying to get back to Mexico through the United States, he was apprehended in New Mexico and put on his word of honor not to leave El Paso. There he died.

Pascual Orozco also was a familiar figure in El Paso. His name, his blue eyes and red hair, and his tallness are reputed to come from one O'Roscoe, of Doniphan's Missouri Volunteers. A man of no education, General Orozco was highly intelligent and many El Pasoans came to admire him. The United States got him, finally, for conspiring against our neutrality. He jumped his bail, spent an afternoon with his family, and by the time the federal officers got wind of it, General Orozco had gone. But he, too, died in El Paso, and four different revolutionary armies marched in his funeral procession.

El Paso is a bilingual town, and in spite of much undercover bad feeling and its occasional flare-ups, it continues to profit greatly by its large Spanish-speaking population. Mexicans are more popular in good times than in bad. El Paso has shipped in thousands to work in the cotton-fields, on the railroads, even as far north as the Colorado sugar-beet fields. When work fell off and the El Paso district tried to get five hundred and eighty-eight Mexicans off the relief rolls, it was found they had all paid their poll tax. Even now some seven hundred Mexicans who live in Juárez work in El Paso as domestics, as clerks in stores and offices. This naturally annoys the gringo, especially as the Mexican is generally quicker at languages and much of El Paso's business is done in two tongues. An editor told me that the young American-born Mexican who has just emerged from high school, the first generation to do so, is more employable than his Nordic schoolmate. His English is purer, his Spanish is good, and he reads the newspapers. This editor was amazed to find that his paper had a circulation of between three and four thousand in the Mexican quarter. The young Mexican is on the up-and-up. He is steadily raising his family standard of living, moving them out of the long rows of adobe rooms which are the typical tenement, and into separate houses. Mexicans have real family solidarity; as one improves, so do they all. These people will not be an exploitable class much longer.

Perhaps this bilingual heritage keeps El Paso more tolerant, and more amused by itself, than the rest of Texas. El Pasoans chuckle about how expeditiously they got rid of the Ku Klux Klan in 1921, when white sheets dominated Texas politics; how they gave Al Smith a majority, when Protestant Texas had stampeded against the Catholics; how they withstood the seductions of Governor O'Daniel and his hill-billy band. All this is nicely reflected in a recent episode. The Methodist ladies, organizing for Chinese relief, rented from the Knights of Columbus a hall which the Baptists had recently occupied. And there, in a closet, they found a set of Ku Klux Klan regalia!

In its two languages El Paso does business in four c's: cotton, cattle, copper, and climate. The South's " King Cotton " has moved West with irrigation, and El Paso has grown into one of the great cotton markets of the country.

Cattle brings less money to El Paso than cotton does, but more flavor, for cattlemen's conventions still like the ornate, marble-lined Hotel Paso del Norte; and its reach is international. Many herds from Mexico are brought into the States to fatten for the market.

Copper mines in New Mexico, Arizona, and Chihuahua ship ore to El Paso smelters, which in big times have vied in importance with those even of Montana.

Cotton, cattle, and copper are business anywhere. In the Southwest, climate is also business. El Paso advertises sunshine for eighty per cent of the possible hours; and without mentioning dread diseases, suggests sunshine as a cure-all. Juárez, just across the international bridge, offers night clubs, old missions, Mexican markets, and bull-fights. The outdoor man can fare farther into Chihuahua to hunt big game or to see strange Indians. Big game also range in the Big Bend, where the Rio Grande has swung south and scooped a hundred square miles of Mexican mountains into Texas. Deer and turkey and even bear offer fine sport in the Guadalupe Range in New Mexico, and there, too, El Pasoans find relief from their summer, too sunny at last, on noisy trout streams and in the coolness of eight- and nine-thousand-foot peaks. Desert quail scurry through the mesquite thickets along the border, and ducks and geese rest on the Rio Grande, or winter there. The Carlsbad Caverns and Elephant Butte Lake's boating and fishing (both a hundred miles up into New Mexico) figure as part of El Paso's lure for the sun-seeker.

The little city's situation is still her destiny. More Western than Southern, she is international too. Four states, one in Mexico, meet and amalgamate at the ford of the Rio Grande, the pass through the mountains where the crossroads hamlet has grown into a center of international business and culture.

The road

from El Paso to Tucson unrolls like a preview of Arizona.
Forty-niners and settlers plodded in that sand, weary foot
after weary foot, so slowly that the mountains seemed always
a week away. It was the Apache's perfect raiding-ground,
where he could elude soldiers of both republics by slipping
across the border, back and forth, like a ghostly, gray coyote,
or make himself invisible by standing still against a cactus
or crouching behind a creosote bush.

It was a prospector's paradise, too. The old Spanish silver-
workings at Santa Rita were developed by the Chino Copper
Company into one of the world's greatest producers of copper. Their engineer, James Douglas, gave his name to the
town which, with its twin, Agua Prieta, straddles the border.
Douglas advised the Phelps Dodge Company to buy the Copper Queen in Brewery Gulch for forty thousand dollars and
lived to see them take a hundred million out of it. He lived,
too, to see Brewery Gulch become Bisbee, the most vicious
and sordid town on the border, and finally a model mining
town. It still climbs up the canyon's sides, with a hotel on
a level with the church steeple. But it has forgotten the
lurid days of the Hog Ranch and its famous old girl who
gave her name to the Irish Mag Mine.

VI

TUCSON:
DESERTS AND DUDES

TUCSON, PERHAPS MORE THAN ANY OTHER SPOT IN THE Southwest, and certainly more recently, has come the whole way from a wilderness of terrific hazards to a winter resort for pampered plutocrats; from a town where one's own blanket in the open plaza was a better bed than any in the infested hotel, and one's own cookery preferable to the " Shoo-fly Restaurant," to dude ranches of metropolitan luxury. Arizona, after centuries of tricking the explorer onto waterless wastes, of tantalizing the prospector and letting him starve, of subjecting both to the savagery of Indian attacks, now lies purring like a tamed tiger to be clambered all over by people who wouldn't normally venture beyond a cottage garden-gate.

Tucson's encircling mountains look bare and rugged from the plain. But over their hard contours the changing light runs modulations of color as rich as organ tones. Pale and stark at midday, mellow afternoon shadows make their cinnamon-colored flanks stand out from purple canyons. At sunset a glow fills the valley bowl, surges up the mountainsides, and shoots along the crests above tree fringes brushed in in blue. Even midnight on the Tucson desert is filled with color. The sky is never black — just deeper blue, as though the thick-set stars illumined more than the sun could show. All around Tucson one may turn off the paved highways and follow illy marked tracks over silver-golden sand and among leafless shrubs and stunted trees, whose need for water has made shapes stranger than a dream. And, like a dream, it fools you every time. The fuzzy nap on the elkhorn cactus turns out to be vicious spines; the cholla's fish-hook barbs jump out to dig at your flesh. The flat, smooth beavertail has hidden prickles that leave an angry smart. But quick eyes will see delicate white poppies, fragile primroses set in a scalloped plate of leaves, and holly bushes with silvery leaves and berries.

Later, when the heat has driven off the dudes, the desert, as though relieved to be alone, stages its glory-show of bloom. The tun-like barrel cactus lifts its red flower-crown, ocotillo cracks its coachman's whip into tips of flame, and low-growing cacti set magenta, pink, and purple blooms like roses in cushions full of pins. And everything is scented by the all-green palo-verde, when its leafless stems and twigs flower, honey-colored and sweet. The saguaro bears yellow blossoms, too: Arizona's state flower. Here the saguaro reaches such height and such dense profusion that a forest growth of it has been declared a National Monument. Magnificent always, when the setting sun or the moon throws a tangle of blue-black shadows on the sand, the saguaro forest fully refutes the error that a desert is unlovely. Dangerous and inhospitable, yes; death for men who do not know it; meager living for those who depended upon it exclusively. But for the traveler in today's security, the desert has a beauty no fabled wood ever equaled.

This desert's fabulous quality has marked its history too, for southern Arizona has repeatedly vanished from man's ken and had to be rediscovered. In 1539 Fray Marcos de Niza short-cut across it, guided by Cabeza de Vaca's black companion, Estevan, whose tales of golden cities with turquoise-studded doorways had all Mexico abuzz. The monk was to spy out the land and report to the Viceroy. Leaving Culiacán, Sinaloa, on March 7, it was early in May when Fray Marcos and his Indian guides came down the little San Pedro River and crossed into what is now Arizona. Estevanico had gone ahead, prancing among Indians he made to serve him, choosing the most comely girls, freeing his slave's inhibitions, and finally getting himself killed in Zuñi. But he had sent the monk crosses bigger than a man, the sign of great wealth ahead. So Fray Marcos went on across the southeastern corner of Arizona and from a hill saw one of the Zuñi villages — Hawikuh. Estevanico was dead and the chopped-up pieces of his body portioned out among the chiefs, so Fray Marcos only looked, and returned to report in Mexico that from his hilltop the town he saw looked " greater than the City of Mexico."

The next year Coronado, the Conqueror, followed him, dazzled by the monk's hearsay reports and the fabulous rumors they grew into in Mexico. Twenty years after Cortez's conquest of Mexico young men were bored with peace and spoiling to conquer another Montezuma and his treasure. The Viceroy, Don Antonio de Mendoza, who saw wisdom in getting restless lads out of Mexico, equipped an expedition and named Francisco Vásquez de Coronado its commander. On February 3 the Viceroy himself launched the expedition from Campostela. It was a magnificent display. Coronado, in gilded armor, rode ahead of two hundred caballeros with helmets, breast-plates and armor sparkling. They quickened or reined down spirited horses and dipped their standards to His Excellency and the general's pretty young wife beside him. Seventy foot-soldiers swung briskly by, armed with crossbows and arque-buses and protected by heavy leather jerkins and steel helmets. They were supported by three hundred Mexicans (as Mexi-can-born Spaniards were already called) and a thousand Indian and Negro servants to drive the spare horses, pack animals, and the cows and sheep for food.

That splendid send-off was the prelude to a long series of disheartening disappointments. Glittering armor was hot in that tropical region, and so heavy that men heaved it off, or sank under it. The historian Obregón, writing in 1584, said: " Coronado's army marched through very hot lands full of rocks, mosquitoes, and crags." They were young men and vigorous, but they suffered between the grueling sun and the hot sand slithering under their thinning boots. They, too, came down the San Pedro River. Coronado, the first white man to conquer in our Southwest, had entered what is now the United States. Disappointment met him everywhere. Fray Marcos's great city turned out to be a mud-walled village, where the only turquoises were ornaments, and only the maize was golden.

The stories of Fray Marcos and of Coronado are the theme of a four-hundredth anniversary celebration in the four modern states Coronado saw. Though it has the stuff of high romance and drama, the tale has been told only by sober historians, and in books for children. The best account for one who wants the story free of entangling scholarly disputes is *The Adventure of Don Francisco Vásquez de Coronado* by G. P. Hammond and E. F. Goad.

After Coronado, explorers followed the route through El Paso del Norte, and southern Arizona slipped out of memory for over a hundred years. Coronado's captains had looked aghast into the Grand Canyon; Espejo and Oñate had crossed Arizona's northern plateau; and Oñate had satisfied himself that California was a peninsula and not an island. But the Papago and Pima Indians remained untroubled in their desert except by their perennial enemies, the Apaches, until 1687, when Christianity came along in the person of the Jesuit, Father Eusebio Francisco Kino.

A cultivated Austrian, Father Kino had come to Mexico asking for the farthest and most dangerous missionary post. But martyrdom was not to be his fate, for no more docile Indians ever bowed to baptism than the Pimas and the Papagoes. One historian marvels at the courage of the " *Padre on Horseback* " in traveling with only Indian servants. But Padre Kino had trouble with Indians only when the military tried to protect him; and an experienced traveler in any age would prefer Indians to soldiers as guides over such country. During his twenty-four years in *la Pimería,* Pimaland, Father Kino made fifty journeys of from a hundred to a thousand miles. He knew all of Sonora and Arizona, and enough of California to learn again that it was a peninsula. He observed everything, understood much, and baptized forty-five hundred Indians. But he was greatest as a builder. Across the Pimería he erected nine missions which dot the map like a necklace of crosses. All still stand and all are beautiful; none more so than the northernmost one at San Xavier del Bac, nine miles from the present Tucson. Padre Kino had only time to lay its foundations before he died; after the Jesuit Order had been expelled from Mexico, the Franciscans put on its ivory-toned dome and towers.

THE JOSHUA TREE. DESERT GROWTH MAKES BEAUTY
OUT OF ITS STRUGGLE FOR WATER

[photo, Ruth Frank]

IRRIGATION DITCHES CAN TURN DESERTS INTO
FERTILE FIELDS

[photo, Ruth Frank]

Meanwhile Spain had established a presidio at Tubac on the Santa Cruz River. That shortlived town is most notable for two who set out from there — Juan Bautista de Anza and Padre Francisco Tomás Hermengildo Garcés. The soldier, de Anza, crossed to the Golden Gate, where he built a small fort, Yerba Buena, which grew up into San Francisco. He also brought word that California was part of the mainland. Garcés covered as much territory as Padre Kino did, but on his own sandaled feet, in the humble Franciscan way, and without the servants who were an inevitable part of the scholarly Jesuit's missionarying. He was killed at last in his own mission at Yuma.

Tubac went into desuetude in 1776, when presidio and mission were moved to San José de Tucson, which may glory in the founding date easiest of all to remember. Spain maintained only a handful of troops there, and the few settlers who stayed cowered in the adobe-walled town, fearful of Apaches, or made desperate sorties against them. Spain had found neither mines nor Indians that were worth exploiting, and Arizona was terra incognita again. It was half a century before the United States entered it, pushed first by expanding population, then by interest in her conquest from Mexico, and finally by the lure of California's gold.

The forerunners of the Nordic invasion typically went alone or in twos and threes. Mountain men appeared as early as the twenties, trapping beaver along the streams, killing deer and elk, and making good money as long as the market lasted. At home in Bent's Fort, in Taos, and in Santa Fe, they soon crossed the divide into New Mexico's hinterland and trapped down the Gila, the Salt, the Verde, and the Colorado. They pushed their patient burros along all the trails the Indians and the missionaries knew, laying out future stage and railroad routes. Most mountain men stuck to the piny plateau in northern Arizona. Only a rare and venturesome one went across to California, like James O. Pattie, who in his *Personal Narrative* recounts a romantic tale of his trek across the desert, his arrest in San Diego, and his rescue from jail by the jailer's sympathetic daughter. But generally Tucson was off their route, and nothing disturbed its dusty quietude until after the Mexican War.

Commissioner Bartlett refers to Tucson as " the most northern town in Sonora," with adobe houses, " a majority in ruins." But Gadsden's Purchase added it to the United States, and the discovery of gold in California shook it awake. Few gold-seekers went by El Paso and Tucson compared with the thousands who streamed along the northern trails. But Tucson was soon bustling with wagon-yards and blacksmiths, merchants, and a wide assortment of drinking, gambling, and whoring places. Then, in 1858, the first Butterfield stage dashed through on its phenomenal twenty-five-day run from St. Louis to San Francisco.

By the middle of the fifties the whole country was demanding a regular mail and passenger service across " the Great American Desert " to the gold-fields. Routes were discussed with acrimony. Both sections wanted California, in case of the war all foresaw. Southern influence won and swung the route far south by way of El Paso and Tucson — a distance of nearly twenty-eight hundred miles. The North raged about the " horseshoe " or " ox-bow " route. But Mr. Butterfield bought a hundred Concord spring wagons and square-bodied coaches, four-horse teams for each; he built stations, dug wells, and armed his drivers and special guards. It was said that so many drivers were killed by Indians that the company saved more

100

in wages than it paid. But the line kept on. The desert had been jumped, if not conquered.

Arizona never disappeared from human cognizance again. Indeed, its doings became so spectacular that it stayed on the front pages for generations. Every wildness of the West was heightened in Arizona into a grandiose extravaganza. Its Indian depredations were more fiendish; its Indian wars fiercer and longer; its bad men more daring and desperate; its wild towns wilder than anywhere else. This was partly because Arizona's magnificent peaks and crags, stupendous canyons, and upland valleys were perfect hide-aways for raiding Apaches or cattle-rustlers and desperadoes. And partly because, as Texas and New Mexico cleaned their bad men out, they moved over into Arizona. Then, as Apaches and bad men were rounded up or stamped out, Arizona prospectors began to strike mines of stupendous richness. Arizona was no longer terra incognita; it was *Helldorado*, as W. M. Breakenridge called his book about Tombstone.

Tucson, as Spanish and then Confederate capital, Army post, and stage station, was too busy to clean up, as J. Ross Browne's *Adventures in the Apache Country* makes unflatteringly clear:

" If the world were searched over, I suppose there could not be found so degraded a set of villains as then formed the principal society of Tucson. Every man went armed to the teeth, and street fights and bloody affrays were of daily occurrence. Since the coming of the California Volunteers the state of things . . . has materially changed . . . volunteer soldiers are stationed all over town — at the mescal shops, the monte tables, and houses of illfame. . . . Citizens in small parties of five or six go out whenever occasion requires and

101

afford aid and comfort to unfortunate travelers who happen
to be waylaid in pursuit of their legitimate business. Papago
Indians do good service also by following up and killing the
hostile Indians who infest the country. . . . It is confidently
believed, therefore, that so long as the troops are kept within
the precincts of the ancient Pueblo of Tucson, they will not
be molested by any enemy of a more deadly character than
mescal."

Whether Mr. Browne was right, or merely piffled, soldiers
in blue wool, encumbered by heavy accouterment and slowed
down by commissary trains, had a lot to learn before they were
a match for Apaches. Unhampered by clothes, the Apache
always managed to procure excellent guns and ammunition
from someone. He rode his horse until it dropped, and then
butchered and ate it. He traveled faster afoot, knew how to
find water, and throve on a diet of prairie mice, rattlesnake,
and lizard, varied by mescal root, mesquite beans, the fruit
of the Spanish bayonet and the prickly pear. He did so well
in his country and was so a part of it that the primary difficulty in fighting Apaches was finding the Apache. The Army
was also greatly embarrassed by capricious changes of policy
in Washington.

After the Mexican War, Apaches were ready to treat with
the United States. Mangas Colorado asked Commissioner
Bartlett for terms which would allow the Apache some land.
Cochise made friends with the Butterfield stage agent. Many
trappers, prospectors, and ranchers had Apache friends who
protected them even from other Apaches. But neither race
could control its own, nor understand the other's point of view.
The Apache found the bluecoat utterly incomprehensible.
First he fought Mexicans, then he protected them. Then he
fought his own kind. And he never could distinguish between

peaceful Apaches honorably keeping a treaty, and a warring lot who drove off cattle and murdered innocent people. Apaches ran in small bands, and one knew nothing of the doings of the others; but to many white men every Apache was " a lying skulking thief," due for a killing on sight. Such men, even Army men, invited Apaches to powwows and filled them with shot or poisoned pinole. General George Crook, commanding in Arizona in the sixties and seventies, said: " The American Indian commands respect for his rights only as long as he inspires terror for his rifle."

General Crook was a soldier. " They sent him out to get them, and of course he went and did." But once he had captured the Apache, it was his policy to treat him like a human being; to give him land, teach him to dig ditches, to farm and to handle stock; and to pay him for the work he did. Crook might have civilized the Apache if it had not been for the political power of men who wanted to sell food to the government for Indians on rations, and arms to Indians on the warpath. Then, when mismanagement, private peculation, and failure to differentiate between good and bad Apaches had driven that whole people into a fiendish frenzy of war, Quakers got the ear of President Grant, and a policy of conciliation was adopted. The Apaches naturally took that for weakness.

A readable side-light on the whole question is given in *Apache Agent*, the story of John P. Clum as told by his son, Woodworth Clum. John Clum went to Arizona in 1874, when he was twenty-one years old. He liked Apaches and made them his friends. He organized the first troop of Apache scouts and with them actually captured the redoubtable Geronimo in Hot Springs, New Mexico. Then, as Mr. Woodworth Clum writes me, " He marched him back to San Carlos, Arizona; put him in the guard-house and gave the key to the army. The army saw fit to unlock the door and give Geronimo his freedom — in 1877. For the ensuing nine years Geronimo committed arson and murder at will and defied five thousand troops under Crook. He was never captured — before or after 1877. In 1886 Geronimo surrendered for the eleventh time, and Miles, who had succeeded the impotent Crook, simply put the renegades into a railroad train headed for Florida. . . . The tragedy of it all is that if the army had not turned Geronimo loose in 1877, some two or three hundred innocent people would not have been murdered; there never would have been an Apache campaign, and a half dozen army officers would never have achieved doubtful reputations as Indian fighters."

All this activity made a good market for beef. During the fifties New Mexico (including the present Arizona) was dotted with forts, manned by about seventeen hundred men and costing about three million dollars yearly. Even before the Civil War a few herds had been driven over Apache Pass to Tucson, and even on to Fort Yuma and into California. Soon after the war John Chisum made good profits on a herd of his " jingle bobs " and many Texans followed him. Arizona's cattle business was pretty lawless at the beginning. Southeastern Arizona offered an alluring field for the rustler. Well-stocked Mexican haciendas across the line; well-watered valleys in the Chiricahua and Huachuca mountains where brands could be altered; a good market for beef in the booming mining towns, and a public opinion which thought stealing from Mexicans was no great crime. Paul I. Wellman, in *The Trampling Herd,* estimates that the Clantons and the McLowerys commanded more than three hundred outlaws in their hangouts in the San Pedro and Sulphur Springs valleys. Many cattle fortunes founded in those days do not bear much looking into. A man might be a law officer or an outlaw, according to political changes, and many who started as outlaws became most law-abiding as their herds grew. Big outfits were built up all across New Mexico and Arizona. Haggin and Hearst had one near Engle, New Mexico, that included eight hundred thousand acres. The Hashknife ran sixty thousand head up around Flagstaff and Holbrook in the eighties. And the Chiricahua Cattle Company, popularly called the Cherry Cow, claimed as many on the southern ranges. Such outfits naturally wanted peace, and cattlemen's associations sprang up all over the West. Arizona followed Texas' example by founding a ranger troop. Its first captain, Burton C. Mossman, still sits on his front porch at Roswell, New Mexico, and tells salty tales of the good old days; and Wyatt Earpp, whose story Stuart Lake wrote as *The Frontier Marshal,* spread law and order over a wide area out of Tombstone.

Tombstone was the gaudiest of Arizona's mining towns, though not the first. Charles Poston had mined silver at Tubac in the fifties, and maintained a baronial establishment, which he himself described as " a community in a perfect state of nature. We had no law but love, and no occupation but labor. No government, no taxes, no public debt, no politics." But when J. Ross Browne came along in '64, it was a deserted village again. Frank C. Lockwood's *Pioneer Days in Arizona* lists dozens of spectacular strikes; every Arizonan can tell how many times a millionaire he would be if only his forebear had held on, or sold out, or done something a bit different. But Tombstone is the best of all, perhaps because the town is so amusing today, with the newspaper John Clum founded, *The Epitaph,* its Boothill Cemetery, and its Bird Cage Theatre, which in its day was the biggest and best between San Francisco and St. Louis.

Tombstone's rich ore-body was discovered by Ed Schief-felin, one of those inveterate, undauntable prospectors. For years he roamed with burro and pick, working only when he needed a stake, sure he would some day strike it rich. Finally he turned up a bit of ore in the Huachucas which interested an assayer; at Tucson John S. Vosburg, a gunsmith, staked them to three hundred dollars' worth of groceries; and the great Tombstone strike was on. Schieffelin called it that because doubters had told him he would find only his tombstone. What he found was a series of gold mines, which produced millions before water drowned them out in 1909, and the Phelps Dodge Corporation bought the property in 1911. Ed Schieffelin and his brother had sold out for a mere six hundred thousand dollars. As usual, the original discoverer did not make the biggest profits.

Neither gold nor silver, however, was to be Arizona's biggest source of wealth. The copper which had attracted little attention until 1875 became immensely important as the increasing use of electricity demanded it, and Arizona's most extravagant tales deal with copper mines. They have been told by Ira Joralemon in *Romantic Copper* with the sound knowledge of a mining engineer and a rare and racy humor. Especially his chapter on Bill Greene of Cananea shows how the grandiosity of Arizona went over into comic extravaganza. In 1890 Bill Greene was a forty-year-old roustabout who punched cows, drove government teams, worked as a miner in Tombstone, even sold wood by the burro-load; but Bill was a gambler who wanted to make big money as the men on Wall Street did. Once when he was trailing steers in Mexico he saw copper on Cananea Mountain. Bill was a big, good-looking fellow, and he knew how to get along with Mexicans. So he acquired the rights to mines which the widow Pesquiera had inherited and could not work. Bill organized a company of old mining friends at Tombstone, and went to New York to sell stock. In a Prince Albert coat and huge black Arizona sombrero, treating to drinks and black cigars and tipping bellhops with five-dollar bills, plain Bill became Colonel Greene. But the millions eluded him until he cleaned up twenty thousand dollars at Canfield's. Then he shook down Tom Lawson for a million dollars. After that, Colonel Greene's ups and downs would seem incredible, even in the movies. At the up, in 1905, he was riding around in his private car, *The Verde,* and to three mining companies he had added a cattle ranch which extended a hundred miles along the Arizona-Sonora border and sixty miles south. His Herefords were the finest in the country; and Bill was the greatest feudal lord in Mexico and the Southwest's greatest financial wizard on Wall Street, where his four companies were quoted at a hundred million dollars. Then Colonel Greene collapsed with a reverberating crash. The Amalgamated Copper Company took over the mines and let Bill live out his life as a sort of pensioner.

Bill Greene was the last of Arizona's theatrical giants. Mines are now owned and operated by large companies and directed by scientific engineers. Nobody's burro falls into an old Spanish mine shaft which turns out to be a great silver lode. Prospectors spend their time giving Frank Dobie material for his books on lost mines. And Arizona's ranches have gone over from cattle to dudes. They may still run cattle, but " staying on a ranch " implies a cabin with private bath, innerspring mattresses, and Mexican pottery and Indian rugs. Even the name " dude ranch " of such good Western tradition is being replaced by " guest ranch."

In the beginning the dude was an Easterner or a European who went west to hunt. Often experienced hunters and horsemen, they slept in the bunk-house, ate at the ranch table, did their own roping and saddling, and "made a hand" at the rodeos. Payment was out of the question. Such places as Wetherill's at Kayenta, Hubbell's at Ganado, and scores of others hospitably offered what they had and "learned the dude the West." His status was implied by the fact that the man set to look after him was called a "dude-wrangler." The horse-wrangler was the green hand who looked after the extra horses.

Who would have dared, thirty or even twenty years ago, to tell a stockman that his ranch's casual visitor would one day be its mainstay? Yet as times grew harder and dudes more numerous, money changed hands. The whole spirit of the Southwest changed with that first dollar, but it took an Easterner to see the possibilities. In 1898 a New Yorker advertised the Triangle T near Oracle, Arizona, as a place for riding and getting Western atmosphere. From that simple start grew a business complicated beyond all foreseeing. Ranch people, having lured them out, began catering to their dudes. Table-cloths and window-screens appeared. Then fruits and vegetables had to be trucked in over roads that made broken springs a daily expectancy. For a long time dudes could be kidded into the notion that a wash-bowl and pitcher and an outhouse were atmosphere; then somebody put in a bath, and every dude rancher saw his profits disappear underground in pumps, pipes, and septic tanks. City sanitation is now expected forty miles from a railroad and in an arid land. Trying to pump enough water out of a desert to satisfy city folk who cannot imagine a water shortage puts that look of desperation in the dude ranch manager's eye.

Dude ranches dot the whole Southwest, but they differ widely. Texas does little more than take in summer boarders.

Goat ranches in the hill country provide cabins and horses to give Houston, Galveston, and San Antonio people a chance to escape their steaming summers. Cattle ranches in the brush country or out on the high plains offer dudes the old sort of hospitality and wrangling. Only a couple of ranches bid for winter business from the North, though San Antonio's wealthy winter people doubtless will soon begin to demand similar accommodations on ranches.

New Mexico, with a few exceptions, is summer country to the Easterner; places above four thousand feet altitude are too cold for winter vacationing. An ardent ski fan hoped to make Santa Fe rival Sun Valley. There, he said, one could only ski and get drunk; in Santa Fe one could ski, get drunk, and go to Indian dances. But the snow turned out to be undependable, and perhaps skiers are seldom Indian fanciers as well. So New Mexico's dudes are put up in log cabins on trout streams, well mounted, well fed, and taken to Indian dances.

Only desert Arizona and California have raised dude wrangling to a high, almost an esoteric art. Still called a ranch — a guest ranch — places named from old cattle brands, Flying V, Forked Lightning, Cross Anchor, and Circle Z, offer not only all the comforts, but all the luxuries of both city and country club. Elaborate suites of rooms or separate cottages are supplemented by tennis courts, golf links, and polo-fields; swimming-pools and sun-decks, card-rooms, bars, and dance floors. Today's wrangler needs the gifts of a kindergartner, a dietician, and a psychiatrist. Often the role is divided between a hostess, operating under a dare to make the " guest " have a good time, and the cowboy, who leads his dudes over fool-proof trails on steady, sure-footed ponies, who obliges with song and dance at night and with romance at all hours. Marriages between cowboys and debutantes have become standard stuff for Western fiction. One ranch — in Texas, as it happens — has started a colony of such young couples, who add atmosphere to the parties and come in to help at rush times.

All this naturally costs money. Simpler places come within the reach of the average traveler. But big places think nothing of asking a hundred dollars a week. Often rates are figured to include one's choice of cigarette and liquor, and the diet the doctor ordered. Roughing it on a ranch is on a par with life in a sanatorium for nervous wrecks. I looked at one — from a respectful distance — where they had just installed a filtering plant for the swimming-pool. In northern New Mexico mountain water must be processed before the dudes could swim in it. Surely it will be scented by another season.

Tucson, above all, lives primarily by and for dudes. Little is left to suggest the dusty desolation Mr. Bartlett and Mr. Browne knew. Less is done to preserve the buildings of Spanish or pioneer days. " The Governor's Palace," unlike the shrines in San Antonio and Santa Fe, is baited for dudes with a smart clothes shop, a restaurant, and a curio store. The old Ornadorff Hotel, a two-story adobe with a patio the four-horse stages dashed into, has been cleared out of the way. The Church of San Augustin served as a garage for several years, and finally was mercifully torn down and its carved stone façade bought by someone for his home. In their place are smart hotels, restaurants, and bars, frequented by *Vogue* and *Esquire* people, who leave their yachts in Guaymas Bay and dash across Sonora to a polo match or rodeo in Tucson.

From the center, long, straight, tree-topped streets run out for miles onto the desert. Houses in town take boarders.

Tourist camps make a fringe. The university covers miles with its buildings and athletic fields. And all around and up into the foothills are mansions of stone or stucco in the styles of Spain, Morocco, Italy, California, and Mexico. Many canny Tucsonians have built expensive houses which they rent in winter for as much as a thousand dollars a month; in summer the family lives comfortably, air-conditioned against the furnace blasts of desert heat.

The children of these plutocrats are served in schools which charge around two thousand dollars for a nine months' term. The whole business, according to Chamber of Commerce figures, brings Tucson something like four million dollars a year. The whole state of Arizona profits no less than seventy-five million dollars annually. That is good business in any Western state. And it is pure " carriage trade." Arizona's deserts, so often forgotten and of so desperate a history, have come at last to figure most frequently on the nation's society pages.

Dudes

have pre-empted central Arizona. But relics of prehistoric life are all around as reminders of how transitory every people's culture is. One might imagine an earnest archæologist of some race, whose scattered ingredients have not yet begun to mix, puzzling his head over an unmistakably female skeleton in spurs and riding-boots dug out of the rusty wreck of a tourist wagon. His conclusions might be no farther from the truth than the guesses of the early Americans who misnamed Montezuma's Castle and Montezuma's Well.

Such monuments, however little understood, impress even the most thoughtless with the length of the Southwestern pageant in which we, with all our noise and trumperies, are just one episode. Sound archæologists are slowly piecing together a picture of many peoples. Each one has built its walls, molded its bowls, hammered its copper and silver, polished its stone, and disappeared, leaving only trash-piles to yield up hints of its comings and goings. There is no crossing the Southwest, in any direction, without somebody's showing you a ruin, a picture on a rock, or at least a broken pot.

VII

BROKEN POTS
AND PREHISTORIC PEOPLE

ADRE KINO, BUSY BAPTIZING AND BUILDING, HEARD HIS converts speak of a *Casa Grande*, a great house, on the Gila River. The insatiably curious priest went to see. No wonder the simple Pimas, living in brush jacales, spoke with superstitious awe of such solid magnificence! The padre described it as: " A four-story building, as large as a castle and equal to the finest church in Sonora . . . there are thirteen smaller houses, somewhat more dilapidated, and the ruins of many others which make it evident that in ancient times there had been a city here." In an eighteenth-century account, *El Rudo Ensayo*, its author reported: " A roof made of beams of cedar or tlascal and with most solid walls of a material that looks like the best cement." Padre Garcés, wandering the desert in search of souls needing saving, saw the Casa Grande and mentioned a tradition linking its buildings with the Hopis, whose stone villages he knew. But the Spaniards only speculated and went on.

113

Mountain men reported too, and Pauline Weaver scratched his name on a wall in 1832, the only visitor brash enough to do so. United States government expeditions noted, mapped, and described many ruins, but made no close study of them. Colonel William Hensley Emory in his *Notes of a Military Reconnaissance* reported on Casa Grande: " Along the day's march were remains of acequias, pottery, and other evidences of a once densely populated country. About the time of noon halt a large pile which seemed the work of human hands was seen to the left. . . . We made a long and careful search for specimens of household furniture but nothing was found except the corn grinder or metate."

After the middle of the century students like Adolph F. Bandelier, Frank Cushing, and J. Walter Fewkes with their scientific observations brought the Casa Grande out of the realm of superstitious awe and into that of sound archæology. Even such men did not realize how wide a background that one ruined city had. Where did its builders come from, where did they go, and when, and why? Answers to such questions are still being sought. Only in the twentieth century by slow digging, sifting, collating, comparing, and compiling, anthropologists are beginning to weave the scattered remains of many peoples into a pattern more or less complete. Happily it is so far from complete that it will keep many generations of students busy and entertained.

For half a century ruined towns, cliff and cave dwellings were studied separately. Then Dr. N. C. Nelson, working in the Galisteo Basin in New Mexico, discovered that potsherds in abandoned rooms or refuse-heaps could tell a consecutive story which connected modern Pueblo people with their ancestors back to the dwellers in cave and cliff who made baskets, but had not yet learned pottery-making — the Basket Mak-

MONTEZUMA'S CASTLE, ARIZONA.
MANY PREHISTORIC PEOPLE MADE HOMES IN CLIFFS
[*photo, U. S. Forest Service*]

ers. Dr. Alfred Vincent Kidder, using this technique in the ruined pueblo of Pecos, worked out a chronology for the whole pueblo area. Dr. Kidder's work, explained in *An Introduction to Southwestern Archæology,* was valuable not only for what it told, but for the clearness with which it showed up the gaps in knowledge. Broken pots, lying in layers in prehistoric kitchen middens, revealed the order of happenings, but not the length of any period. We know now that most of the guesses allowed too much time for every period. Later explorers also have shown that the Pueblo culture and its predecessor, the Basket Maker culture, developed over most of modern Utah, northern Arizona, southwestern Colorado, and most of New Mexico, were contemporaneous with another development in desert Arizona, and a third in the Mogollon country in southeastern Arizona and southwestern New Mexico.

The Salt River Basin, center of the desert culture, was inhabited long before the Casa Grande was built. The Pima word *Hohokam,* " the people who have gone," is applied to its ancient inhabitants. Three excellent institutions are studying them intensively. The Department of Anthropology of the University of Arizona, headed by Dr. Emil Haury; Gila Pueblo, near Globe, a research institution owned and operated by Mr. and Mrs. Harold Gladwin and open only to qualified students; and the Phoenix city museum, Pueblo Grande, headed by Mr. Odd S. Halseth. The most cautious students date the Hohokam remains as far back as A.D. 500. Mr. Gladwin would place it as far back as 200 B.C. In any case, the Salt River culture began as long ago as a consecutive human story can be traced anywhere in the Southwest. The Hohokam lived in scattered villages of perishable material; they met for ball games, as primitive people of all ages do; they wore ornaments of shell; they made buff-colored pottery decorated

115

with little figures of men and birds and beasts in red; and they cremated their dead. One might assume that they made baskets as well as pots, and wove cotton as well as reeds, though no specimens have been found.

The Hohokam pottery may indicate a relation with a people who lived along the Mimbres River in southwestern New Mexico. Apparently they ranged from the Mimbres westward beyond the Santa Cruz; their era was from 1000 to 1200. Their widest modern public is travelers on the Santa Fe's crack train, the Super-Chief. For the tiny birds, beasts, and human figures which appear on its dishes are copied from Mimbres pottery. When Miss Colter of the Harvey System decided to use those amusing figures, she went to the Museum of Natural History in New York. They had, she found, no end of Mimbres pottery in a warehouse over in Brooklyn. A day's taxi-fare, a long search for the man with the key, hours of copying in a huge loft undisturbed for years, and these vivid and humorous running quail, inquisitive rabbits, and tender fawns were brought out for the joy of modern travelers. Perhaps their predecessors were the turkeys and snakes, antelopes and nameless birds and beasts on early Hohokam ware.

What happened to the early Hohokam people is still in dispute. Some archæologists believe they were the ancestors of the modern Pima and Papago folk who still live in brush shelters on the desert. These are the gentle people whom every white man has loved. Every writer has mentioned them with affection and appreciation. Peaceful and trustworthy, they welcomed thirsty wanderers in their wattled huts of ocotillo wands; they helped and comforted many wounded survivors of Apache raids; they even fought with white men against Apaches. Pimas and Papagoes speak languages so nearly alike that they must have the same ancestors. They have not been much studied. Ruth Murray Underhill, in her *Singing for Power*, describes the Papago as " a tribe of Indians who have never fought with the whites. As a consequence, they are a people whom the whites hardly know." Her book is a rare combination of sound ethnology and readable prose.

Whatever the disagreements about the end of the Hohokam, there is no doubt that they were great canal-builders, the Southwest's first reclamationists. Perhaps as early as our year one they were irrigating the valleys of the Gila, the Salt, and the Verde. An aerial survey of the region near Phoenix located a hundred and twenty-five miles of canals, some as wide as thirty feet, ten feet deep, ten miles long, and as well plotted as a modern engineer could do. But as agriculturists the Hohokam faced the same problems that plague today's farmer. Engineers figure that about one-fifth of the water brought to the Salt River Valley from the dams is lost through seepage. This would cause an annual rise in the watertable of from three to five feet, waterlogging the soil and putting the ditches out of commission. So the prehistoric Indians dug deeper and raised their floors, building ever higher mansions — if only to keep their feet dry. This makes the Pueblo Grande at Phoenix look like a house of many stories, though it was probably never more than one. Finally they had to give up and move away altogether. But before that end their land was invaded by a people from the northeast. Nothing indicates that it was a warlike invasion; the two peoples seem to have lived amicably together.

These newcomers were called the Salado people, and the invasion is calculated at from 1200 to 1350. They came from the valley of the Little Colorado, through the White Mountains and across the Tonto Basin. These " salty " folk buried instead of cremating their dead, a custom which may link them with the Pueblos. They made a polychrome pottery and a polished ware. But their greatest achievement was as builders. They built the Casa Grande, whose towering walls are still a splendid sight, in spite of the long-legged roof with which the Park Service protects them from further washing away. It is not of adobe bricks, such as we still use along the Rio Grande, but of plastic mud, puddled in as a child might do, allowed to dry, and more piled on top. This makes the solid cement wall noted in the *Rudo Ensayo*. These people also built the heavy, buttressed walls at Pueblo Grande. They probably used their great buildings for storage or for ceremonial purposes. Some students believe they were fortresses — the last strongholds of a people driven out by invaders. The bellicose Apaches may have been pressing in from the North during the fourteenth century. But there are no signs of battle. Where these people went, and why, is one of the puzzles. It has been suggested that their descendants live in Mexico's great Chihuahua Basin.

Mr. Odd Halseth, working in the Pueblo Grande, has found few skeletons, and those suggest a pitiful and tragic tale, for they are all of seniles or infants. Whether the place was abandoned because of superstitious dread or because water-logging had ruined the land, only those who could walk and carry their share took part in the exodus. Nothing indicates that the deserted babies grew old enough to cope with such a losing situation.

Whatever caused it, this southward movement of the Salado people was probably accelerated by the Great Drought, which modified all Southwestern prehistory and is readily traceable in the migrations. It lasted from 1276 through 1299.

How can one be so sure of dates in studying people who disappeared long before white men had touched this continent, who left no written record and no consecutive body of tribal lore? The answer opens up one of the most astonishing chapters of our story.

The dating of prehistoric sites by potsherds, which has proved reliable as to relative chronology but inaccurate as to actual time, has been supplemented by a study of tree-rings. This method was hit upon by an astronomer studying sunspots, and with no thought of its applicability to archæology. Dr. A. E. Douglass, of the University of Arizona, discovered that coniferous tree-rings show great variations. In a wet year, a wide ring; in a dry year, a narrow ring. All trees in a given area show the same general pattern. By comparing and charting the rings in young trees with those in old trees, exact dates can be determined for as far back as the life of the oldest tree. When Dr. Douglass asked for data on beams in prehistoric ruins, archæologists came slowly to realize that he offered the solution of one of their toughest problems; because it was soon discovered that the sequence of dry and wet years overlapped between standing trees and cut beams in the ruins. Even bits of charred timber can be read, now that a technique has been perfected. Step by step, accurately determined dates were pushed back; newspapers often carry news of newly uncovered ruins, giving older dates. Perhaps the oldest generally conceded date is A.D. 438, determined by a beam found in Mummy Cave in Canyon del Muerto in Arizona. That was a very dry year. So when an archæologist states that the Great Drought began in 1276 and ended in 1299, he knows exactly what he is talking about.

The Basket Makers, who cut those beams away back in the first centuries of our era, can best be studied in Utah, Colorado, and the brilliantly colored and fantastically eroded desert in northern Arizona. In spite of their name, Basket

Makers made pottery. By the fifth century they had that craft and were building houses as well; perhaps they had acquired both from the Mogollon or Hohokam people. They lived in temporary structures or in caves, and used caves for storage or burial places. They had no cotton, but they wove yucca fiber into sandals, bags, and baskets of many shapes. They had not domesticated the turkey, but they raised corn and squash. Generally unhampered by clothes, they made light, warm blankets by twisting rabbit skin around threads and weaving them together. A few such blankets have been found in their burials.

The most exciting Basket Maker discovery is that of Esther, found in 1939 by Earl Morris near Durango, Colorado. Esther is an extraordinarily well-preserved mummy, with unbroken if not quite unblemished skin, perfect teeth, and every bone intact. Five feet and three inches tall, she now weighs sixteen pounds, but in life she probably registered over a hundred. Her *September Morn* pose would indicate that Esther was a nice girl, and modest. Why she died does not appear; but near her, in the same crevice, lay the mummy of a young man. His relationship to Esther is a mystery, but the maiden's expression — contorted face with protruding tongue and one closed eye — might indicate to the pure that she died defending herself from worse than death. The other seventeen people who lay near her and Jasper (her young man was Jasper) have left no record of what they knew or gossiped about.

Anyhow, Esther's people were the first known inhabitants of the Mesa Verde in southern Colorado, the ruins most thrillingly beautiful and intelligible to the layman. They have been much written about; for the casual reader of any age, no book is more pleasing than *Deric at the Mesa Verde*, by Deric Nusbaum, who spent his childhood there. A clever mother, directing his education, suggested that he write his compositions about the cliffs and ruins he knew so well; a publisher saw them and suggested the book. The boy, given such an early bent, quite naturally grew up to be one of the Southwest's soundest archæologists.

The Mesa Verde National Park was a wonderful place for a boy to grow up, or for a vacationer of any age. It is a high plateau, where sun and wind coax out and sweep along the scents of pine and cedar, where deer bounce to a stop as a car passes, piñon-jays scream, and fluffy-tailed squirrels scold heatedly. On the mesa are many of those round little hillocks which a student spots at once as hidden houses. The archæologist finds at the Mesa Verde remains of the whole archæological field, from earliest Basket Maker to the peoples who immediately preceded the historic Pueblos. But for most of us the wonder of the place is to step out to the edge of a cliff and see, across the tree-filled canyon, perfect ivory-toned houses sheltered in shallow caves, which have been eroded out of its friable sandstone walls. Cliff Palace, Spruce Tree House, Balcony House — any of them — fill one with mystery and awe from afar. But they are no disappointment after the observer reaches them by a stiff climb, all a-puff, and studies the well-cut stone, laid in even courses with well-turned corners.

Everything is made easy by the National Park Service, which provides cabins, good food at reasonable prices, lectures by learned gentlemen by the nightly bonfire, and for guides fresh-faced young college boys, who recite their pieces with enthusiasm, accuracy, and stern determination to instruct. But even they do not know just why the people left these lovely homes, so easy to defend, in a country so rich in game. Few burials have been found, and nothing to indicate a major disaster. Their granaries were full of corn stored in well-made jars. They had good stone tools and weapons, and plenty of domesticated turkeys to yield feathers for robes. Perhaps Old Devil Drought discouraged them into leaving, a few at a time. The Utes may have had something to do with it. It is known that the Mesa Verde was abandoned between 1250 and 1300. Such dates are not easy to determine, because people did not all pick up and go at once; they drifted out; first those quickest to be inspired or frightened. Perhaps some of the old mossback conservatives never did go — just died where they were, leaving the stores of corn and turkey feathers we find today. But if we do not know why they went, or precisely when, we do know where.

Apparently the Mesa Verde people divided, some going southwestward to the Canyon de Chelly, and others toward the southeast and the San Juan River drainage. To the west, ruins in Canyons de Chelly and del Muerto indicate a relationship with the Mesa Verde. The many cliff and cave dwellings which dot northern Arizona were already occupied, but a migration from Canyon de Chelly may have added its bit to the amalgam which was to evolve into the modern Hopi. It may be proved, too, that the people who abandoned Montezuma's Castle on the Verde River in the fourteenth or fifteenth century went on into Tusayan, which we call Hopiland. The first settlers there did not scale the rocky tops of those pale, stark mesas, but settled around them, where ever living springs make patches of green. Later the combination of Spaniards and Navajos forced them onto the arid heights. Only old Oraibi was occupied before recorded history, making it Acoma's rival as the oldest inhabited town in the present

United States. This district also includes the famous Seven Cities of Cíbola, our modern Zuñi.

The Museum of Northern Arizona is making a detailed study, which promises the whole story of the Little Colorado region. Founded in 1917, this museum is maintained by the citizens of Flagstaff, and directed by Dr. Harold S. Colton. Dr. and Mrs. Colton, always interested in strange places, went to Arizona on their honeymoon in 1914. He was a zoologist, she a painter. Both liked Indians. The first thing they did was to climb the San Francisco Peaks, whose tips support a subarctic flora and fauna. They descended into the Grand Canyon, in whose depths are exposed the oldest geological strata we know. And they visited the Hopi villages, traveling on horseback, with mules packing food, bedding, scientific instruments, notebooks, and painting materials. No people ever knew their country better. First they made a summer camp at Flagstaff, where their children could be cared for while they explored the desert and its denizens; then they decided Flagstaff was the place and built a home of stones picked up on their chosen hill, of pines cut down to make place for it and to open a view of the San Francisco Peaks. Near it now is the museum of the same construction. What more perfect living could there be?

The museum, as stated on a board framed in Hopi tiles, shows " ideas, not things." It is designed to tell the story of the region in graphs, charts, pictures, and actual articles. There are also words, simple unscientific words which a child could understand, but one looks rather than reads. Here are stones from the Grand Canyon, placed to show how they rise, one above the other, through the ages. Here is a cross-section of the San Francisco Peaks, revealing the rocky insides, the

123

growth on the surface, even the birds and beasts that frequent
them. Actual bits of salt-bush, juniper, and fir are stuck on
at the right point, as are dead birds and lesser beasts. One
could only wish the birds and squirrels had been mounted in
more lifelike form. But here, as in every good thing, enough
money is lacking. What could be done by sound knowledge
and cultivated taste has certainly been done.

Human life is as well displayed. A picture shows how prehistoric people lived in a cave, a pit-house, or a village. How
they dressed; the game they brought in; how they stored and
prepared their food; their weapons and ceremonial objects.
And enough of the actual finds — half a moccasin, a potsherd,
a scrap of figured cotton, an arrowhead — to indicate how the
archæologist arrives at his certainties. An original contribution is drawings of ancient pieces to show their pristine beauty.
A blackened shell inlaid with turquoise and jet is not very
convincing to the tyro; but seeing that design completed in
colors as bright as the originals were, he thrills to realized
beauty as the archæologist does to the worn fragment. The
whole museum is planned to share with the layman the specialist's delight in his work. This sharing includes annual con-
ferences and picture exhibitions, and a summer show of
Navajo and Hopi crafts. Mrs. Colton is particularly interested in a revival of the best old Hopi weaving. Indians work
about the place, as do students from the Arizona State Teachers College at Flagstaff, getting invaluable training.

Local museums like those at Flagstaff and Phoenix mark a
big change from the beginnings of archæology in the Southwest. The first men to appreciate the richness of the field and
to explore and study it were foreigners. Adolph Bandelier,
the Swiss, explored as many ruins as he could get to between
the Casa Grande and the Rito de los Frijoles. Cosmos Min-

deleff made valuable studies in the Canyon de Chelly, Count Gustav Eric Nordenskiold studied the Mesa Verde cliff dwellings and sent a priceless collection of artifacts to the national museum of Sweden.

Archæological riches appeal only to the truly cultivated mind; most Southwesterners were panning for gold or scratching for a living. They entertained the odd but always interesting strangers, guided them about, sold them old blankets, or pots, or strings of wampum. Many of these men, it is true, made their reports and turned over their finds to American museums, or to the Smithsonian Institution in Washington. Among them were Americans. J. Walter Fewkes reported on the Mesa Verde and the Zuñi region. Frank Cushing studied the prehistory of Zuñi as well as its legends. But what they found went into Eastern collections. To a great extent much of this wealth still goes east. It was not until the turn of the century that the Southwest woke up, or grew up, to an appreciation of its own treasures.

The first Southwesterner with the vision and the energy to do anything about it was a young professor in the Normal School at Las Vegas, New Mexico. Edgar L. Hewett had two qualities which were to contribute much to American archæology. He was a go-getter. And he could inspire young people. Through his efforts the Museum of New Mexico was founded; and the Archæological Institute of America, which then maintained schools at Rome and Athens, placed its first American establishment at Santa Fe. Dr. Hewett did some excavating at the Rito de los Frijoles, and there some of our leading archæologists got their start. Sylvanus G. Morley, Jesse Nusbaum, Earl Morris, Kenneth Chapman, and Neil Judd have gone out from the School of American Research at Santa Fe to range the whole hemisphere.

Soon after that, Byron S. Cummings of the University of Utah went down into Arizona. With John Wetherill of Kayenta, he explored the deserts, where drifting sands had preserved records of centuries of prehistory. A Piute Indian led them to the Rainbow Bridge. One of them (which is still unsettled) was the first white man to see that marvel. Dr. Cummings soon transferred from the University of Utah to that of Arizona, and founded the State Museum, which was affiliated with the university. The University of New Mexico in 1928 established its Department of Archæology and Anthropology, with Dr. Hewett as its director.

The sparsely settled Southwestern states are no longer fields from which foreigners take their finds; its own institutions rank high in anthropological work.

Two other institutions make specialized contributions. The Laboratory of Anthropology at Santa Fe undertakes to coordinate the work of the whole field through its collections and studies of Indian arts, both modern and prehistoric, its work with tree-rings, and the facilities it offers to white and Indian students. It attracts not only academic doctors, but Indian schoolchildren, wide-eyed before the work of their ancestors, and sober Indian craftsmen seeking to improve their own technique and design. Near the laboratory is the House of Navajo Religion, wherein is housed Miss Mary Wheelwright's matchless collection of Navajo sand-paintings and a library of explanatory material.

All these institutions perform an invaluable work in teaching the value of archæological remains. There are thousands of sites in the Southwest. Any day the most unimpressive mound may yield the one vital link in a chain of evidence. It is impossible to guard them all, and much irreplaceable material has been and continues to be lost through ignorant pot-hunting. In spite of laws against it, vandals will dig recklessly into ruins, crashing down walls, removing artifacts to sell, or merely to keep awhile and then throw away. As though a child who could not read were turned loose in a fine library and allowed to cut out any pages that tickled his fancy.

As an educator, nobody is better than Uncle Sam. Many of the most important sites in the archæological Southwest — which includes Utah, southern Colorado, Arizona, New Mexico, and part of Texas — are now national parks or monuments. Visitors are welcome, but they are well watched; given a chance to enjoy it, but required to take decent care of what they see. It is now possible for a motorist to trace the whole course of human development, from the earliest known pithouses in Utah down to where its culture met that of the canal-builders in Arizona, or across the Mesa Verde and down into New Mexico.

The southeastward migration through the San Juan Valley leads first to Aztec. This misnomer, like Montezuma's Castle and Montezuma's Well, only indicates that somebody, fifty years or so ago, had heard of the famous Aztecs and their last ruler. Many ranchers still refer to archæological sites as " them Aztec ruins." At Aztec, New Mexico, the Park Service has an excellent museum, with a map of the whole region, and a cross-section of a dump showing how potsherds, bones, bits of textile, and worked stones are found in layers. Rooms have been left with furnishings and utensils in place, and even a skeleton with food-bowl and water-jug beside it. A small kiva has been restored to show the entrance from the underworld, the fireplace where the new soul was warmed, and the vent through which it rose to the sunlit world above. This is the work of Earl Morris — he who found Esther — and of his wife, who works with him. Ann Axtel Morris, in *Digging in the Southwest,* has written an amusing account of archæologists, their vicissitudes and triumphs, and of why it is such fun to be one.

Though we trace a migration from the Mesa Verde to the Rio Grande, the whole region shows remains of earlier cultures, as well as of the great period. It will take many years of digging, sieving, and co-ordinating to work a definite pattern out of what still lies tumbled like a mammoth jig-saw puzzle. Chaco Canyon, for instance, was abandoned a hundred years or so before the Great Drought; yet its masonry is unsurpassed; it represents the highest stage that Pueblo culture ever reached. Its Pueblo Bonito, with a hundred rooms terraced up from one story in the patio to five which form the outer wall, is as impressive as a palace. Its many kivas indicate a rich ceremonial life. Excavations have yielded excellent pottery, strings of turquoise and shell beads finer than most modern needles could string, and exquisite inlaid work of turquoise, jet, and shell on bone or wood. No burials have been found. Every archæologist dreams of stumbling some day on the Chaco Canyon cemetery. They must have buried far from home, and what treasures must have gone into those unknown graves! Pueblo Bonito is only one of many villages in the Chaco, which is now the scene of the University of New Mexico's summer school for embryo archæologists.

The abandonment of such splendid homes may have been due to erosion. The Chaco River is now a stretch of dry sand between high, sandy hills. In mentioning a Southwestern river, one always states whether it does or does not contain water. The Chaco in its better days certainly did contain enough water to support a population of thousands. That does not mean as white men use water, but as the modern Hopis, for instance, do. The Chaco may well have meandered along

a flat valley floor, depositing enriching silt, leaving underground moisture which a patient Indian would know how to
use. At least this is Dr. Kidder's conclusion.

Again, nobody knows where the Chaco Canyon people went.
They might have drifted as far west as Zuñi. Perhaps they
were the ancestors of the Acoma people on their rock. It is
clear that some of them got themselves across, or around, the
Jemez Range and into the Rio Grande Valley. Their best-
known sites are on the Pajarito Plateau, which thousands of
tourists have visited. Always accessible, the Rito de los
Frijoles is now practically unavoidable, with a road of easy
ascents out from Santa Fe, and a rocking-chair descent into the
canyon instead of the old trail which used to make such good
boasting.

Bandelier wrote his monumental *Delight Makers* about the
Rito de los Frijoles. Every traveler since has had his say.
But nothing is more original and pleasing than Gustave Baumann's *Frijoles Canyon Pictographs.* " When Gustave Baumann first came to the Southwest many years ago he was so
delighted by the cave drawings at Rito de los Frijoles . . .
that he made drawings of them for himself; and he has now
put together a book of that first excitement and delight of his,
with a running text and two-color cuts of the drawings."

The people of the Pajarito Plateau are the immediate ancestors of Pueblos who live along the Rio Grande today.
Santa Clara people see ghosts among the cliffs at Puyé, the
Cochitis keep alive the cult of their stone lions; every pueblo
uses ancient dress and prehistoric articles in its religious rites.
Nowhere in the world does remote prehistory touch today so
closely.

A vivid, visible bridge between the two worlds is now being
studied for its full significance. In 1935 Gordon Vivian of

the University of New Mexico, excavating at Kuaua, near Bernalillo, began work on a square kiva. He glimpsed color under the plaster. Thousands of kivas have been excavated; few paintings have ever come to light. It was a treasure-trove unique in Southwestern archæology. For as meticulous, prayerful care took off eighty-five layers of plaster, preserving each intact, seventeen painted layers were found. As exposure threatened the color, they were copied as rapidly as Indian painters could work, and the originals stored safely in a vault. The Kuaua murals were done on earth walls with earth colors — true frescoes. They represent human figures, masked, and carrying ceremonial objects; birds and animals; and symbols familiar in modern Indian life. Indian shamans are now working, unknown to each other, at their interpretation. Perhaps through them will come a clear message from the world the Spaniards were at such pains to destroy, for modern Indians may be able to read what their ancestors said.

The great historical importance of these Kuaua murals is that Villagrá describes them in his *Historia de Nueva Mexico*. Writing of the Tiguex villages where Coronado spent the winter of 1540–1, he describes " paintings of the demons they worship as gods." But the frescoes everyone longs most to find have not yet come to light. Writing of his own visit in 1598 to Puarai — a village which has not been positively identified — Villagrá said: " The Indians took the priests to the quarters which had been prepared for them. The walls of their rooms had been recently whitewashed and the rooms were cleanly swept. The next day, however, when the whitewash had dried, we were able clearly to see through the whitewash paintings of scenes which made our blood run cold. God always finds a way to make known the glory of those who suffer for His holy faith. There pictured upon the wall we saw the details of the martyrdom of those saintly men, Fray Agustín, Fray Juan, and Fray Francisco. The paintings showed us exactly how they had met their death, stoned and beaten by the savage Indians."

That will be the epoch-making discovery! Meanwhile the Coronado Cuarto Centennial Commission has restored one set of the seventeen murals to its place in the kiva, and erected there the Coronado State Museum, which is designed as a monument, not to Coronado, the conquering Spaniard, but to the three cultures which have come together as the result of his *entrada*. New Mexico is still deeply marked by the three peoples who have made her history — the Indian, and the two white cultures, which have been modified by him in many ways, and which have come at last to value the great gifts he has brought to them.

Central Arizona

*is not only a storehouse of material for the archæologist and
a play-place for the visitor. Because of its situation — on
the way to California — of its deserts — terrible — of its
people — savage, warlike, all but invincible — and, finally,
because of its potentialities, central Arizona has been the
constant concern of the federal government for almost a
century: to help people who tried to make their way across
it, or, even more daringly, to live in it; to defend them from
Apaches; and, finally, to make the desert productive.*

*It offers also a fascinating contrast between the ways of
the aborigines and of the modern, with perhaps some in-
dication that civilization is better, in the long run, than primitive living close to nature. The whole story revealed by
archæology is one of peoples harried by disaster. We pass
lightly over hundreds of years, because peaceful and quiet
living leave little trace. But sooner or later every prehistoric
group was defeated by nature — a cataclysm like flood or
drought, or slow attrition from misuse of land or water. The
ruins tell a tale of the migrations of discouraged peoples.
So, perhaps, does our own history. But modern man, having
made all the mistakes of primitive man, seems capable of
profiting by them. Free of the superstitious fears which ham-
pered primitive man, he can study his situation and evolve
ways to meet it. The story of that honorable, though still
undecided, effort is well revealed by what the United States
has done in the Southwest.*

VIII

UNCLE SAM'S SOUTHWEST

UNCLE SAM, ESPECIALLY UNDER OUR FRONTIER President, Andrew Jackson, coveted his neighbor's house (and land), his neighbor's ox and ass. He even looked with favor on his neighbor's wife, whether she was of pure Castilian blood, of the uncontaminated Indian race, or a blend of the two. What he most wanted, perhaps, was California. But California, appropriately for a land of promise, was guarded by the Great American Desert, by mountain ranges like solid stone ramparts penetrable only at a few points and defended by savage warriors.

After Mexico had freed itself from Spain and was trying to make a republic out of the unlikeliest human material, increasing numbers of buffalo-hunters, beaver-trappers, and traders pushed ahead into Mexican territory and pre-empted it. Almost without firing a shot Uncle Sam acquired the Southwest. Texas, having been a republic under her own lone star, reserved her public lands " to squander in her own way," as one Texan put it. But New Mexico, which then included all of Arizona, presented a major national problem. Desert country, overrun with the fiercest tribes Uncle Sam ever dealt with, and bordering on Mexico for two thousand miles of desert and sandy, shifting river — what to do with it?

The Army knew the answer, then as now. In 1855 Jefferson Davis, Secretary of War, shipped from Egypt to Texas about seventy ships of the desert, and a camel-driver, Hadji Ali, to teach his art to Western mule-skinners. From their headquarters at Camp Verde, Texas, the improbable animals were sent across the barren wastes as far as Palm Springs, California. But as the beast of the hour, Egyptian camels could not compete with the ox or the burro, so they passed on, leaving only their bones to plague future archæologists, and their driver's name perpetuated, as the mule-skinners pronounced it, in " High Jolly," Arizona.

The Army was more practical in encouraging settlement, " for occupied territory is easier to defend than an unsettled region," and in guarding the border and protecting explorers and settlers. With the settled Indians, like the Pueblos of New Mexico and the Pimas of Arizona, Uncle Sam continued the policy of Spain and had no trouble. But the warlike tribes whom Spain had never subdued fought desperately and savagely as they saw their land invaded. White men made reprisals just as savage. Uncle Sam doubtless meant to do right by the Indians as he conquered them, but three things worked against him: Indians who persistently got off the reservations and committed outrages, white men who violated treaties even faster than Uncle Sam could revoke them, and the fact that the government did revoke its treaties, as it pushed the Indians back, and claimed more and more of their lands.

Gradually the tribes were overpowered and penned up on reservations, where Uncle Sam not only had to feed them, but, largely because of Christian pressure from the East, to look to their manners and morals. They must be educated, Christianized, and civilized. Before the end of the century Uncle Sam, in New Mexico and Arizona alone, was bewilderedly operating twenty-two reservations, sixteen boarding-schools, trying to keep the peace among hundreds of competing missionaries, and doing it all through hundreds of employees procurable at a very small stipend. All his efforts were subjected to criticism, abuse, and free advice from various organizations founded for that purpose. Meanwhile he kept right on chasing savages until the last recalcitrant Apaches were reduced.

When Uncle Sam had time to forget his problem children, he dealt with land, and, arising from it, a confusion equaled only by the dust-storms of a later era. The whole Southwest had become public domain, except what our treaty with Mexico had guaranteed to its previous owners. The Pueblo Indians retained some of the best valley lands in New Mexico, granted them by Spanish kings and confirmed to them by the Republic of Mexico. Many white people also held such " grants " from the Spanish crown, or from the weakly apprehensive Mexican government, which hoped they could defend it, not only against Indians, but against Yankee encroachment.

The rest, millions of acres from the Missouri to the Pacific, was thrown open to homesteaders. In that way the whole West, from tidewater to the plains, had been settled. The General Land Office, created in 1812, allowed a man to acquire a hundred and sixty acres by living on it for thirteen months. That was a very decent farm back east, but altogether inadequate in the arid West. Major J. W. Powell, in his report of 1879, estimated that in grazing-country a man needed two thousand five hundred and sixty acres to make a living, using some of it for farming and raising fodder. Major Powell's recommendations of sixty years ago embody many suggestions now being put into operation. " The redemption of all these lands," he wrote, " will require extensive and comprehensive plans, for the execution of which aggregated capital and co-operative labor will be necessary. Here individual farmers, being poor men, cannot undertake the task." Major Powell might have been writing for the New Deal. But the Congressmen who read his report were quite unable to understand it, and for generations they tried to govern the arid and treeless West by laws applicable to the humid and forested East. The man actually in the West was forced by conditions into new patterns of living, and he broke most of the laws before he convinced Congress that his needs were unlike those of the farmer on rolling, grassy hills, with ample water.

By the seventies the East, suffering the depression that followed the Civil War, was demanding ever quicker ways to California. Transcontinental railroads were the dream, and eloquent gentlemen went to Washington. They wanted only to serve the people, but no railroad could be expected to maintain itself across the uninhabited Great American Desert. They needed government subsidy. So the Congress awarded the road-builders a bonus of land. The Atlantic & Pacific, now the Santa Fe, got alternate sections for fifty miles on each side of its tracks, all the way from Albuquerque to Los Angeles, a total of about seven thousand, five hundred square miles of territory in New Mexico, and over fifteen thousand in Arizona.

Meanwhile, government agencies were established, one after another, to study the new territory, to adapt it to man's uses, and finally to adapt man to its way. The names of the new departments are significant. First came surveys — geological and biological, even ethnological — for studies of Indians were made. Then followed bureaus of animal industry, of plant industry, of agricultural economics, and others designed to help the pioneer make a living. Bounties were paid on wildcats, mountain lions, wolves, and coyotes, which preyed on lambs. As they also preyed on prairie dogs, those prolific little marmots increased prodigiously and partook so freely of the roots of crops that they had to be blacklisted and gone after too. Salaried government men have succeeded bounty hunters, but rodents have never hurt the range as much as man's bad practices.

Overgrazing has long been recognized as an evil. Cattlemen blamed sheep, who cropped so close they ruined the range for cattle. Sheepmen complained that cattle cut the country down into arroyos. Their differences led to several of the meanest "wars" of the West. But, according to impartial students of the land, both were guilty of denuding the range of grass. Thousands of acres which might have renewed themselves interminably were eroding down into future and unforeseen dust-bowls. And lumbermen, too greedy for quick profits to care, or too ignorant to realize the danger, were stripping the mountains of their pines and removing the natural cover that held rain-water back and prevented its tearing the country down into the silt which aggraded the rivers, made marshes of good farmland, even threatened towns with floods. It all came about insidiously. No private owner, cutting timber on a mountain, could see his connection with a farmer, washed out years later, and many miles away. He could not even see that he was abolishing his own future income.

I know of one example out of my own experience and distress. In the 1920's I used to take parties to see the Shalako at Zuñi, driving out across the Zuñi Mountains. If we did not bog down in snowy mud and have to spend the night keeping up the fires and each other's spirits, it was a journey of glistening beauty through a noble forest of pine, packed with snow. Miraculously, the trees had rooted themselves in a broken lava flow, and in the hollows quaking aspen protected the infant pines until they were strong enough to crowd out their guardians ungratefully. A new stand of pines was always coming along where old trees had died, or, in a few places, had been burned out. Burning is a devastation, for after a forest fire it takes many years to bring back a productive stand of timber. But the Zuñi forest had suffered little.

So it was with much anticipation that I offered to take my sister through there in 1935. As we drove along, I boasted of the lovely forest she was to see. . . . Well, it was gone. No trees stand there now. No noble pines sough gently and scent the air. No groves of aspens make dells of shimmering light and shadow. No infant pines show sturdy promise. Only bare lava rocks bake under the untempered New Mexico sun. Students tell me that a forest cannot come back to beauty and to usefulness under two hundred years. Our nation has not lived as long as that. Something had destroyed timber that, by proper lumbering, might have produced wood forever. Not a natural holocaust, forest fire, or tornado, but a private company had laid low everything that grew in one regardless gesture. They had taken not only matured pines, ready for cutting, but young pines that would have profited by the removal of their elders. What could be used was hauled to the mills. What could not was burned. And the company went on to seek other lands to devastate.

This is typical. The Nordic, marching heavy-footed across the continent, is Paul Bunyan. Though that " first real American " never saw our Southwest, our treatment of it suggests his doings, in kind and in scale. He, you remember, logged off a magnificent pine-clad mountain so thoroughly that he left only the Dakota Badlands. Of every township, formerly of thirty-seven sections, he let one whole section wash away down the creek. The hoofs of his blue ox, Babe, sank four feet into the earth; he tore down hills, leaving only piles of sand. And in Kansas he leveled a rich and rolling country, full of streams and woods of whisky trees and beer vines, into a dry, flat cornfield. " His desire," so says James Stevens, who collected his lore, " was to make history; his imagination rose above mere industry." And when he had destroyed the forests, and no timber remained for his loggers to cut, he summoned his inventiveness and resourcefulness and devised something even more complicated to offset the evil he had wrought — as when he built his smoke-stacks so tall he had to equip them with hinges to let the clouds go by.

The parallel with the energetic and inventive Nordic is probably too obvious to need laboring. The trails over which he drove his steers and his covered wagons are now deep and dangerous arroyos. He has leveled not only Kansas, but many states; and not only into flat fields, but into bowls of dust. He has made badlands not only in the Dakotas. Like Paul Bunyan, he has been more eager to make history than to use a land where man's industry could make a modest living. And when all else failed, he could move, couldn't he? That a day might come when there would be nowhere to move to, no " farther west," was quite beyond his limited ken. He was, and still is, the most trying problem Uncle Sam has to solve.

As early as the nineties, doubts arose as to the advisability of giving away all public lands, and the government withdrew quietly from the real-estate business. Informed men knew that the resources of the West, popularly considered infinite, were seriously threatened, and in 1891 certain lands were set aside as forest reserves, now known as National Forests. Another act, in '97, provided for their administration, but the idea did not grow popular until Theodore Roosevelt, who loved the West and understood its problems, injected two new concepts into the national consciousness: service, and conservation. In 1905, when he was President, the Forest Service was established under his friend Gifford Pinchot, who could inspire young men to a great ideal of service. It had, of course, no control over privately owned land. So the great forests of northern Wisconsin and Minnesota continued to go under the saw to enrich their fortunate owners, while millions of acres of timber-producing land were laid waste, watercourses ruined, people deprived of farmlands, and the Mississippi and its tributaries overfilled with waters which have caused floods all the way to the Gulf.

But in the West, where so much land had remained public domain, the federal government could, and did, prevent much similar waste. In New Mexico and Arizona the forest boundaries were drawn to include watershed and mountain grazing-land, as well as commercial saw-timber. The purpose was to control use of forage as well as lumber, and so to prevent erosion. Travelers today love to joke about the signs: " You are now entering Forest So-and-so," when there is not a tree in sight. But there is usually a good stand of grass, land is protected, men miles away are benefiting. The Forest Service increased its control by buying back all the railroad land it could. Miles of country, which had been denuded of trees, are growing back into forest. Along the highway near Williams and Flagstaff, Arizona, one may see how sturdily young pines reclothe bare hills when they have a chance. Another result of good forestry is that, except for one small, arid corner of

New Mexico, neither that state nor Arizona is included in the Dust Bowl.

At first the Forest Service was naturally greeted with derisive howls. Imagine a great, he-man Westerner, used to destroying his country as he went, being told how to run his business by "a little squirt from some college back east." But the college foresters turned out to be one of the best-selected bodies of men that ever served Uncle Sam. They have a record now of thirty-odd years behind them, unmarred by any scandal. Chosen for knowledge and efficiency, and not politically, they are men who could hold more lucrative jobs in private industry, but who like to live and work outdoors, with assurance of decent living and security. It is the first civil service in which the United States approached the British ideal.

As time went on and they gained experience, the foresters made a striking success. They slipped easily into the social life of every Western town and took part in community affairs. They dealt with armed and angry stockmen; more than one forest ranger risked his life to adjust a grazing problem. They disproved the old theory that sheep and cattle require different ranges, though dual grazing as generally practiced is nothing less than double grazing, and double trouble for Uncle Sam. They recognized the rights of elk and deer, as well as domestic stock, and they sympathized with the sportsman's contention that killing might be beneficial. In the Kaibab Forest of Arizona, the earlier policy of no hunting was modified into regulated hunting when it appeared that the famous deer herd was eating itself into suicide. Overstocking of the ranges was gradually eliminated, and millions of acres responded with greatly improved forage. Constant watching and quick action greatly reduced the hazard of forest fires and saved wooded canyons and mesas for recreational areas. All this adds up to the Forest Service's principle of " multiple use." The same land gives the camper and the hunter forest and game, and the lumbermen saw-timber; produces forage for game as well as cattle; and proper protection keeps streams fresh and clear for trout, as well as saving the watershed and reducing the fire hazard.

The private owner has always complained, with much reason, that too much was expected of him. Why should he limit his stock, when his neighbor's bad practices might endanger his entire holdings? Why should he conserve timber for the benefit of posterity, when one carelessly thrown match might burn down more than he could save in a lifetime? The Forest Service has met this criticism with long campaigns of education. Lectures, and movies, and cartoons, warnings on trees, and posters by the running brooks. I once saw a camper pollute a sparkling stream with a dishpan of dirty water, and drive off, leaving a brisk fire under a tree. Not many such vandals remain. And lumbermen are apt now to take Forest Service advice about when to cut, and how. Years of education through demonstration have taught owners that careful measures result in actual profit. Recently a lumber company has employed a firm of forestry experts to work out a long-term program to improve their forest and make it more productive at the same time. Uncle Sam could have told them how twenty years ago, when that same lumber company ruined a fine stand of timber. But Uncle Sam is merely smiling in his beard, and none of his employees will hint at anything except admiration of the experts' excellent and expensive plan.

The National Park Service, with a comparable personnel and an equally honorable record, has a longer history, and serves a different need. The Forest Service works primarily to protect land and to make it more widely and steadily profitable. Our National Parks are great, inviolable stretches of country, preserved in their virgin state — an idea which germinated in campfire talk as long ago as 1870. In that year Henry D. Washburn and N. P. Langford crossed Wyoming with a military escort. How they must have reveled in magnificence, as their horses bore them slowly across canyons, through forests, among lakes and geysers, sighting big game and ever grander vistas! One of them, foreseeing a West cut up into farms, rattling with railroads, and booming with towns, remarked that such country should be set aside as a national preserve, where grizzlies and elk, deer and buffalo, might live forever. In time they got to Congress with the idea, and Yellowstone National Park was created in 1872 and put in charge of the Army. Estes National Park followed in Colorado, Grand Canyon National Park in Arizona, and, eventually, Carlsbad Caverns in New Mexico.

About 1906 it was decided that certain sites of archæological or historical importance should be preserved also. This was to discourage private pot-hunters from carrying away priceless records, and lazy builders from using beams and cut stone out of old forts and prehistoric ruins. There are now more than twenty-five National Monuments in New Mexico and Arizona. They include prehistoric sites, like the Rito de los Frijoles and Chaco Canyon in New Mexico, Canyon de Chelly and Casa Grande in Arizona; freaks of nature, like New Mexico's White Sands and Arizona's Petrified Forest; and extraordinary growth, like the Saguaro and Organ-pipe Cactus Forests, near Tucson.

All the parks and monuments were administered by various government departments until 1916, when, Franklin K. Lane being Secretary of the Interior, the National Park Service was created in his department. In 1933 they were all brought under uniform control, and park rangers now assiduously police almost two million acres of land for over a million visitors annually. Much of this may be seen by motor, but many miles of wilderness are accessible only on foot or horseback. The parks are for people who can appreciate them, and they are subjected only to such rules and regulations as a vandalistic public requires.

The newest and one of the most significant projects of the National Park Service is the Big Bend National Park in Texas. Roads have been built to the edge of the Grand Canyon of the Rio Grande, which, while only half as deep as that of the Colorado, is splendid. The Big Bend National Park has, besides, an international importance, for Mexico is matching it with a similar preserve across the river, and we may now greet our southern neighbor, as we do Canada, when we picnic.

Meanwhile other practical services had been established. A generation to which the plow was the emblem of civilization naturally thought of irrigation as a way to turn the arid West into farms. Prehistoric Indians had irrigated fields along the streams. Spanish settlers all lived on rivers, or on ditches. The all-conquering Nordic proposed to water the whole West and make it bloom. Streams which rose into destructive torrents in summer and dried away in winter should be harnessed, and great stretches of country irrigated. The Reclamation Service, founded in 1902, undertook to water the public domain in seventeen Western states.

Most of these projects have dealt with from seventy-five to three hundred thousand acres, and they now include Boulder Dam, the most stupendous irrigation scheme the world has ever seen. The Elephant Butte Dam made a great lake in the middle of New Mexico, and turned the lower Rio Grande

Valley from small farms, owned and operated by independent farmers, into cotton-fields worked by hired hands. Roosevelt Dam in Arizona watered the desolate Salt River Valley. Imperial Valley, one of the most terrifying deserts on the globe, has, by the damming of the Colorado River, been turned into one great truck garden. Eager town-builders, thrilled by all this, undertook state or municipal projects, of which New Mexico Middle Rio Grande Conservancy Plan is the perfect type. By a series of dikes and drainage canals, and by damming the Rio Chama in northern New Mexico, they proposed to irrigate thousands of dry acres, and to reclaim as many waterlogged ones. Dreamers dreamed of great orchards and truck gardens, of great fortunes. They failed to consider the very evils which had waterlogged the alluvial land and left so many dry acres above the reach of the irrigating ditches. The muddy Chama, still pouring red silt into the Rio Grande, might endanger the usefulness of the whole project within a man's lifetime. And the Rio Puerco, dumping mud into the lower river in the ratio of about forty parts of silt to one of water, can choke the Elephant Butte Lake long before the disputes about its water can be settled. Even Boulder Dam is doomed within a calculable term. An engineer, faced with that question, said: " Have you no confidence in progress? By the time this dam is choked up, somebody will have invented a way to eliminate silt." Paul Bunyan, that is, will again summon his resourcefulness and invent something.

Reclamation, in almost every project, had fairly well demonstrated that it could not work alone. What had been done was the best that could be done at that time. We were, even in the twenties, still filled with grandiose ideas. Every man had a chance to be president — the go-getter won. Every boy was taught to take a long chance and, by implication, to let the devil take the hindmost. It took a major national depression, a four years' drought, and an agricultural crisis to convince us that the basic resource of the United States, the very land itself, must be saved, and quickly, and intelligently. And the way is by controlling erosion where it starts. It is a fearful monster when grown, but not too difficult to strangle in its cradle.

This is one of the meticulous, unspectacular jobs which cannot be done until public opinion is ready for it. The Forest Service had done what it could, but it controls only the headwaters of the stream, and high, timbered country. However good a job is done there, overgrazing and bad practices down the creek can cause a lot of havoc, and do. No adequate program was possible until national disaster brought the cry — it was a universal cry then — that government must do something. Out of this need came new agencies, whose high standard of personnel and fine achievement promise to assure their permanency. They deal with a variety of technical phases of land use and range management, and much of their work will be of more use to later generations than to us. But two of them are doing jobs of such immediate and obvious importance that anyone can see it.

The Grazing Division, under the Taylor Act of 1934, which put an end to homesteading, controls the public domain and can enforce measures to arrest its deterioration. Trained men calculate the number of animals which may graze without endangering the range, and lease lands accordingly. The Department of the Interior, under which this division operates, is empowered to exchange government for private or state lands in order to facilitate its control. And it co-operates with committees of local stockmen who understand regional conditions. The complications — personal and political — may be

THE PATIENT PLODDING BURRO HAS HAULED
WATER ACROSS THE DESERT

[photo, Ruth Frank]

BOULDER DAM, THE MOST STUPENDOUS
IRRIGATION PROJECT

[photo, Ruth Frank]

imagined. A " grass counter," as grazing reconnaissance men used to be called in the Forest Service, must be a very smooth diplomat as well.

The Soil Conservation Service works with this and with all government departments which have to do with land, as well as with private owners. All these services have the benefit of years of experience, filed away in careful plans and accurate specifications. And the Civilian Conservation Corps provided man-power for projects too expensive and too far-reaching for private enterprise. Nobody who saw those forlorn skeletons on their way to the first camps, and the brown and husky youths they became with food, cleanliness, and outdoor work, will ever forget them. If nothing had been done but to make healthy men out of derelicts, it would be worth it. But their work has gone a long way toward saving the Southwest.

The great problem is the typical mind. Give the American something big and costly to gaze upon, and he thrills. Tell him that he, personally, must plow in curves rather than in straight lines, reduce his flocks and herds, vary his crops, or let certain fields lie fallow, and he becomes heatedly resentful. He has always stubbornly refused to learn from the farmers whom he found making a living in all the irrigated valleys. Spaniards who had farmed arid Spain knew that every wet cycle would be followed by a dry cycle, probably longer, and very sure. In the fat years they hoarded their harvests for the lean years; and always they used water sparingly. But the Nordic accepted every wet year as proof that the climate had changed; borrowed money to enlarge his holdings, buy machinery, and put up a better house; and when he went broke he cursed God and started for California. The whole Southwest is dotted with abandoned shacks which government reports list as " visible evidence of failure."

Recently this problem has grown into a national disaster with the coming of the dispossessed from the Dust Bowl. California's fertile valleys are overfull. And, for the moment at least, she is failing utterly to administer her fabulous wealth to prevent such hideous want as her Mexican laborers suffer in the Imperial Valley, such maladjustment as is caused by recurrent unemployment and hunger on her fruit ranches, such violence as her ports know. California can absorb no more people. Yet people continue to strive to reach that land whose promise has failed; are turned back at her border and head east again, begging gas and food along the roads. In *The Grapes of Wrath* John Steinbeck has told a tale which must surely shock the most callous and torpid imagination. And his facts are borne out by every impartial survey.

Uncle Sam's new services are trying to prevent the continuance and recurrence of such horrors. His success, even in five years, has been so striking that he can now count on public approval. Poor men who had been often tricked by politicians have learned that the government technician is as scientific about saving land as a doctor at a sickbed. Rich men who could afford herd reduction that would be disastrous for a small owner have seen fewer animals produce more wool and more meat. Both classes are beginning to suspect that Uncle Sam knows best.

In a typical dry-farming area near Mountainair, New Mexico, terraced fields yielded one hundred and seventy pounds of beans per acre, and unterraced fields only one hundred. It is as simple, and as inexpensive, as that. In the same region, farmers who had tried rotation of crops and contour plowing found their fields secure after torrential spring rains, and with enough stored moisture to carry them through the dry summer.

On the Navajo Reservation, Indians who counted their

wealth by heads of stock and rickety horses, as well as wool-bearing sheep, were astonished to see the Steamboat Canyon area produce almost twice as many lambs, and lambs of seventy pounds on the average instead of forty-five, after five years of Soil Conservation practices. Any Navajo can see the difference between the grass where the range has been protected and that on overgrazed areas.

Such jobs are matters of careful doctoring. Nature will rush to the aid of the earth as she does to a wounded man. Rest for the patient is usually the main desideratum, but even if complete rest is not possible, much can be done. Anyone driving across New Mexico and Arizona will notice wire and brush entanglements along the arroyos, which check the rush of water, permit vegetation to root, and so narrow the channel. Jetties help to hold the stream, catch silt, and prevent cutting. Anyone may have the eager company of a soil-conservation enthusiast to show him many such evidences of success, which are replacing the old evidences of failure.

Uncle Sam, through all these experiments, has discovered a couple of facts which may weigh heavily in the future. One is that much of the Southwest is not suitable for commercial agriculture. In a number of areas commercial agriculture is fairly successful. In others the choice lies between large-scale operations enriching a few, and subsistence farming supporting a large population on their own land. Subsistence farming sounds like a pretty slim diet, until you realize how much real living can go with it. He thrives best who does not plan to make a fortune, or even to make money, but who is willing to work to make a living.

Uncle Sam has discovered that (contrary to the Horatio Alger books) everybody is not a potential millionaire. There is simple Mr. John Doe, who can do well enough, if he is not overburdened with debts and taxes, if he has good land, and a fair chance to work it. But he cannot rise above too many failures. And now his old recourse of packing up and moving on is denied him. His individual failure has grown to the stature of a national disaster. From the hardest and most ruthless point of view, we must realize that when he fails, he does not disappear. He lives on, breeds on. So Uncle Sam, through his Farm Security Administration, is helping this rather futile, but inevitable, person to make a living and support his family.

The result of all this, so the unreconciled insist, is that Uncle Sam owns and controls the entire Southwest. They complain that the Southwesterner, once monarch of all he surveyed, can nowadays do nothing without asking permission. The hard-riding, quick-shooting frontiersman, who could look every man in the eye and tell him, is now a meek citizen who consults a man in an office, fills out blanks, and signs papers before he can even carry a gun, cast a fly, gaze into the Grand Canyon, or climb Pike's Peak. How much game he may kill, how many fish he may fry, how many head of stock he may graze, where and how he may build a house, how much land he may put into what crops, all depends upon the say-so of some federal service or other.

The Southwesterner, whose plight begins to bring tears to the eyes, does not even hold title to his land any more. What with Army posts, Indian Reservations, National Forests and Parks, and Reclamation Projects, Uncle Sam controls something like seventy per cent of Arizona and almost thirty-five per cent of New Mexico. The states own so much that only a paltry eighteen per cent of Arizona and forty-nine per cent of New Mexico belong to the private citizen who pays taxes, growling a good deal.

What he fails to calculate, in his growlings, is that Uncle Sam's payroll produces much of the cash on which the Southwest lives, and the taxpayer would be the first and loudest howler if it were threatened. Without the federal payroll the Southwest would be the Great American Desert indeed. This is just the point the Eastern congressman makes when another appropriation is sought for the Western states. What he does not remember is that much of this expenditure, sidereal as its figures are, benefits not only the Southwest, but the country as a whole.

The Southwesterner came from the East. People in any numbers could not survive in the desert as it was. So the desert has been reclaimed and every project, from the smallest to the largest, is a center — not only of trade and business, but of social life in all its phases. Thanks to the dry air, people who would be invalids elsewhere live out a span of usefulness here. And the whole country comes west to play at being a man who can fend for himself, saddle his own horse, weather a sudden rain, build a fire, even sleep on the ground. And that is important. To save our sanity, we must have relief from the too complicated civilization we have made. This intangible advantage of Uncle Sam's upbuilding of the Southwest may be one of the most valuable.

The Southwest is also a demonstration area of mammoth proportions, for here the federal government owns and controls enough land to show how our magnificent national heritage may be made forever productive. Within the memory of living men our preoccupation has swung round from ridding the country of Indians, through oversettlement and overuse of what was considered exhaustless wealth, to conservation of resources, to service. In a century the conquering Anglo has met the Southwest and been conquered. Almost all his ideas have been proved wrong. Millions of people hold out still in their refusal to see what is actually going on. But the object lessons of the last ten years have scared enough of them to make possible some really far-reaching experiments.

The Southwest has long served as a museum for the geologist and anthropologist. It has now become a laboratory of experimentation in bringing mistreated land back to usefulness. Perhaps some of us will live to see it the proving-ground for an experiment in the simplest tenets of democracy: a land governed for the greatest good of the greatest number, where every man may have a chance to enjoy life, liberty, and the pursuit of happiness.

Not until Arizona

was a state and wealthy did white men succeed in doing what both Indians and whites had tried and failed to do — harness the Salt River and make its waters turn the barren desert into an oasis. The Salt River Valley Reclamation project was also Uncle Sam's first successful effort at large-scale remodeling of scenery to suit.

Phoenix, center of that great, irrigated area, is also the most populous center of Arizona, and of what it is easy to believe is the most magnificent natural beauty in the world. In Arizona, only superlatives will serve. Most roads lead to Phoenix. One may approach it across the desert as stagecoaches made it from California, or from the east across the mountains. The Apache Trail, extravagantly beautiful in the springtime blossoming, is not so thrilling as the drive from Safford to Globe and into Phoenix by Superior. There one drives for hours along roads which wind, climbing and descending with glorious vistas of deep-cut canyons and breathless drops below. And north of the Apache Trail one may skirt the Tonto Basin and drive all day through sheer beauty, by way of the little towns of Pine and Payson, and on into northern Arizona. The Apache Trail, of course, crosses Roosevelt Dam, and its bare-sided lake made possible the taming of one of the toughest landscapes in our country.

IX

PHOENIX AND
THE DESERT RECLAIMED

N 1870 FRANZ HUNING OF ALBUQUERQUE TOOK A WAGON train out to Prescott, and on down to Wickenburg and " Salt River, now Phoenix. . . . The country," he wrote, " is dry and dreary, and after leaving the Hassayampa we could water only about half way to Salt River at a well in the Agua Fria wash or creek. . . . In the Salt River Valley the firewood is very scarce, and almost the only living thing available for fuel at that time was the mesquite root. . . . The valley produces a tarantula of a very large size, and I had more than one scare on their account, because they are generally considered poisonous."

At that time white men had known those dreary stretches for almost fifty years and had found welcome shade and water in the thin line of cottonwoods and sycamores along the Salt River and the Agua Fria. But they had all gone on, pursuing their various mirages. A few struck pay dirt, like Henry Wickenburg, who, chasing his burro, stumbled onto the Vulture Mine, which produced more than three million dollars in ten years. And the nameless German who never told where he got the burro-loads of gold he used to bring out of the Superstition Mountains. Nobody has ever found his lode, though thousands have searched; even now the Don's Club of Phoenix makes an annual pilgrimage in search of the " Lost Dutchman's Mine."

But for every success, hundreds died in torments of thirst on the Arizona deserts, or were killed by Indians. What most white men thought of Arizona was best summed up by that gay cynic J. Ross Browne: " With millions of acres of the finest arable lands, there was not . . . a single farm under cultivation in the territory; with the richest gold and silver mines, paper money is the common currency; with forts innumerable there is scarcely any protection to life and property! With extensive pastures there is no stock; with the finest natural roads travel is beset with difficulties; with rivers through every valley, a stranger may die of thirst. Hay is cut with a hoe and wood with a spade or mattock. In January one enjoys the luxury of a bath as under a tropical sun, and sleeps under double blankets at night. There are towns without inhabitants, and deserts extensively populated; vegetation where there is no soil, and soil where there is no vegetation. Snow is seen where it is never seen to fall, and ice forms where it never snows. There are Indians the most docile in North America, yet travelers are murdered daily by Indians the most barbarous on earth. . . . Mines without miners, and forts without soldiers are common. Politicians without policy, store-keepers without stores, teamsters without teams, and all without means form the mass of the white population. . . ."

Mr. Browne ought to see it now. In fact, he missed the beginning of the new day. Farms were under cultivation when

he was there — not only the hoed cornfields of the Maricopa
Indians, but farms put under ditch by men who could foresee
great possibilities. The first of them was Jack Swilling, who
began his ditch in 1867. Within ten years a dozen other canals
had been dug, and thirty thousand acres were under cultivation. In some cases the prehistoric Indian's ditches were found
to be so well graded that they were cleaned out and put into
operation again. The Salt River Valley was filling up with
farmers who appreciated the rich soil and were willing to dig
and delve to make it bear.

Among them was Charles Trumbull Hayden, who once sat
on the bluff overlooking the valley where Tempe was to be,
and dreamed. Mr. Hayden·had been shipping flour up from
Guaymas to his store in Tucson. It was not very good flour.
Why not use the stream's fall to turn a mill as well as to irrigate? Mr. Hayden had visions of making the " desert bloom
like a rose." The phrase was less trite then. So he put in a
dam, built his mill, and in time put water onto six hundred
and forty acres which he planted with alfalfa, grain, orchards,
and gardens. He announced that he would employ anybody
who wanted a job. He could use millers and mechanics; teamsters, horse-wranglers, and blacksmiths; carpenters and stone-
masons; farmers, dairymen, and sheepherders; ditch-diggers
and bookkeepers; even teachers were needed. The only draw-
back to teachers was their tendency to get married as fast as
the stages could bring them in. This perhaps accounts for the
wide, if thin, dissemination of learning in the Southwest. Mr.
Hayden even brought a one-legged doctor back from one of
his trips to St. Louis. Such an establishment would be incom-
plete without the English remittance-man; Mr. Hayden's was
Darrell Duppa, who figures in a recent romance concocted by
Clarence Buddington Kelland. Mr. Duppa left tag ends of

his classical education all over the map. He rechristened Hayden's Mill Tempe, because he found the valley as lovely as the Grecian vale. And Salt River, he prophesied, would rise from the past like the phoenix bird from her ashes. So Phoenix it was. Mr. Hayden, a New England gentleman who spoke only yea and nay and took no liquor, must have warmed to such highfalutin nomenclature. Mr. Hayden is credited with bringing the first plug hat into Arizona. Most Southwestern families boast of the first grand piano freighted out across the plains; the plug hat is a welcome variation.

In time Mr. Hayden met an adventurous Arkansas lady in California, married her, and brought her home across the deserts. From Morgan's Ferry on the Gila there was not a house until they got to Salt River. Somewhere along there Mr. Hayden asked his bride what she thought of Phoenix, and she had not even noticed it! Poor lady, she had been jolted and bruised for days, her eyes burned from dust and glare, and she had a " rising " in her ear. Still, this story is more successful in Tucson than in Phoenix. In Tempe, Mrs. Hayden found a stately adobe house with water piped in, an osage orange hedge around an orchard of peaches, plums, figs, oranges, and pomegranates. There she lived out her life and raised a family still prominent in the nation. Arizona's Senator Carl Hayden is one of the babies the one-legged doctor brought, and another is Miss Sallie Hayden, who has kindly shared her memories with us. Servants there were none, but strong Mormon girls could be hired to help, and Maricopa Indians brought in sticks of wood neatly built into heavy wings on tiny burros. Mrs. Hayden, with a general's strategy, commanded the turning of rough foodstuffs into meals served on a table laid for thirty, as a matter of routine. What could not be used daily was dried, preserved, pickled, or jellied. Nobody in her neighborhood went hungry; every mother in childbed, every household in illness or grief, was her personal charge. Any stranger passing by was asked to eat before he was ever asked his name or business; a desert rat with a keg of water and a sack of beans on his burro, needing only a small grub-stake to assure the richest of all strikes next time; soft-footed Indians with nothing to say; men driving a herd of cattle up to Fort McDowell or Fort Whipple; a covered-wagon family resting up in the grove by the river; and, as well, Army officers, judges riding circuits of hundreds of miles; the first distinguished scientists and writers studying the wonders of Arizona. Mr. Hayden stuck to his Puritan principles, but the lady from Arkansas entertained at brilliant, candlelit parties, cheered and made famous by perfectly blended mint juleps and egg-nogs.

Such women as Mrs. Hayden were the real civilizers of the frontier. Courageous and resourceful, they were never more so than in their insistence, in a raw, new land, upon the graces that had made life dear back home. One up in northern New Mexico cooked for years over an open fire in a lean-to, but she set her bare table with silver candlesticks from Virginia, and taught her children correct syntax. Another, left widowed, bestrode a horse herself and kept the cattle together until she made them produce college educations for two daughters and a son. The roughest men respected such women, and built them the churches and schools they demanded. In time they even cleaned out the gamblers and prostitutes, planted trees in parks, put on white collars, and submitted to imported lecturers and singers. Children of such families were sent all over the United States to school, carrying with them the democratic feeling that came of the Mormon girl in the kitchen and the desert rat on the porch, and a sense of responsibility due to taking care of the woman in childbed down by the creek, and sharing the milk with the Jewish peddler's family.

During the seventies the Latter Day Saints reached the Salt River Valley. They had first gone into Arizona with Colonel Sterling Price as the Mormon Battalion. But fighting men, accompanied by their women and children with carts and cattle, had a pitifully hard time; soldiering was not their forte. Later, as colonists and missionaries to the Indians and the gentiles, they were more successful. Mormons always got along well with Indians, whom they considered one of the lost tribes. Approaching Arizona by the hardest way, they moved south through Utah's Kaibab Forest and crossed the Colorado River at Lee's Ferry. Generations of the Lee family poled people back and forth there, charging a pony, a Navajo blanket, or a piece of wrought silver. Recently the government has spanned the river with a spectacular bridge, which daily buses cross on their run from Tucson to Salt Lake City, making a comfortable ride through what was so long invincible country.

The followers of Brigham Young built towns like Holbrook and St. Johns, with solid brick houses and rows of poplar trees along the streets. They were, and still are, a sturdy folk, and good farmers. They use neither strong language nor strong drink — not even tea or coffee. They practice thrift, hard work, and the tithing system, and on gala days they test their strength at races, wrestling matches, tugs-of-war, and dancing. In the Salt River Valley they settled Lehi in 1877, and dug the Utah Ditch. Later the town of Mesa grew up to become an ecclesiastical center second only to Salt Lake City.

The entire development of the Salt Lake Valley was, contrary to the general experience of the West, without speculative advertising, without a boom. Every canal was financed by one man, or by a small group; and in only two cases — the Arizona Canal financed by W. J. Murphy, and the Consolidated Canal, built by Dr. A. J. Chandler — did outside financing figure. By 1892 sixteen diversion dams were in operation — mostly structures of brush and stone, which went down like so many matches when a cloud-burst in the mountains discharged itself in a mighty torrential rush. Often irrigation was halted by too much water while ditch headings were repaired. But people kept coming. Inevitably, too much land was put under cultivation, and disaster followed over-sanguine development. With an annual rainfall of only seven inches, one could hope to irrigate only a limited number of acres every year. Theoretically, those would be the acres first used. Under irrigation laws common to the whole West, the man who first puts the water of a stream to beneficial use has a prior claim to it. If the stream should ever fall so low that only his land could be irrigated, he would have a legal right to deprive his neighbors of all water. This is the theory; actually, all sorts of things happened in the dark of the moon. A water-gate might be left open. A farmer enterprising enough to arise and irrigate at three in the morning might look like a trespasser to his neighbor with the prior right. The " first beneficial use " right became something to be schemed for at best; at worst, Arizona had not outgrown the old gun-toting ethic.

Still population continued to grow, wet years were mournfully followed by dry years, and on two tragic occasions wet years turned out to be more disastrous than dry. In almost any rainy season the Salt might rise into a torrent half a mile wide and ten to twenty feet deep, washing out small dams, inundating fields and orchards. But in February 1891 there came a flood unequaled before or since. Even the substantial dam at the head of the Arizona Canal was so damaged that it could not be repaired for several months.

After that, there followed thirteen years of drought, prob-

ably worse than any since the Great Drought, which shifted the
Indian tribes around in the thirteenth century; and that was
succeeded by another flood in 1905, only less devastating than
the first. It was clear to everybody that something more than
individual enterprise was called for. With fifty independent
canals, and two hundred and thirty thousand acres of land
under ditch, about one-fourth of the farmers were in a precarious position in dry seasons, and the great floods had respected nobody. Even if spring rains were promising, a dry
summer might destroy carefully nurtured crops. The obvious
answer had occurred to some Salt River Valley farmers prior
to 1890. Why not dam the river and impound even the
heaviest rainfall of the wettest years for use in the drought
sure to follow? Engineers estimated that for a paltry four
million dollars, repayable at a dollar an acre a year for twenty
years, a storage reservoir could be constructed which would
hold enough water to irrigate the whole valley, and make
everybody rich. The only question was: where to get the four
million dollars?

Just then, by a lucky stroke for Phoenix and the Salt River
Valley, Congress was considering the Reclamation Act. Some
very brisk and effective lobbying by Arizona's lone territorial
delegate, and the personal assistance of President Theodore
Roosevelt, got the law amended to permit the use of government funds to reclaim private lands. Then the advocates of
the dam undertook the organization of a legally constituted
body to do business with the government, and to assure repay-
ment of money advanced.

Far-sighted and public-spirited men went patiently up and
down the valley, showing graphs and charts, explaining, ex-
horting. They met all sorts of opposition. Poor men with few
acres were suspicious of rich men with many. Holders of

" A " land, that preferred under the prior-right clause, saw no reason to co-operate for the benefit of less-favored neighbors. Old feuds and personal animosities awoke. One gentleman chuckled to remember the funniest dissenter he met — an old Confederate soldier, who was suspicious of any " Yankee proposition." He was finally shamed into signing by the assurance that he would never see an armed Negro soldier guarding his ditch head. In time more than a thousand farmers had signed, and the Salt River Valley Water Users Association was incorporated. It really was a case of join or go broke. And even the most ruggedly individualistic farmer, it seems, can be forced into co-operation if the pressure is heavy, and general, enough. At that, a few held out until as late as 1924. Stock in the association was subscribed on the basis of one share for each acre to be benefited. Each landowner gave what amounted to a first mortgage on his land to cover construction costs. But the sum of fifteen dollars an acre could be made to look like nothing at all, against the marvelous advantages to accrue with an assured water-supply. The original organizers would doubtless have been appalled if they had known what they were really in for. Happily, nobody could foresee that vastly expanded development would push that fifteen dollars up to over one hundred and fifty dollars an acre. Nor could anybody prophesy that such a mammoth investment could retire itself through revenues for a by-product like electric power.

Work was begun on the Tonto Dam, later to be called the Roosevelt Dam, in 1903. A Texas company, which got the first contract, hauled out two hundred and fifty thousand dollars' worth of machinery. Heaviest freighting was from Globe, on the railroad; twenty-six miles of stupendous mountain grades, over which six- and eight-mule teams strained and

THE GREATEST YELLOW PINE FOREST IN THE UNITED
STATES CROSSES NEW MEXICO AND ARIZONA

[*photo, Ruth Frank*]

sweated. Old teamsters unlimbered their long lashes, and even longer vocabularies, and gee-hawed as they had not done for years. Actual construction work brought together a collection of characters, and left a mass of tales that still delight the engineers who worked on the project.

Jack Whitney was a " pick-handle foreman," who enforced his orders by knocking the handle out of a pick and sailing into his man with the club. Jack was described as " a walrus-mustached, hawk-nosed individual with the keen, pale-blue eyes of a typical fighter, and with an absolute contempt for any show-off. On one occasion a new inspector was strutting his stuff for city friends. He stood aloft, bawling orders to riggers, carpenters, mixer men. Jack watched him for a few minutes; he stopped the mixers and the cableway, told all the carpenters to lay off, made the laborers stand still, and reduced the job to absolute quiet. Then he hollered: ' Now, you so-and-so, you give your orders so your friends can hear them good and clear, and then we'll go on with this job.' "

The use of Indian labor almost started the Indian wars again; members of various tribes had to be carefully segregated. Even college-bred Indians had a way of reverting to type. Upon one occasion an Apache, wearying of his marital relations, cut his wife's throat and threw her over a cliff. A young engineer, shuddering with horror, remarked to a Carlisle graduate on the heinousness of the crime. " Yeah," replied the educated Apache, " you bet. A knife's a damn poor way to kill a woman."

L. C. Hill, United States Reclamation Engineer in charge of the work, was a beloved and revered example to every young engineer fortunate enough to work with him. The magnitude of the Salt River job was attracting the attention of the whole world. It would make or break the man in charge of it.

163

Once a visitor looking at the completed structure said to Mr. Hill: " I'd hate to be at the foot of that dam if the thing washed out; wouldn't you, Mr. Hill? " To which Uncle Louis replied with the wry smile that made him loved: " If that dam washed out, I'd rather be under it than any place I know."

When the job was finished in 1911, President Roosevelt attended the dedication of the greatest dam known up to that time. In his speech he commented on the size of the structure, the wildness of the country, and the unusual difficulties of the construction. He said: " Undoubtedly a monument should be erected to the men who have accomplished this great and useful work of construction. What they will get, however, will probably be that reward of faithful public service — a Congressional investigation." So stated, so done. But that does not come into this story.

The engineers made a phenomenal record, not only of the original dam, but of the subsidiary operations it entailed. The original estimate of four million dollars had risen to fifteen million before they had a dependable working system. Impounding the water was only the first step; it had to be put on the land that needed it, and at the right time. The old rock and brush dams, still being given to washing out when most needed, would not serve. Two diversion dams were constructed on the Salt River, and old privately owned canal systems were acquired and improved. Finally the project was extended to the development of hydro-electric power, with the result that the ten thousand farms under the project can all be electrified. The sale of surplus power to mines, municipalities, and other markets has made the power system so profitable that it has defrayed much of the cost of the project.

But all was not yet well. Waterlogging, the old devil of the prehistoric Indian, with his primitive wooden hoe, rose again to bedevil the modern white man with all his scientific engineering methods. The Water Users Association found that it had to install extensive pumping plants. It is now the boast that the Salt River works for man three times: it makes electric power, it irrigates land, and its surplus water, which waterlogs the land, is pumped out and made to irrigate more land.

By 1917 the entire project, a successfully going concern, was by contract turned over to the Salt River Valley Water Users Association, which is recognized as one of the most successful co-operative undertakings in the world. Ten million dollars, due the government at that time, was to be repaid in twenty years, without interest. Other dams and engineering works, undertaken alone, bring the total capital investment up to about fifty-three million dollars. That investment waters two hundred and forty thousand acres of land under the project, and incidentally furnishes some water for ninety-five thousand acres outside the project.

All this disciplining of nature has resulted in farming which goes on for twelve months a year. Vegetables, including lettuce, which is one of the biggest crops, are shipped out during January, February, and March. During the spring months alfalfa is ready for its first cutting, berries ripen, corn fills out, and cotton is picked. The hottest summer months are the only ones during which no cotton is shipped. Citrus fruits go right on maturing among their blossoms, and northern fruits, like apricots, peaches, plums, and grapes plump out into marvels of perfection. Figs and dates, along with melons and the unwearying grapefruit, orange, and lemon, carry on into December, when the worst of the heat is over and vegetables again come in. An ardent Phoenician reminds me that: " This does not count livestock, poultry, dairy products, bees, ostriches, sweet-peas, or tourists." One generally thinks of tourists as the one thing central Arizona must import from without, but it seems not.

T. A. Hayden, spokesman of the Water Users Association, answers a question about the success of farmers: " Commercially successful? Now, Miss Fergusson, to ask such a question! According to the Chamber of Commerce, all; according to the railroads who are paid for hauling, yes; according to the grower, some crops, some years; other crops, other years; no crops, all years; and all crops, no years. There is always the element of chance, but the law of averages operates to eliminate the gamble to the greatest extent from the operations of the farmer who raises diversified crops. On the average, he gets along." In 1920, on the same authority, two-thirds of the project plunged into long-staple cotton, for which the farmers expected to get a dollar a pound. The bottom fell out, and most got less than thirty cents. In that year over a quarter of the project farms changed hands through mortgage foreclosures, and so on. In any case, seven thousand farmers are now operating project farms, so there must have been a good many transfers in thirty-six years. By law, one man is now permitted to own only a hundred and sixty acres under the project, which was designed for the small farmer. But many men in Arizona have large families, and large ideas. It appears that many assist an extensive family circle. One man told me that he had sixteen hundred acres in oranges; he spoke of another who owned three thousand acres. The best land, in mature citrus trees or otherwise highly developed, is worth as high as three hundred dollars an acre.

On the whole, the Salt River Valley belongs to modest farmers who make, on an average, about twenty-six hundred dollars a year. They live in tidy little houses, hidden under bougainvillea and climbing roses, many with electric lights, fewer with city plumbing. They are all close to town, and the movies. Most of them drive cars. The manager of a mortgage company in Phoenix said that men seeking loans never mention crop failure as a valid reason for needing help. A hundred causes are cited: children must go to college, new equipment is imperative, illness has struck, a death demands immediate funds. But when you can telephone for water when you need it, as Reg Manning so effectively puts it in his *Cartoon Guide to Arizona,* crops do not fail. On the whole, the Salt River Valley farmer's difficulties seem to be largely man-made. Driving through Phoenix's residence district, where spacious homes are set in orange groves and bowered in lantana, roses, and oleanders, I asked if those were the farmers' homes.

" Oh, no," said my Phoenician guide. " These houses belong to the people who hold mortgages on the farms. And the shippers who contract for crops and sell them in the Eastern markets."

Even here, where co-operation has staged such a telling proof of its effectiveness, individualists are still too stiff-necked to sell co-operatively; they support a large class of middlemen. Nevertheless, the Salt River Valley farmer is probably better off than his like elsewhere. But his tribe will never increase just here. The Salt River Valley has reached its human saturation point. Paradise is closed. There is not, and never will be, enough water to irrigate more land. Future development of this valley, as in so many parts of the Southwest, depends upon people who bring incomes from other states. One observer said: " This is going to be a pensioner's paradise. With a little pension, and five or ten acres, an oldish man and his wife can do very well, and live out their lives in a balmy climate."

167

Besides this, there is the ever growing winter invasion of wealth. Years ago Dr. Chandler built the Desert Inn at a town which took his name. A fine and conservative old resort, it continues to attract its original clientele, mostly from Chicago. Families have grown up there. Phoenix, like Tucson, has its ranches of all sorts, from real cow outfits to the most splendiferous of them all — the Arizona Biltmore. Before it was built, months of testing had determined the warmest spot in the valley. A company was organized, rocked along, weakened, and was saved in the nick of time by Mr. Wrigley, who had decided to invest his chewing-gum nickels in stately pleasure domes. Putting out more money to save his original two hundred and fifty thousand dollars, Mr. Wrigley finally found himself the almost sole owner of a hotel extravagant beyond all computation. Sand-hills were converted into a famous golf course with ice-water on every tee, into tennis courts, gardens and pools, patios and terraces — everything it takes to make a wealthy man forget how hard he labors to support an ungrateful population. At last Frank Lloyd Wright was induced to work his magic, and out of plain, gray cement he produced a rambling structure which fits into the hills without a jar, and a decoration of simple geometric forms that lend a lacy lightness or a richly embroidered note where cement alone might be too heavy. Cement also has been rolled out over the hills — thirty miles of cement trails for sturdy walkers who long to stride across the desert without leaving the pavements. Indoors, wonders pile on wonders, until they reach their acme in the gold-leaf ceiling laid on by hand in four-inch squares — acres and acres of gold ceiling above cement walls. And one can, with scarcely an effort, spend a hundred dollars a day for just the right accommodations.

Phoenix, defying the desert, has not failed to develop water-sports, too. The dams have made a string of lakes, which offer miles of boating between precipitous canyon walls, and mountain resorts advertise swimming, as well as conducted rides over old desert trails. The Apache Trail, most glorious in spring, when its bare hills burst into brilliant bloom, leads one into a land of complete unreality, where lakes are starkly set in desert with no softening fringe of trees or grass, no reeds in the shallows. Strangers always ask why so much water has not made sheltering shade for itself. The answer is that the water-line goes up and down too fast to permit growth. Along the canals and small diversion dams, growth is quick. All around Phoenix one sees miles of grassy, tree-shaded banks sprinkled with wild flowers. But a big lake, filling with water in a rainy season, may rise a hundred feet or more. Then, when its waters are sent down to irrigate the valley, the shore line falls many feet below the high-water mark. Any little tree, ambitious to grow in such a situation, might find itself drowned one year and dying of thirst the next. It is as though Nature, obliged to submit to all this regimentation, refused to be gracious about it. The desert holds its own, even among mountain lakes.

The cultivated valley seems as artificial as the lakes set in sand and reflecting cholla and saguaro cactus; as incongruous with its desert matrix. One drives onto this man-made oasis as onto a stage-set. Aridity, and then, without warning, wheeling platoons of citrus trees like soldiers in dark green, with brass buttons. Avenues of plumy palm mark off tidy truck farms, fields of melons or berries, vineyards, and orchards of figs or peaches. All that moist greenness has affected the atmosphere, too. Dampness drains the buoyancy even out of Arizona's air, and mists its clarity like a breath on crystal.

The Salt River Valley, which the Chamber of Commerce is trying to alter into the more advertisable " Valley of the Sun," feels, as well as looks, like California. Near the city are hundreds of tourist camps, invariably " air-conditioned." They advertise ice-water, shady swimming-pools, sun-bathing pavilions, and one, at least, " sea breezes." Emulation of California could go no farther. Californians used to refer to Arizona as " back in the desert." The desert has been converted into California. The dream of Arizona's visionary prophets has indeed come true.

Once when

children in the Indian School at Phoenix arranged a pageant, they presented it in two parts. The act depicting the Pimas, the Papagoes, and the Maricopas they played on the floor of the auditorium. Those, they explained, were the lowland people. But the Navajos, the Hopis, and Havasupais they presented on the stage, for these were upland tribes. Little Indians understand what every traveler feels in his ears as he mounts from desert to forested Arizona.

A rocky shelf bisects the state from southeast to northwest. Below it is desert which makes nothing of a temperature of a hundred and twenty in the summer, which revels in days of sunshine all winter. Above it, on a plateau more than four thousand feet above the sea, the greatest forest of yellow pine in the United States crosses western New Mexico and eastern Arizona. But that plateau is never flat. Its misty peaks, high above timberline, point bright silver tips into a cerulean sky. Its Grand Canyon is without a peer, or even a lagging rival; its lesser canyons are marvels of color and form where streams between high rock walls have worn deep pools or formed tiny, grassy parks.

At Wickenburg an arch over the road reads: "The Dude Ranch Capital of the World." Beyond that the road climbs two thousand feet in seven miles, from the transparent jade of mesquite and the oily green of greasewood, through the smoky gray of live oak to piñon and shaggy cedar trees. Then, in thinner, higher air, they are replaced by yellow pine. Upland Arizona is a different world; even a motor seems to frisk in bright, dry air a mile above the sea.

X

PRESCOTT AND TWO WOMEN

RESCOTT SEEMS TO SIT ON THE VERY TOP OF ITS WORLD, in spite of the pine-clad hills which surround it. It is fresh, clean, and quiet. Pine trees stand guard along its wide streets and above its small homes, with their tidy gardens and picket fences. Its broad square, with brick buildings all around and a modern court house in the middle, makes the customary Southwestern word "plaza" a misnomer. But even Prescott, so new it seems of yesterday, and so Northern in feeling that it suggests New England, introduces its history with an act from the drama of Spanish exploration.

In 1582 Antonio de Espejo, marching up the Rio Grande and westward through Cíbola, kept hearing of mines ahead. His scribe, Pérez de Luxán, wrote: " If there are good mines, this will be the best land ever discovered, because the people of these provinces are industrious and peaceful." But when they got out on their *Río de los Reyes*, later called the Verde, Luxán wrote: " Many of them (Indians) came with us to the mines, which were in a very rough sierra; so worthless that we did not find in any of them a trace of silver, as they were copper mines, and poor." They were indeed copper mines, and none richer were ever found, but almost three centuries were to pass before that was appreciated.

After the flash and clank of Espejo's armor, nothing disturbed the great forests except soft-footed wild animals, and Indians whose moccasins moved as quietly over pine needles, until men in coonskin caps and buckskin leggings came along with beaver traps and long guns. Even they made little change until they began to lead the Army over trails they and their burros had long known. The decade of the surveys was also the beginning of Arizona's mining fever, for as the mountain man joined the Army as a scout, the prospector took over the burro and the center of the stage.

The burro has never been properly celebrated. I've asked every historian I know, and none can tell me who brought the first of them into our country, or into Mexico. Yet Southwestern civilization rode a long time burro-back. Where horses cannot go, a burro can. In long, patient files he hauled ore from the Santa Rita mines down into Chihuahua; he grunted under casks and chests all the way from Mexico to Santa Fe; trappers and prospectors packed the little beast with water-kegs, supplies of bacon and beans. Around mines and haciendas the burro has moved the creaking crusher wheel, worked the pump, carried supplies in and ore out. He is a willing enough worker, resigned to the common fate; but he has his dignity, too, and cannot be driven farther nor faster than seems just to him. His day is done, now that motors go everywhere, and even Santa Fe gets its piñon and cedar firewood in trucks. But children still like to ride a burro before their legs are long enough to bestride a horse; and his gentle, fuzzy face, with eyes of deep reserves and ears forever cocked to express amused doubt, is stabilizing in a whirl so fast that

173

we forget how silly speed is. Surely we owe the burro a monument at the top of some crag that only he could climb.

Long before there was a town of Prescott, burros and prospectors had staked out hundreds of claims on the Agua Fria, the Verde, the Granite, and the Hassayampa. Of that stream they say that one who drinks of it will never tell the truth again; or never need to, probably. In the early sixties war brought distrust. The Walker Weaver party, which seemed innocent enough, and probably was, was reported to be on its way to join the Confederacy. Whatever their original intent, all those men actually did was to pan out gold in the gulches around where Prescott was to be, and stay there long enough to deserve consideration as the town's first settlers. But the Army was suspicious, and in '63 they established a barracks above Prescott, and named it Fort Whipple for a young lieutenant who had made brilliant surveys along the border. Wood was plentiful, and they soon put rushing Granite Creek to irrigating grain-fields, fruit trees, and vegetable gardens. Other supplies were shipped from Fort Yuma up the Colorado River by steamboat to Ehrenburg, and freighted across from there in big army wagons with expert mule-skinners handling twelve- and sixteen-mule teams.

Meanwhile Congress had decided to cut the vast territory of New Mexico in two and call its western half Arizona. John N. Goodwin of Maine was appointed Governor, and when he got to Santa Fe, General Carleton, who knew the temper of Tucson, advised him to strike straight into the wilderness and found his capital well to the north of both Mexicans and Secessionists. So the Yankee Governor set out for his province, escorted by troops under the command of Lieutenant-Colonel J. Francisco Chaves. They paused near the present railroad station of Navajo Springs, and on December 29, 1863 they formally organized the Territory of Arizona.

Days later, they found the perfect spot for a capital, and called it Prescott in honor of the historian of *The Conquest of Mexico*. At once they set about building log cabins with the steep, pitched roofs so suitable to the cold, snowy winters. By May they had a government house where the council met and adopted a great seal. Secretary McCormick, its designer, described it: " A stalwart miner, standing by his wheelbarrow, with pick and shovel in hand, the up-turned ' paying dirt ' at his feet, and the auriferous hills behind him." Though the seal has since been changed, the motto: " *Ditat Deus*," God enriches, still reminds the Deity what Arizona expects of Him.

One of the earliest houses was a hotel. Frank C. Lockwood, in *Arizona Pioneers*, prints its first menu, which indicates that Prescott was quite independent of the outside world.

BREAKFAST

Fried Venison and Chili

Bread and Coffee with Milk

DINNER

Roast Venison and Chili

Chili Baked Beans

Chili on Tortillas

Tea and Coffee with Milk

SUPPER

Chili, from 4 o'clock on

175

But northern Arizona was not going to depend forever on venison. Like every Western state, sheep were to be an important source of wealth. Even in the fifties, sheep drives from the Rio Grande to California had begun. Sheepherding has never caught the imagination, as has everything connected with cattle. But it has been vital to the West through its entire history, and it has its romance, too. It even has one book, written by a Wyoming sheepherder, which expresses a comfortable feeling of superiority to the poor cowboy, who could never know the herder's freedom alone with his woollies, his dog, his gun, and his philosophic thoughts. Archer B. Gilfilian in *Sheep* may claim to be the only articulate sheepherder so far recorded.

Columbus brought the first sheep to the Americas, and Coronado to our country. They were *charros*, and not much good for either meat or wool, but the rams were picturesquely crowned, even to clusters of six and seven horns. Every later expedition brought *ganado menor*, lesser cattle; and even when the Spaniards were driven out, the sheep stayed, throve, and multiplied on the scantily grassed hillsides. Sheep can graze on steep and rocky ground where cattle lose their footing or cannot reach the grass; they can last several days without water, and after a particularly bad drought the few survivors build the flock back to full strength quicker than cattle ever do.

The padres at the missions taught Indians some principles of animal husbandry, and Indians, in every ruction and between times, stole stock freely. So sheep spread clear over into the Hopi country. But the sheep business was primarily a gentleman's business. In 1800 Governor Baca's two million sheep were herded by twenty-seven hundred peons. As late as 1890 Charles Lummis estimated that four-fifths of the

Caucasian male population were sheepherders at five to eight dollars a month. In addition, of course, the herder got his handful of beans and chile. It is still said in New Mexico that if you own sheep, you are a Spanish-American; if you herd, you are a Mexican.

In the early nineteenth century the *partidario* system developed. It is a " sharing " so popular with owners that it persists to this day. Certainly the owner can hardly lose. He farms out ewes to a herder, who agrees to return the same number, in the same condition, after a term, usually of five years. The partidario pays all expenses, even taxes, and, of course, takes all the risk of flood and drought, blizzard, disease, or other losses.

Colonel Edward N. Wentworth, writing for the *New Mexico Stockman*, comments: " The Spanish possessed a distinct genius for complexity." A ranch staff included a *mayordomo*, who went the rounds of camps to check the condition of the flocks, to hire and fire, to oversee monthly accounts. Under him came a *caporal* to supervise three *vaqueros*, watch for disease, seek strayed or stolen sheep, and supervise the moving of the flocks to other pastures. The vaquero had his little dignity, too, and rode a horse. The *pastor*, shepherd, was at everybody's beck and call. But he had the constant companionship of his dog, and no finer beast was ever known than a well-trained sheep-dog. Tireless, sagacious, resourceful, and faithful — often unto death — he, like the patient burro, ought to have a monument.

The *ricos*, until the Mexican War, drove sheep south to supply mining towns as far away as Vera Cruz. Profits of three and four hundred per cent were usual. But after the Mexican War and the gold rush, it became more profitable to drive to California. Many followed the Tucson-Yuma route, but Colonel Francisco Chaves, who had marched across with Governor Goodwin, and his neighbors, the Lunas, preferred the northern way. The first flocks to reach California sold, according to Bert Haskett, writing for the *Arizona Historical Review,* for $16 a head. In the sixties the price dropped to $3.75.

Those drives were lordly junkets, as well as business ventures. Superbly mounted, dressed in tight-fitting buckskin trousers and jacket, with silk shirt and hand-made boots as soft as a glove, the hidalgo rode from ranch to ranch, sending a vaquero ahead with word of his coming, staying for days of regal entertainment, until the slow-moving flock caught up. Such a trip was expected to take a year, what with the time spent in California, where life was lazy, lovely, and luxurious beyond believing.

It is told of one young Luna that he had been gone two years, and his mother had grieved in crepe for months, when he came riding gaily home again with jewels from Los Angeles, and a bride from a California hacienda. They brought good merinos from California, too, and did much to breed up the scrubby New Mexico herds.

The first white man to settle with sheep in northern Arizona was Juan Candelaria. In 1866 he drove seven hundred head from Cubero, in New Mexico, to Apache County, where he lived until his death in 1930. His were the finest merinos in New Mexico, and he was one of those astonishing men who could live at peace with Indians. His example was followed by many others, and for a couple of decades sheep fed all summer against the cool, fresh flanks of the San Francisco, Mogollon, and White mountains, and were drifted down in winter to the warmth of the Salt River Valley. But cattlemen soon began to encroach, and one of the ugliest of all the sheep-

cattle wars was fought over the beautiful Tonto Basin. It was a
long-drawn-out feud between the Graham and Tewksbury families, filled with harsh romance and such conflicting claims that
its truth would be very hard to come by now.

Prescott, Arizona's capital, shared in all this, growing
prettily among its pines, and maintaining its New England
dignity. A Masonic lodge was promptly organized — perhaps in protest against Catholicism — and the newspaper
boasted that it was the only one in the great bilingual Southwest that was all English. But Catholic and Spanish-speaking
Tucson got the capital in 1867. The Yankees won it back to
Prescott in '77, and when John C. Frémont, the Pathfinder of
the West, was Governor of Arizona, he lived in Prescott. The
old gentleman was past his prime, and poor, and Arizona
finally requested his removal, as he was devoting more time
to his own money-making schemes than to his governing.
During the next decade fast-growing Phoenix played a shrewd
political game, and by '89 she captured the capital, and has
held it ever since.

Still, Prescott prospered through mines. As mines boomed,
and speculators put out tons of lying prospectuses, Prescott
continued to take in cash for supplies, for hauling goods and
machinery in all directions. Its greatest growth was due to
the United Verde Mine. In '77 Al Sieber, an Army scout,
thought that all that copper-stained iron ore in the Verde
Canyon ought to mean something, so he staked a claim; others
followed. Like all immensely rich mines, this one is reputed
to have been sold for a burro, a quarter of venison, a one-
eyed mule, or a plug of tobacco; so George Wharton James
reports in his *Arizona the Wonderland*. Mr. James may have
drunk of the Hassayampa, and his name has been jocosely
mispronounced as George Whopper James. But even the ac-

curate Mr. Joralemon states that the famous engineer James Douglas advised the Phelps Dodge Company not to buy the Verde, on the ground that a haul of a hundred and seventy-five miles to the railroad would forever prevent its paying. But the United Verde Copper Company, with Eugene Jerome of San Francisco as secretary, took out eight hundred thousand dollars' worth of copper before the price dropped and they had to shut down. It was not until '88 that W. A. Clark, Montana's Copper King, came along with enough money to make the United Verde pay.

The Copper King was active also in promoting a proposed railway to connect Prescott with Ash Fork, on the Santa Fe main line, and so shorten the haul by wagon train. A bill to provide a subsidy had been introduced into the territorial legislature of '85, known as the " thieving thirteenth." Swapping was brisk. Tucson wanted the insane asylum, but was put off with the State University. Phoenix got the coveted asylum, and other counties what it took to bring them into line. Negotiations were further complicated by the fact that the Southern Pacific, then building across southern Arizona, had no wish to be brought into competition with the Santa Fe at Phoenix. The battle was long and acrimonious, but it resulted in the building of a line, which was finally acquired by the Santa Fe.

So Prescott realized the universal dream of small towns and got a railroad, even if it was only a spur. In other ways, too, it developed as a normal frontier town. When the whole log and frame village took fire in 1900, the leaping flames consumed all of Whiskey Row and left only two of its thirty-five saloons. Prescott's citizens made a great field day of the event, set up tents, knocked shacks together, organized contests at rebuilding, and in no time had a better, sounder town, and a water system for fighting future fires. Its Yankee atmos-

phere was not changed; it still has a serene and quiet aloof-
ness which is more delightful to the visitor than the brisk
bustling its men of business might prefer.

In front of the pillared court house an arrestingly vigorous
Rough Rider in bronze reins his horse to a stop. On the
granite base is inscribed:

> " Erected by Arizona in honor of the 1st Volunteer
> Cavalry, known to history as Roosevelt's Rough Riders,
> and in memory of Captain William O'Neill and his com-
> rades who died while serving their country in the War
> with Spain."

Captain O'Neill in the Army and on the monument, his
neighbors knew as Bucky O'Neill, famed all over Arizona,
who lived at the Grand Canyon, and whose stained and battered hat hangs there now in Bright Angel Lodge.

In the court house I found the Yavapai County Chamber
of Commerce. There a brisk, heavy-set woman was dictating
sonorous phrases, which she later explained were designed
to encourage Congress to lend Arizona's mining men more
money, and quicker.

" Just a minute," she called politely. " Just look around."

I had not got far with the cases of ore samples, shelves of
Indian potsherds, racks of photographs, and piles of pamphlets, when she swiveled toward me.

" I can talk now. I'll be glad to."

With little prompting, she enlightened me. Prescott is the
center of the cattle business (cf. Fort Worth, San Antonio,
El Paso, Amarillo, Tucson). It is the center of the sheep
business. " Flagstaff may, of course, actually have more
sheep, and New Mexico runs some, but we are the real center
of the industry. Prescott is the center of a mining region

which produces all the ores: copper, silver and gold, lead, tungsten, and manganese. A few large mines are found elsewhere, but Yavapai County has the greatest number of small mines in the world.

" The dude business? We don't use that word. *Guest ranch* is correct, and Prescott is the center of that region. We have twenty-six guest ranches in Yavapai County."

" The first, they tell me, was in Oracle."

" They are," the lady said crisply, " in error. The very first lay-out was Mrs. Sturrett of the Cross Triangle, the ranch Harold Bell Wright used in his *When a Man's a Man*. Mrs. Sturrett had always done as everyone did, taken in all comers and made them as comfortable as she could. But people really prefer to pay their way. So finally Mrs. Sturrett began to let them pay thirty dollars, and gradually raised the rate to fifty dollars."

" A week? "

" A month. And she thought that was high. But it included horses, of course, and everything. That was about 1909 or '10. Then Romaine Laudermilk started his ranch at Wickenburg, and later he moved over into the Verde, where he is now. So, you see, Prescott is the center of the guest-ranch business, and its beginning."

I did not mention Wickenburg, nor allow myself to think of Tucson.

" This is really the heart of Arizona, you know. The area from Flagstaff north to the Utah line has all the flora and most of the fauna native to temperate and frigid zones. From Congress Junction south is found everything — animal and vegetable — that grows in tropical and subtropical zones. And here around Prescott we have both. And this is the one spot in the great Southwest where we have four distinct seasons: spring, summer, fall, and winter."

I bow to the Yavapai Chamber of Commerce. Weeks of travel had accustomed me to centers, but pre-empting the seasons was " tops " in my experience.

I referred to Bucky O'Neill, whose back was toward us, showing his hand reaching for the gun.

" That statue was made by Solon Borglum, and it is the greatest equestrian statue in the world." That was no surprise. " Sculptors come from everywhere to see it. Bucky O'Neill raised the first company of Rough Riders, you know, right here in this plaza. . . . Teddy Roosevelt? Oh, no, he just took over what Bucky had done. It was all right, of course; he could popularize it. But the first company was raised right here."

I was curious about the first rodeo, and I remained calm at the answer: " Right here, in Prescott. This is the cowboy capital of the world, you know. The first rodeo was on the Fourth of July, 1888." She produced proof in the form of a silver plate, backed by a wooden shield. " Citizens' Prize," it read. " Contested for and won by Juan Leiva over all competitors for roping and tieing steers. Time 1.17½. 100 yds." The medal had been turned in by an unknown patriot as scrap silver during the World War. Fortunately, it caught the eye of one whom Juan Leiva had taught to rope in his younger days. So he bought it and presented it to the Yavapai Chamber of Commerce.

My arms filled with literature, I strolled out onto the plaza, thrilled to feel that I was in the center of almost everything. In what one of my pamphlets described as " the pine-laden, health-giving, natural-air-cooled sunshine," I sat upon a bench to contemplate Prescott's manifold uniqueness. Naturally I looked at Bucky O'Neill, whose fine profile was stern under the soft Rough Rider hat. Two men of his kind balanced on their heels between the cement and the grass.

" Good, isn't it? " I ventured.

" Sure," said the younger one. " It's good all right. Look at Bucky a-lookin' off to the west where he must a seen a Spaniard, and a-reachin' for his gun. But he didn't quite reach it in time, you see. They killed him."

" Is it right? The pose and the gun? The horse reined in like that? "

" Well, his reachin' for his gun is all right, I guess, and his face turned like that. . . . He sure must a had a good horse to rein him in that a-way without upsettin' him."

" Is it a portrait? Did you know Bucky O'Neill? "

" Well, no, I didn'; but *he* did."

The older man squinted against the natural-air-cooled sunshine.

" Well," he admitted, " I wouldn't call it a particular likeness, but as a resemblance it ain't so bad."

Later I sought the " Governor's Palace," which turned out to be two log cabins firmly and newly cement-chinked and roofed; and between them the square stone building recently put up by PWA funds to house the Sharlot Hall Museum. To me, Sharlot Hall was an infinitely more important experience than any quantity of old furniture, branding irons, prints, and even books. For no more Sharlot Halls are being produced, and no book will ever convey the living feeling or the true importance of this one.

Her room was not in order; my visit was too early. But Sharlot Hall does not apologize, any more than she makes unnecessary gestures with her worn and shapely hands. She stood firmly on adequate feet, and so erectly that a body no longer young rose like a fine tower to a heavy twist of hair still brown above the graying temple growth. Manner, voice, and enunciation were of a correctness not often met, but without pedantry. When she needed a racy word or provincial expression, she used it with the finality of a Dr. Johnson admitting it to the English language.

"Yes, the pioneers stuck together all right. They knew they'd better, or they'd be planted."

Miss Hall seldom smiles, but when she does, light travels across her strong, rugged face slowly, from eyes to lips.

"I am not 'co-operative,'" she smiled to say, but let it go at once. "So as long as I live this place is mine, and I control it. Most of the exhibits are mine, and I keep things up. The men who built this house were not very competent, so the roof leaked, and I had it done again."

Scorn is closer to Miss Hall's speech than humor. "Competency is no longer valued by a generation that expects a living without working for it. I offered a job to a high-school boy, and he said no, he'd get a government job at eighty-five dollars a month. I said: 'What can you do that would be worth eighty-five dollars to anybody?' But all these boys want is money, a bright car, and a new girl every twenty-five miles. And the girls are willing to be the new girl. . . . Well, when I get really impatient, I read Washington cursing God and wishing to die like Job."

Then she showed me around. "Tucson was the Spanish capital, of course, but it was only a small garrison, and they were scared to death of Apaches all the time; so when the Territory of Arizona was created in 1863, the capital was located here. Most of its inhabitants were New Englanders, and you can see that the house, 'Governor's mansion,' is pure Cape Cod. They built what they knew, and the winters are cold enough here to justify it, in all conscience. The log walls are all that is left of the original; and it has suffered a good deal. They put in new doors and larger windows, and one architect, who wanted it to look like Mount Vernon, put on a portico with a graveyard fence around the top. Nobody cared, of course. But finally the state bought it, and we have tried to restore it to some semblance of the original log cabin."

Miss Hall was reluctant to talk about herself, but I got a sketchy history anyhow. Her mother's family had moved from Iowa across Colorado, prospecting for placer gold.

" But the Utes were bad. And when Governor Goodwin came along with a sufficient military escort to assure some safety, they decided to try Arizona. . . . The country offered nothing, of course. There were no agricultural possibilities, no way to make a living; there isn't now." (" Dear, dear," I thought, " and the Chamber of Commerce sent me here! ") " Even sheep suffer from our frequent droughts. . . . There is ideal sheep country around Congress Junction, and in extreme drought the Basques from California used to drift their sheep into Arizona from the Owens Lake country. But when the first pioneers came in here, everybody was looking for gold, and there wasn't any to compare with the California gold finds. Placer mining developed along the Hassayampa as a backwash from California. The first miners here had failed out there, but learned their business anyhow."

Miss Hall, I found, was not born in Arizona, but in Kansas, where her mother's family had returned. Father Hall, apparently, just happened to be there in his wanderings from the Missouri to California and back again. He took his family west in '81. Sharlot, then a girl of twelve, drove a herd of thoroughbred colts. " And they were quite a nuisance.

" Yes, we went through Albuquerque. I remember it well, because the alkali water made the horses sick, and two of them died. But it was a pleasant town — shady — and the people were kindly. I remember one white woman who called to me as I went by. She was lovely, with a sweet voice. She was taking her bread out of one of those Mexican outdoor ovens, and she gave me a loaf for my mother, who wasn't well."

We could not establish the fact, but I should like to believe that the sweet-voiced woman was my grandmother. She lived there then. She probably baked her bread in an outdoor oven, and it would have been like her to give a little girl a loaf. I remember that nobody ever came to her house that she did not offer something — a glass of wine with cookies; coffee with thick, ropy cream and sugar — and cinnamon-sprinkled coffee cake; and for children, tall glasses of milk from the coolroom. And nobody left without a gift: a pat of butter in a catalpa leaf, new-made cheese, fruit or berries in an Indian basket, or a bunch of garden roses from the thicket by the gate.

" Yes," said Miss Hall, after I had reminisced, " people not only knew how to take care of themselves, but they helped each other, too. Many people were kind to us, I remember. No, we were not a large party; just two wagons with four-horse teams. Travel was safe enough then, and my father and uncle knew the frontier. We children had to do our part; there was no coddling in those days. Even the youngest gathered firewood, and if there were no sticks, no excuses were accepted. You could always find buffalo or cow chips."

So Sharlot Hall was grounded in the realism I found so inspiring, and by living close to it she had gathered her sense of the Southwest, which she expressed later in poetry. When Charles F. Lummis founded *Out West* in California, she worked with him as associate editor. She did not talk much about the bustling little man, but she spoke of his wife's gentleness, and of the boys. In 1910 Sharlot Hall's collected poems were published as *Cactus and Pine,* a good title for her. Thorny cactus makes marvelous beauty out of its struggle for existence, and pines are invincibly straight and true.

I decided not to return to the Chamber of Commerce. My mood was spoiled for more assurances of the priority and centrality of Prescott. I preferred to meditate on the two women, and on what they exemplify of the changing Southwest. Miss Hall so completely personifies our matter-of-fact ancestor, who had no illusions about a land that was hard to live in, but that he chose all the same. The Chamber of Commerce secretary sees all that rigorous past through a rainbow, which is also a magnifying glass. One presides over a museum, whose exhibits faithfully set forth the paucity of the life they served. The other animates an institution devoted to putting the best foot forward, to making everything look richer, bigger, easier, more romantic than it is. I wanted to leave Prescott remembering most sharply a woman who is herself as worthy a monument to the old Southwest as the bronze Bucky O'Neill in the plaza. Spectacular as he is, he is not a shade more gallant.

Northern Arizona

is dominated by the Grand Canyon, and who can describe the Grand Canyon? The Spaniards found its cliffs taller than the tallest towers of Seville. James O. Pattie noted it only because it got in his way. After days of following the canyon, he said: "A march more gloomy and heart-wearing to people hungry, poorly-clad . . . cannot be imagined. April 10 we arrived where the river emerged from these horrid mountains which so cage it up as to deprive all human beings of the ability to descend its banks and make use of its waters."

A modern poet, from a comparatively gentle New Mexico valley, wrote of the drive in from Cameron: "Forty miles," he groaned, "of terrific unrelieved geology! Not a human thought or emotion, not a shred of human experience anywhere among its awful rocks! At the Grand Canyon we leaned over the edge until the indisputable blurred our vision. . . ."

All northern Arizona is powerful. Size, like the Grand Canyon; age, like the Petrified Forest; impersonality, like the Painted Desert, are sure to give man a sense of his own proportionate puniness — if only for a minute — or to throw him into violent revolt against it. Perhaps a kindly Providence has seen to it that several northern Arizona towns offer the refuge of a Harvey House. Nothing could present a more soothing contrast to too much geology or too much travel than the quiet restfulness, the sense of being at home again, that a Harvey House gives. No picture of the Southwest could be complete without a sketch of that genius, Fred Harvey.

XI

FRED HARVEY, CIVILIZER

N 1850, WHEN THE SOUTHWEST WAS FAIRLY WELL COV-
ered with trails, every night women clambered out of creaking covered wagons to fry up one more greasy step toward
national dyspepsia. In that year the frying-pan's doom
stepped ashore in New York. Nobody would have thought
then that the gangling British youth was destined to be the
great civilizer of the wild and woolly West. He was tall and
spare, light-complexioned, and he spoke with the British accent the West was to find so funny. He had little education
and no money, but he had energy, and the first job he found
was in line with his destiny, if he had only known it. For
Fred Harvey's career is said to have begun in a restaurant,
washing dishes. Judging by his later achievements, he doubtless washed them phenomenally clean. At any rate, his beginning wage of two dollars a week rose steadily until he had
the price of a ticket west. In St. Louis he owned a small restaurant where he cooked such good food that it made a reputation and a success until the Civil War ended it. Broke again
and ill after a round of typhoid, young Harvey returned

to kitchen and pantry jobs, but the Western bee was in his bonnet, and he became a mail clerk on the westbound Hannibal & St. Joseph Railroad, which was soon absorbed by the Chicago, Burlington & Quincy.

With that road, and for many years, Fred Harvey rode the line, getting business. His specialty was shipments of cattle driven up from South Texas over the trails, and there he learned to judge beef. But Harvey was a restaurant man by destiny. He liked good food, and he must have had a tender heart for the traveling public, eating soggy sandwiches out of paper boxes or acquiring indigestion in fly-infested eating-places along the route. He suggested to the Burlington management a series of eating-houses where well-prepared good food should be cleanly served. The Burlington had no time for visionary notions, and finally, to get rid of him, said: " Why don't you take your scheme over to the Santa Fe? "

" That's a good suggestion," said Mr. Harvey, and followed it.

At the Santa Fe he found encouragement and in 1876 the first Harvey Eating House was opened at Topeka. By that time he had been married for sixteen years and had a family of four lively children, growing up in the shadow of that first little red-painted eating-house. The Topeka House was followed by others as the tracks were laid westward until now they dot the line at convenient intervals all the way to Los Angeles. Travelers on the A., T. & S. F. no longer had to bother with lunches in boxes. At every meal-time the train stopped at a Harvey House and a dinner gong pounded by a white-coated man announced such a meal as was seldom equaled in those days.

Good hot food, well cooked and served, and plenty of it. Breakfast consisted of oatmeal, steaks or chops, eggs, hot cakes, and coffee, with liberal second helpings. And all for seventy-five cents. Dinner, for a dollar, included soup, a roast or fowl with vegetables, potatoes, dessert, and a drink. The manager passed around with sizzling steaks, urging more food, and waitresses reached the long-armed coffee-pot over every shoulder to keep the cups filled. One might, of course, have tea or great brimming glasses of rich milk. Passengers were seated at tables for eight, and served as quickly as they could eat, but without feeling hurried. Who can ever forget the managers intoning: " Passengers will be given ample notice before the departure of the train "; " Passengers still have ten minutes "? And for a slow eater many a train has been held, while conductors stood, watch in hand, and the engineer panted with his locomotive.

Those were the happy days for railroads and their related enterprises. All forward-looking towns wanted the railroad and bid high to get it. Santa Fe, some of whose citizens foresaw fortunes for themselves in the Denver & Rio Grande Railroad, gave that line the advantage, whereupon the Atchison, Topeka & Santa Fe built directly from Las Vegas to Albuquerque and left its namesake off on a spur. Down the valley, Bernalillo was chosen for the division point, but Don José Leandro Perea, the great patron of that town, did not want the disturbance of shops and switch engines, so he supported stagecoaches as against trains, refused either land or cash, and Albuquerque citizens gave the Santa Fe enough land for all their buildings. In eastern New Mexico the little town of Portales refused to " co-operate," and Clovis, a perfectly new town of fresh frames, was built.

Fred Harvey rode along with all these undertakings, for the Santa Fe gave him land and built his eating-house alongside its station and hauled his freight and express free of

192

charge. One who knew young Fred at the beginning of his career said: "These fellows think they know how to ask for things, but they ought to have seen Fred when he was building up. He used to ask for everything, he asked and kept on asking, and finally he got it. He paid no freight or express, no telegraph bills or traveling expenses. He even shipped his help around without paying for them. No wonder he could buy better food than anybody else and serve it cheaper. No local place could compete with him, possibly. They still can't."

These helpful privileges no longer exist, but Fred Harvey is still unrivaled, for he had such ideas as no local concern could equal. His roasters and broilers ended the supremacy of the frying-pan. Knowing good meat, he replaced the thin slab of beef, pounded and fried hard in fat, by the thick juicy steak, broiled over coals. He even began to offer rare steaks and roasts. "I've seen many a critter," said one cowboy, affronted by pink meat, "be hurt worse than that and get well." He bought beef and mutton in the Kansas City stockyards, where his early arrivals and canny eyes got the best every time. His meat is still bought so, on the hoof, by expert buyers, in Chicago now as well as in Kansas City. He bought poultry and eggs from farmers along the way and contracted for milk. So the cattle country drank its first milk fresh from the cow and not from cans. Harvey even saw the possibilities of game and fish, and mountain trout, quail and rabbits, venison and bear meat appeared on the menus. He made his own blend of coffee and offered both black and green tea, a curious innovation. It is a mark of the man that the system he founded still deals with many individuals and firms he started with sixty years ago. No rival can come in and undersell an old dealer. Vegetables were, of course, the last to come, even in the Harvey Houses, for this universal browsing on green is a new fad. Even today a green salad in a wooden bowl is an innovation at the Alvarado at Albuquerque, though in any house direct communication with the chef will produce a crisp salad properly tossed in an oily dressing with a hint of hidden garlic.

The Harvey idea went beyond good food to include cleanliness unprecedented and such service as the West had never known. It began that way and has never changed. Waitresses appear in fresh striped uniforms every morning and in snowy white at night. Every detail is supervised with military severity. Kitchens are impeccable, and all employees know they had better be. During his lifetime nobody knew at what hour, day or night, the big boss might appear. Before a train had well stopped, Fred Harvey might appear behind the counter, in the kitchen or the pantry. His methods were direct, and his vocabulary adequate. Let his keen eye detect one spot on table, floor, or cloth, one smear on coffee-urn, one chip in a cup, and he might upset the table, yank out the immaculate linen, send china and silver crashing, food spilling, coffee splashing in a steaming flood. At least such stories have long been current in the West, perhaps because that country could not imagine such excellence as Fred Harvey achieved without violence. And he made nothing of firing anybody, from bus boy to manager.

Once Tom Gable, who now lives in Santa Fe, was with him when " old Fred " lit like a bomb in Raton. Negro waiters were employed then and the Raton force had got involved in a midnight brawl. Several darkies had been carved beyond all usefulness, and the manager was distracted. Fred Harvey had no use for distraction in managers, so he fired that worthy along with his entire force and appointed Tom Gable to the

WHO CAN DESCRIBE THE GRAND CANYON?

[*photo, Laura Gilpin*]

vacancy. Mr. Gable had had no restaurant experience at the moment, but one did not argue with Fred Harvey. Anyway, Mr. Gable had an idea. Women, who had been used in houses farther east, he hoped would prove less likely than Negro men " to get likkered up and go on tears." He would take the job if he might have waitresses. So wires were sent off to Denver and Kansas City.

" And that," says Mr. Gable, with modest recognition of his historical role, " is how I brought civilization to New Mexico. Those waitresses were the first respectable women the cowboys and miners had ever seen — that is, outside of their own wives and mothers. Those roughnecks learned manners."

Fred Harvey was an autocrat, and from his decisions there was no appeal. But he was a beneficent despot who cared for his people. Even before he began to build hotels, he rented, cleaned up, and furnished houses for his waitresses, who were provided not only with decent quarters, but with chaperonage too. When hotels were built, they included rooms for the girls with laundries, ironing-rooms, places to sew and to receive their beaux. The latest and finest is at the Grand Canyon, where a stone building with timbered second story houses one hundred and fifty girls in quarters much better than many hotels offer their guests. Girls start as waitresses in small-town lunchrooms and are promoted to better houses, to dining-rooms, and to the swankiest hotels. For many years El Tovar at the Grand Canyon and the Alvarado at Albuquerque were preferred; nowadays La Fonda at Santa Fe runs them a close second. And many a " Harvey girl " has lived in the service to be a woman of years, walking a bit gingerly on feet that have suffered much, but still smiling, still remembering hundreds of names, still a recognized part of the life of her town.

Bridget Malone, who was head waitress at Las Vegas for thirty years, knew so many people by name that it was said she was one of the two most popular women in New Mexico. The other was Miss Clara Olson, who, as secretary to several governors, could have run the state quite as well without the political puppets who postured at her manipulation. Miss Jennie Flanagan at Albuquerque rivals Bridget, for the success of many an Albuquerque party depends upon her, and nobody who knows the Alvarado will ever feel a stranger there, passed on from Joe, the bellhop, to Sammie Bowman or Walter J. McNally in the office, to Jennie in the dining-room.

A person of seventy who has never worked for anybody but Fred Harvey is not unusual. And when faithful employees have lived out their usefulness, they are cared for. Fred Harvey's will gave everyone employed at the time of his death a life pension equal to his wage, and assurance of a job as long as he lived. The last beneficiaries of that generosity have died recently: a colored bartender and a porter. But the system has no pension plan, no remotest hint of employee participation. " Cases," they say, " are handled on their merits." And meritoriousness means a complete submergence of the individual in the system. A manager who expressed his opinion of affairs in the town where he lived was removed to another town and made aware that one more such break would end his career. Fred Harvey people are always and forever Fred Harvey people and have no life aside from that. Most of them have never known anything else, and probably never felt its lack.

Most men and women in positions of authority now — managers, directors, supervisors, and heads of departments — started as bus boys or bellhops, began in the kitchen or selling papers on the trains. Chefs and head waiters are usually

Italians, Swiss, or French, who have first served as stewards on dining-cars. Victor Vizetti, who had been a chef in Italy, met Fred Harvey in Chicago, and before long he was supervisor of the whole dining-car service. Once, when Fred was still operating on a shoe string, Victor Vizetti found himself with no chef either in Williams or in Winslow. So he cooked the breakfast himself in Williams, caught the fast train to Winslow, and cooked one there in time to catch another train back and cook dinner in Williams, and get back to Winslow in time to prepare that dinner and make it back to Williams for supper and so to Winslow. Busy times.

Fred Harvey, as civilizer, has had occasion to discipline the public too. Early he decreed that no coatless man should be served in his dining-rooms. Tieless, yes, even with unbuttoned collar, but coats were compulsory at the linen-covered tables. Nobody went hungry. The man in his shirtsleeves could eat in the lunchroom, and he was offered a coat at the dining-room door. They were usually smallish, black alpaca jackets, which strained over the typical Westerner and left his big hands dangling.

Whether because the tight coat irked his brawny shoulders or the prissy rule his spirit, one ill-advised Westerner brought suit in 1921 and carried his case to the Supreme Court of Oklahoma. Mr. Ford Harvey, then its president, appeared for the company. He explained that his father had found rules necessary for the protection of his patrons ever since cowboys used to ride into the eating-houses and demand food for beast as well as man. Mr. Harvey convinced the judge that the rule against horses was no more imperative than the rule against " unsightly, if not unsavory people," and won his case. The coat rule broke down, at last, in Santa Fe, where Fred Harvey, then in the dude business, advertised artists as an attraction. And artists, who then affected an assortment of bright-hued shirts superimposed, refused to wear coats.

Other rules are still inviolable, as anyone can prove any time. One snowy, blustery day a friend and I arrived at a Harvey House, and the Southwest offers no more grateful refuge after a hard trip. Aching with cold and weariness, we longed for tea in front of the roaring fire in the lobby. But no, tea could not be served there, though seven employees stood about, doing nothing, and we were ready to fee a boy to fetch it. The manager said he had no discretion; no authority nearer than Kansas City could grant our plea for tea taken cozily by the fire. So we perched, perforce, on tall stools in the lunchroom and drank our tea like nice children. The Harvey System, on such occasions, is like nothing so much as a good old German nurse, starched and firm. " Now you got everything nice," you can hear her say. " Be a good girl and don't fuss."

But Fred Harvey is not too unyielding. He can change with the times, as your most conventional old aunt finally comes round. The first big change got him into the news business, which has led on to curios, antiques, and finally dudes.

" Before Fred Harvey," as his older employees say, the Railroad News Company supplied the traveling public with its periodicals, chewing-gum, and soda pop. But there was so much complaint of butcher boys as short-change artists and purveyors of " racy packages " that Mr. Ripley, president of the Santa Fe, asked Fred Harvey to take over the news business. Fred Harvey did, and with it a German youth of about sixteen who was to prove a valuable heritage. Herman Schweizer has developed into one of the country's best judges of Indian and Spanish Art. At sixteen he was honest and bright, hard-working, willing to do anything, and he had that gift of the gods, a sure taste for the authentic and the beautiful. Even while he peddled his papers on the trains, he bought what he could, always selecting well-worked Navajo silver and blankets that were firmly woven and of harmonious design.

From butcher boy Herman Schweizer rose to be the one-man force in the lunchroom at Coolidge, New Mexico. There he began to buy old guns and there occurred an incident he rather sheepishly admits to be " more or less true." One night the crew of a freight train came in. Trainmen were tough in those days and accustomed to bully anyone they could. Herman served them from his freshly steaming urn, setting out little pitchers of cream and a big sugar bowl. Doughnuts were handy, of course, and pies and cookies under glass domes. The men ate and then rose to leave without paying. It was a trick they were good at, and what could a slim boy do against so many? The slim boy, as it happened, could do plenty. One he crowned with the sugar bowl, and then, by most effective mischance, he picked up an ancient and unworkable gun which happened to be standing there. The railroaders, no judges of ancient arms, made no further ado about paying. Next day Herman was summoned to division headquarters, where, instead of the reprimand he expected, he was commended and promoted.

Fred Harvey and his good friend President Ripley of the Santa Fe both appreciated the picturesque background of the Southwest with its double cultures, and they had named hotels for Spanish conquerors. But it took the combination of Herman Schweizer, John F. Huckel, who had married Miss Minnie Harvey, and directed the news business, and Minnie, who had designed the hotel at Trinidad, to launch the Harvey System on a career very strange for a purveyor of food. In 1900 Albuquerque was a growing town and it was proposed

199

to erect a good hotel there. Mr. Huckel, a highly cultivated man of wide experience as writer and publisher, proposed a Spanish building. Minnie, with her man's brain, woman's appreciation, and a genius for getting what she wanted from her father, was enthusiastic. So the Alvarado was planned with the wide porches and heavy Spanish-Moorish arches which the irreverent have dubbed " Harvey eating arches." Taste has changed, but the deep porches are still cool on the hottest days and the Alvarado must stand as the first recognition of New Mexico's Spanish background as its name honors the first white man to pass by there.

The Huckels, almost the first to buy with discrimination, had a priceless collection of the best Indian craft of the Southwest. It was proposed to show it in a museum at the Alvarado and to open a curio shop of good Spanish, Mexican, and Indian antiques and modern handicrafts. Who had the first idea it is difficult to say now. One can imagine many glowing, visionary gabfests between Herman Schweizer, with his growing knowledge of " curios," and the Huckels, inspired to make a commercial concern an arbiter of the arts. What they needed was a decorator who knew Indian things and had imagination.

Mary E. J. Colter, teaching architecture in a school in Wisconsin, got a message one day offering her a job to design an " Indian Building " in Albuquerque, New Mexico. It was signed " Fred Harvey."

" Who is Fred Harvey? " asked Miss Colter, whose wanderings had been in the Northwest.

" Fred Harvey," said her adviser, " is the man who made the desert blossom with a beefsteak, and you'd better accept."

Undeterred by the blossoming beefsteaks and eager to handle a fine collection of Indian things, Miss Colter took the chance. Her taste laid out the famous room at Albuquerque with its shelves of ancient baskets, its correct Hopi altar behind locked gates, its petrified woods, carved chests, and piles of blankets. After a couple of turns during her vacations, Miss Colter left the Wisconsin school and became a part of the Fred Harvey System.

A black porter made her welcome. " You've done joined up with a fine system," he said. " This is a patriarch and we're all related."

From the start Fred Harvey's curios and antiques were as good, as well chosen, and as correctly served as his famous beefsteaks. But a public which had never heard of Pueblos or Navajos, of Spanish art or Mexican churches, declined to detour from the straight path to the beefsteaks to see " real Indians at work " or a museum of antiques. Literally for years young Herman stood in front of his Indian building, begging travelers just to step in and look. For years, that is, except when he was touring the Indian reservations for more blankets; making trips into Mexico when another family's treasures came on the market; or negotiating in his office with shawled women for a battered old saint, a dented silver dish with a noble crest, or a low-set brooch or ring that had to be sold to meet the rent. There was no fooling Herman Schweizer as to value, but he gave fair prices. They say only Fred Harvey's confidence in Mr. Schweizer's business acumen allowed him time to turn the tide of indifferent eaters into the steady stream of visitors who now know the Indian Building at Albuquerque if they know nothing else of the Southwest. Charles Amsden in his book *Navajo Weaving* says: " Fred Harvey saw the value of this outmoded article when others less discerning were casting it aside for the new, and I think it is no exaggeration to say that Fred Harvey saved from destruc-

tion thousands of worthy old specimens of Navajo weaving."
This may be said of every other Indian craft of the Southwest,
and of priceless examples of Mexican and European art.

Meanwhile Fred Harvey and the Sante Fe had discovered
the Grand Canyon of the Colorado in Arizona — an event
more momentous than Cárdenas's discovery of it in 1540.
The few who had seen it before 1905 rode out on horseback
or in buckboards, and stopped at Martin Buggeln's Bright
Angel Camp, where one could sleep in a small tent, eat in a
big one, and hire horses to ride down the trail. A railroad,
designed to haul ore out from the Anita Mine, had failed, so
the Santa Fe bought it up. And Fred Harvey built a hotel and
named it El Tovar after the first Spaniard to see the Hopi
villages. El Tovar represents a cross between the log cabin,
considered suitable for a mountain place, and the turreted
hostelry which could ask top prices. Fire seems not to have
occurred to anyone as a danger, but the building was set too
far back for the view, lest the enduring rocks should crumble
and pitch it into the mile-deep abyss. There are more bathrooms now; the best possible fire-fighting equipment could
deluge the whole place at the first flicker of a flame; but old
El Tovar is as it was when people now aging went there on
their honeymoons, and any suggestion of a more modern
building brings protests from all over the world.

Another Indian building was built at the Canyon, Hopi
House. Built of native stone by Hopi Indians, it looks like
one of their villages and it houses a notable collection of Hopi
basketry and weaving and Navajo crafts. Hopis work there,
as Navajos do in Albuquerque, and every afternoon when the
tourist buses come in they dance. But dancing for tourists
with no deeper meaning of their own, they are not averse to
protecting their bodies from the mountain chill with long,

warm underwear. In fact, a visitor's real distinction is established if for him the Hopis dance without their flannels.

For twenty-five years El Tovar has been managed by Victor Patrosso, who began to work for Fred Harvey under his uncle, the famous Victor Vizetti. He is that stately diplomat who greets you with such impersonal suavity, whose manner with European royalty and stars of the stage and screen is no more impressive than his gentle consideration of any grandmother. Mr. Patrosso has known all the great of his time and remains quite unfluttered. He can arrange a mass on Sunday when Al Smith is the guest, provide food suitable for an East Indian nabob, preside at a Rotary banquet, protect a President from annoyance, and spot a bounder in one wink.

The old Bright Angel Lodge had been operated as a more modest house, and near it was a building where one might hear lectures on the Canyon and the daring few who had gone down it in boats, buy postal cards and pictures, or have one's own films developed. In 1936 a new Bright Angel was built. Stone cottages are strung along the rim, many with magnificent canyon views, all furnished in early American style. The lobby contains many old bits of Western life: a Jenny Lind holding a bunch of cigars, worn and stained old sombreros, branding irons, and spurs. Saddle leather and cinches form the upholstery, blue denim buttoned with brass the hangings, and the fireplace is made of stones from every geological era the river has cut through to make the Canyon.

This, like most of the houses, is the work of Mary Colter, who ranks with Herman Schweizer as a Fred Harvey find. Aided and abetted by the Huckels, she has studied Southwestern architecture and all its variants from church to pueblo, from Moorish castle to Navajo hogan, and she has incorporated all their features into Harvey's hotels. She has ravaged antique shops and bid at auctions from New York to Mexico, and she has shipped in or had copied furniture and rugs, curtains, dishes, iron lanterns, tiled friezes, and porcelain cocks. She has bought the work of Southwestern artists, and used rare examples of Mexican or Indian pottery and of hand-carved saints in the bedrooms. The public instinct for collecting has made it necessary to screw such things to the walls, but one may still look at them. One by one, most of the little red eating-houses of fifty years ago have been rebuilt and refurnished in what should probably be called the Fred Harvey style. Their names reflect the Spanish history of the Southwest: Cárdenas and Castañeda, La Posada, and Alvarado; not one celebrates the fame of an Anglo. The only Indian appellation is El Navajo at Gallup, New Mexico, though that too is in the Spanish form. El Navajo is notable for a signal act of courtesy. Its walls are decorated with copies of Navajo sand-paintings, put there with the consent and approval of the tribe's medicine men, who performed a ritual dedication of the building.

As civilizer and educator, Fred Harvey is in some danger of raising the threat to his own supremacy. Every considerable Southwestern town now advertises one or two hotels with all the Harvey features: good beds and food, immaculateness, efficient service, and even the Spanish name and architecture, Indian crafts and decorations. They are as standardized as the old golden-oak furniture and red carpet ever were, and one advertises itself as the " most unique hotel in the Southwest." They have, too, a curio shop to compete with other shops which line the streets offering " real Indians at work," and articles that run from stamped-out tin jewelry to excellent pieces. They all cater to thousands of travelers in their own cars and by motor bus. Neither the Santa Fe nor Fred

Harvey has a monopoly and can dictate terms any more. The Santa Fe pleads with us in full-page advertisements to be safe in trains, it designs new trains to tempt poor purses, and it assures us that its taxes keep our children in school. And Fred Harvey is putting up signboards to remind us that the Harvey Hotels are the best. Those of us who have known them all our lives have no doubt about it.

The Harvey System is a fascinating study in meeting new conditions without sacrificing old character. There has been no let-down. A smear or a spot is as unimaginable now as of old. But Fred's son, Ford, as president, injected a greater suavity into the discipline. He had not known his father's struggle. Always a rich boy and man and well educated, he was an unusual executive and unfailingly considerate. He was quick to catch a new idea, generous in allowing his employees a chance to work things out and in giving credit where it was due. His brother Byron, who succeeded him, has done an equally fine job during a ten-year period of depression and rapidly changing conditions. " Mr. Byron " is known to his employees as quick and sympathetic to understand their problems; those who know him best laugh at his reluctance ever to take personal credit for anything he does.

These men and their sons carry on the old tradition with family pride and loyalty, for the Harvey System is a family affair; not a dollar's worth of stock is owned by outsiders. Its only presidents have been the first Fred, his son Ford, and now his second son, Byron. Byron has three sons, two of whom are now vice-presidents. What would happen if this sturdy stock should produce a waster or a nitwit nobody can forecast. Certainly the system would run for a while on its own momentum, manned by its extraordinary force of employees. But they are all employees, no more. To the Harvey family any hint of democracy in their ranks is not so much anathema as beyond conception. They offer a suggestive example of how capitalistic enterprise might hold its own, remain free of labor troubles, keep its labor turnover below the average, and keep government out of business. If all employers had been as thoughtful about housing their people, for instance, how little we should have heard of federal housing! The Harvey folk as well as the traveling public are content with such treatment as the old German nurse gave her charges. " You got everything nice here now. Be a good girl and don't fuss."

Arizona and New Mexico

*are held together by the Navajo Reservation, which alto-
gether disregards the state line. The railroad and the highways parallel the southern boundary of the country of the
Navajos from a point between Flagstaff and Winslow, Arizona, to a point near Thoreau, New Mexico. It is a country
of colored rocks and of strangeness. The Petrified Forest,
which Arizonans used to endow with petrified birds singing
petrified songs, is amazing enough without that; for the
trunks of its great fallen trees are broken to reveal colors
as lovely and traceries as delicate as a butterfly's wing. And
the Painted Desert's layers of colored sands make a kaleido-
scope that faints at midday into pale tones, and warms at
sunset into richest reds, yellows, purples, and violets; it always shimmers, as though movement were in the sand, not
the air.*

*From a few miles west of Gallup to thirty miles east of
it the road runs along tall sandstone cliffs like battlements.
Streaked with purple, varied with ochres and toneless buff,
their canyons are so concealed that they seem to have no
opening. One might believe the Navajos were forever safe
behind them, protected from the noisy life of the white man,
speeding along the tracks with jettying white steam or rolling
black smoke, honking in motors, or building towns loud with
whistles and bells.*

*But the Navajo is not apart. All along the road one sees
him, riding a pony, driving a wagon or a creaking jallopy,
loaded with his mothers, sisters, cousins, and aunts. (Only
never his mother-in-law.) In every town they trade wool for
canned goods, blankets for clothes, jewelry for the luxuries
they are learning to like. Gallup, especially, is the Navajo's
town.*

XII

GALLUP AND THE NAVAJOS

ALLUP, NOT LONG SINCE KNOWN AS A DULL AND dusty town on the Santa Fe, has, by an inspired stroke of advertising, established itself as the Indian's show town. Since its Intertribal Indian Ceremonial was established in 1922, readers of tourist folders from the whole world head annually for Gallup to see Indians dance.

White men had passed that spot many years before the Santa Fe built a red board station-house there and called it Gallup. Trappers watered at a spring under the hill where Indians had refreshed themselves centuries before that. The Army rested at that spring on their first daring expeditions into the Navajo country. Later it was a way station between Fort Wingate and Fort Defiance, named as a tribute to the dangers of its location. After the tracks were laid, students of the Navajo and sightseers with the fortitude to ride miles and to sit through long winter nights set out from Gallup to attend Navajo ceremonies. Guides could always be had in Gallup. Dick Maddox, dean of them all, whose Ford and his driving of it have grown into a legend of mechanical sturdiness and the tenacity of human life, still twirls his mustache and rolls out his resounding remarks around El Navajo. Most modern travelers choose less picturesque guides with easier cars. Gallup supports several touring companies, and a Chamber of Commerce housed in a Navajo hogan and bursting with information about Navajos. Traders from the whole eastern half of the reservation stock up in Gallup, owe money there, and meet there the visitors whom they proudly jounce off over back country roads for days or weeks in " a real trading post." Navajos and Zuñis trade in Gallup, too, picking up the worst of the white man's liquor, diseases, and habits in exchange, often, for the worst of their own handiwork. To its inhabitants, Gallup is much else. To the traveling public, it is the taking-off place for the Navajo country.

Once, driving toward Gallup, we opened our lunch near a carload of Navajos. The older man wore his hair long; the young fellow's was cropped up to his ears, and he wore neither woven sash nor silver necklace. His wife, giggling shyly, shook round breasts under a velveteen jacket, and bobbed a string-wound chignon on her neck. The older woman wore the traditional dress, too — ruffled skirts, velvet blouse, and a mass of turquoise and silver. We exchanged comments on the Ceremonial. The young man was going to dance the *Yebechai;* the older was a singer, he said.

" I wonder," said my companion, " what those Indians think about when they sit so quietly? " Thoughts no more memorable, probably, than mine, as I watched the shadow slide up Mount Taylor's flank, while the sun lowered itself through horizontal clouds of rose and silver in the west. But they could call up many images out of their racial consciousness — if there is a racial consciousness, and if the schools did not catch them too young. For Mount Taylor, whose shapely crest would be the last to let the sunlight go, is the southern outpost of the Navajo's legendary world. There the sacred twins were born, from there they journeyed in the four directions, defying the unconquered monsters and preparing the world for the coming of the People. *Yei*, gods, inhabit its slopes as they do those of the other mountains which guard the Navajo's land: the San Francisco Peaks on the west in Arizona, El Pelado in the Jemez Mountains to the north, and the San Juan Mountains in the east.

Navajo legends have peopled streams and pools, rocks — wind-wrought into human or animal form — and ruins like the White House in the Canyon de Chelly, with beings as beautiful, as dramatic, as the gods of ancient Greece, and much less licentious. To many Navajos their gorgeous desert is still the home of mystic forces potent for good and ill. The sky-bird may still shake the silver showers or the woolly snow from outspread wings. In kindly mood, his waters soak and vivify the earth, or rest for months, quietly nourishing the roots of plants. In evil temper he may rage across the plain, wrecking man's little house, uprooting his crops, drowning his animals. If a man has committed evil he himself may suffer, or the children whom he loves so much. For the Navajo accepts responsibility for natural catastrophe. The world, as his ancient wise men saw it, was designed harmoniously, and if he attains inner concord, he can life forever at peace with it. All his legends and the course of his ceremonies illustrate this belief. His prayers are not only supplications; they are conscious endeavors to renew contact with the unheard harmony. Every morning he stands a moment facing the rising sun, he clears his mind of all evil before assisting at or even attending a religious rite. His ceremonies are meetings of people whose unified faith shall touch the supernal symphony

THE YOUNG NAVAJO
TRIES TO ADAPT TO A
CHANGING WORLD

[*photo, Ruth Frank*]

NAVAJO FAMILY MAKING CAMP BEFORE A DANCE

[*photo, Franc Newcomb*]

and restore its beauty to the sick one who has lost his own hold.

That Navajos do not always live in harmony with good needs no saying. That they have such an ideal and try to attain it is worthy of respect. That they manage to keep as much of their faith as they do against the white man's schools and churches is phenomenal. Perhaps their gift for changing in externals while they retain their inner integrity is due to their heterogeneity. They clearly show their kinship with every people that has crossed their range. But tall or short, long- or round-headed, even blue-eyed and red-haired, a Navajo is always unmistakably of the People. And he walks with the calm superiority of one who has never doubted his own worth.

Navajos, wanderers of Athabascan stock, have been a problem to somebody ever since they hit the Southwest, about three hundred years before the Spaniards did. Primarily hunters, they always farmed a little in well-watered valleys, and they supplemented their own harvests by raiding the granaries of the sedentary Pueblos. Along with food and stock, Navajo marauders carried Pueblo women and children off into slavery. Many of their clan names indicate descent from Hopi, Zuñi, and Jemez people, and all their crafts stem from Pueblo or Spanish culture. Navajo pottery has never amounted to more than the shaping of plain bottles or cooking-pots, and their basketry, though fine, is used only for certain ceremonial baskets. But Navajo women, with quick, facile fingers, soon learned to weave better blankets than their Pueblo teachers. James Pattie, crossing New Mexico in 1826, preferred Navajo blankets " as an article much better than that produced by the Spanish. They dye the wool of different bright colors, and stripe them with very neat figures." They had been making blankets then for about fifty years. The silversmith's art they were to learn later from the Mexicans.

Legends and ceremonies suggest that the Navajos must have captured shamans as well as women and children, for their religion is full of Pueblo lore and ceremonial art. Like the Hopi and Zuñi, the Navajo tells of his emergence from the underworld after similar adventures in three worlds below this one. Their masks and prayer plumes, sand-paintings, nine-day ceremonies, sacred meal, and altars are all clearly of Pueblo origin. Navajo masks are not so elaborate or so exquisitely made as the best of the Hopi or Zuñi masks, and altars are very inferior. But the Navajo sand-painting is true art in its beauty of design and precision of execution; and his legends are more poetic in conception and richer in imagery. He heightened and intensified every figure as the two dirty, snotty-nosed little boys of Pueblo mythology became the shining twins of the Navajos, bestriding the rainbow, fighting with forked lightning, riding the wind. The Navajos' debt to the Pueblos, so Dr. Ruth Underhill states, is clearly proved by comparison with the Apaches, a related Athabascan group. Apache rites and customs are more like those of the plains Indians than of the Navajos.

Alonzo de Benavides, writing of them in 1630, translates the word *Navajo* as " great planted fields." Later writers caught its resemblance to the Spanish *navaja*, knife. Certainly the Spaniard had reason to use the more bellicose word; the history of every village in New Mexico is marked by gory tales of rape and slaughter. The Spaniard fought back, of course, but until the United States Army faced him along a gun-barrel, the Navajo roamed unconquered and ravaged where he would.

At first the Navajo respected the bluecoat not at all and

continued to break treaties as fast as they were made. Then, in the sixties, General Carleton ordered Colonel Christopher Carson to kill all Navajo stock and round up the people. So ordered, so done. For Kit Carson, trapper, scout, mountain man, New Mexico's redoubtable hero, understood how to deal with Indians, treating them kindly when he could, sternly when he must, but always fairly.

At the *Bosque Redondo,* Round Wood, the Navajos knew such an exile as only a Hebrew poet could do justice to. Far from their deserts of colored rock, their rich valleys, piny hills, and snow peaks where the gods dwelt, the People suffered every ill. They were hungry because they could not hunt, and the food they were issued was often bad and always insufficient. When they tried to farm they were plagued by drought and flood. The alkali water made them sick, and they were smitten with smallpox. They were cold because they had no sheep to give wool for blankets. Their old people died of sorrow and their children of undernourishment. They were filled with dread because of a tradition that the *Diné* (People) would perish if they went east of the Rio Grande.

White men sold the government tainted meat and shoddy blankets for double the price of good stuff. Navajos, observant and quick, could learn a crooked game too. They forged the government's ration cards and managed to live by doubling freely in the weekly count. When metal disks replaced the paper cards they learned the art of making metal dies such as they still use to stamp out their silver and copper plaques. They demanded that zealous young priests should pay for the privilege of teaching their young. Many Indians ran away, especially young women who found men among other Indians and village whites who would feed them well and care for their children.

Those bitter years left a mark not yet eradicated. The Navajo is still a man of spirit, but it is now a smoldering, undercover temper which breaks out only in bitter mirth, in sullen distrust of the government, or in enjoyable outsmarting of the white man. Navajos, as a people, are never pitiful. Tragic, yes, but their strength and cleverness preclude so soft an emotion as pity.

By the treaty of 1868 the Navajos agreed to live at peace with the United States. They were given a small part of their former range — some three million, five hundred thousand acres — and some cattle, sheep, and corn for a start. They were promised schools, and heads of families were permitted to homestead one-hundred-and-sixty-acre tracts of their reservation. Their supervisor was a civilian agent instead of the military. As no Navajo wanted to leave the reservation permanently — few do yet — or understood individual ownership of land or the value of education, the only advantage to the Navajo must have seemed that of getting back to his old familiar mesas and canyons.

There were then about eight thousand Navajos (according to a very inaccurate count), who lived much as they do now. A pleasant and sympathetically correct picture of this life is given by Gladys Reichard in *Spider Woman,* and in *Dezbah.* Dr. Reichard lived with Dezbah's family as they drifted from the winter hogan of mud-wattled logs to the airy summer shelter of juniper. Families do not move far; many clans are known only in their own neighborhood. Relationship is through the mother, whose position is very dignified. Women own the sheep; the maternal grandfather or uncle heads the family. Men do some farming wherever it is possible, herd a few cattle, own far too many horses, trade with the whites, and control the ceremonial and clan life. Medicine men are priests as well as healers, and most of the great chants or sings are for the curing of physical illness.

At once traders and missionaries appeared. The government's first policy was to entrust Indian education to the churches, with the result that Catholics and Protestants staged some ludicrous contests for the souls and persons of bewildered Navajo children. Indians, generally hospitable to other creeds and courteous to other gods, were completely bewildered by the inability of the various Jesuses to get along together.

Traders, licensed by the government, built stone houses sturdy enough to serve as forts. The round house at old Red Rock, Arizona, had upstairs living-quarters with loopholes; and all had counters shoulder-high to protect the trader against his customers. A trader's stock included flour, coffee, tobacco, sugar, and canned goods. He carried bright calico because the missionaries had shamed the Navajo women out of the short wool dress and into the full, ruffled skirts of the period. Both men and women wanted velveteen for shirts. They offered in trade rough wool (Navajo carpet wool was shipped east from Albuquerque in the seventies), woven blankets, and silver jewelry. The ingenious Navajo proved himself a shrewd business man. His deft fingers could forge an I O U, and he could outsmart almost anybody in a trade. He became an expert borrower, pawning his jewelry and wangling it back from the complaisant trader to wear at the sings. The trader may, by law, sell a piece unredeemed after a year and a day, but most old traders can show fine shell, silver, turquoise, and coral that they have held for years. Navajos are honest about returning borrowed pieces and paying their debts — at long last.

Many traders are famous folk. The oldest post at Ganado,

Arizona, was built in 1876 by Lorenzo Hubbell, son of a Connecticut Yankee and a high-bred señorita from the Rio Grande Valley. The Navajos called him " Old Mexican " and as long as he lived he was their unfailing friend. His son Román, who spoke Navajo before he did English and who often seems to think like a Navajo, carries on the place and the tradition. Every distinguished visitor to the reservaton has sat in the long room at Ganado with its priceless blankets and baskets, autographed books, and orginal paintings and drawings, inscribed to the hospitable Hubbells. Many books about the Navajos have been assembled right there.

Ganado is not so far from the railroad, for the Southwest, at only eighty miles. Kayenta, one hundred and eighty miles north of Flagstaff, Arizona, is our most remote post office. When Witter Bynner, the poet, made his first visit there he rhymed in the guest book:

> *I don't forget*
> *And never will*
> *John and Louisa*
> *Wetherill.*

Neither will anybody else who ever knew them. John, gentle, vague, profane old Quaker, stumbled on the Mesa Verde hunting strayed cattle and, by a lucky turn in the trail, was the first white man to see the Rainbow Bridge. And Louisa, whose childhood in Colorado was enlivened by Ute attacks, knows more Navajo songs, legends, superstitions, medications, and spicy jokes than anybody else, and the Navajos so trust her that the head men from her region held up the first council meeting until she came. The Wetherills have raised their own family and a couple of Navajo girls, one of whom was found half dead with cold after she had been turned out of a school.

The best blankets and silver were made before the railroad brought buyers of cheap " Indian curios." The old blankets, of firmly woven stripes in natural tones or colored by vegetable dyes, are harmonious, soft, and durable. And the old bracelets, bowguards, and beads were hand-hammered out of thick, pure silver and set with rough chunks of turquoise. But when twenty-five-cent bracelets and gaudy blankets were demanded, Navajos eagerly bought aniline dyes and wove careless blankets on cotton warp, copying numerals from freight cars and letters from flour sacks. Silversmiths wrought thinner and thinner pieces, marked with arrows and swastikas, and forgot all the old designs. It took outsiders, headed by Fred Harvey, to create a market for good work.

Don Lorenzo Hubbell at Ganado and J. B. Moore at Crystal began to demand, and to get, good blankets. Cozy McSparren at Chinlee would buy only vegetable-dyed blankets. Mrs. Staples at Coolidge spent hours helping old weavers to remember the ancient dye formulas, and Colonel Staples set silversmiths to copying old bracelets, necklaces, and belts. Mrs. Franc Newcomb, at Two Gray Hills, amused herself by studying sand-paintings in the ceremonial hogans and by drawing them afterward. In time she won the confidence of the medicine men, who criticized her work and corrected it. In 1937 her *Sand-paintings of the Navajo Shooting Chant* was published. In 1939 some of John Frederick Huckel's collections were published as *Navajo Medicine Man;* others had been used in the Harvey hotel at Gallup.

Much as traders vary, from storekeepers to people aware of the tribe's wealth of art and lore, no whites have influenced the Navajo more. Trade is sensible, and must seem very steadying in contrast with the vagaries of missionaries and the government. It is not only that government policy has changed with every administration, but that different kinds of men, pursuing different ends, have always operated at one time. The wonder is that the Navajo has developed anything except a tribal dizziness. But his facile adaptability has kept him abreast of the times — almost.

Ten years after the treaty of 1868, the Navajos numbered thirteen thousand people, the beginning of a steady growth which is the root of all the trouble. Stock had increased accordingly; the People were selling blankets as well as wool and had become an industrious and prosperous nation. By 1880 the reservation had been enlarged several times, and the government, by the purchase of merinos, had tried to improve the sheep. The range was good, with miles of tall grama and blue-stem grass; and windmills, dams, and tanks had increased the water-supply so that most families could raise a little grain and some fruit. What else they needed they got from the trader. The government establishment consisted of one agent, one doctor, one farmer, one herdsman, one chief of scouts, and one teacher. That, except for the teacher and possibly the doctor, must have seemed about perfect to the Navajo.

Appalled by today's confusion of governmental agencies, missionary and welfare efforts, and political critics, one is tempted to yearn for those halcyon days. But time was not standing still, and the tribe went on increasing. Every year saw more, and presumably better, babies. And more and leaner stock, grazing on poorer pickings as they ate the grass down faster than it could renew itself. Something had to be done to balance increasing eaters and lessening food-supply; and, as the territories filled up with settlers, to fit the Navajo to meet the encroaching white on something like a fair basis.

In 1887 government Indian schools were established as the

best way round the conflicting claims of the churches. They were designed to make Indians into whites, without considering the Indian's capabilities or needs. Children were taken, by force if necessary, to huge boarding-schools, put through the standard courses, and required to do the menial work of the place. They were forbidden to speak their own languages, and religious toleration was interpreted to mean free election of any Christian faith. Indian parents naturally resorted to every trick to protect their children from education, and the Navajo Scouts were largely occupied in catching recalcitrant scholars.

The railroad brought rough and often vicious men, who sold illicit whisky on the reservation and hastened the spread of tuberculosis and venereal disease. By leasing and selling its alternate sections of land, the railroad checkerboarded the southern boundary of the reservation with white stockmen, who were always irresponsible, often predatory. Sheepmen began to push their flocks into land which had always been the Navajo's range. Public lands became, in the eyes of these gentlemen, their rightful domain, and the Navajo the interloper. And, because the Indian has never asserted his right to vote, with its attendant obligation of paying taxes, he is quite outweighed politically by the white man. His rights have always been the concern of associations, some sentimental, some sensible, all useful in reminding this country that it has promised the Indian a living in return for his land.

The man who has had to face all these conflicting interests — missionaries and traders within, aggressive white voters all around, uplifters and critics at a distance, and a remote and apathetic Congress — is the Indian Service employee. Whether you like him or not — and many do not — one can understand the Navajo problem only by contemplating the government man's fix. The policy now is to understand the Indian and to help him meet actual conditions. It is a policy more difficult to explain than the older systems, and more open to criticism and ridicule. John Collier, appointed United States Indian Commissioner in 1933 after years as the most unsuppressible critic of the Indian Department, moves rapidly on all fronts at once. His appearance lends itself to caricature, and his work has offered a good target for critics of the national administration.

Looked at coolly, his program offers little that is new. Commissioner Collier continually tries to get more land for Navajos. So has every commissioner preceding him. Everyone has known that the tribe must have more land or perish. Father Anselm Weber, head of the Franciscan Mission School at St. Michael's, Arizona, noted as long ago as 1921 that the reservation was twice as heavily stocked as rural Arizona. And he observed that white stockmen who used the public domain had no more notion of paying taxes than the Navajos.

In 1938 the Navajo's territory had been increased to 16,-000,000 acres; but there were 45,000 Navajos. The per capita holding was less than it had been since 1870, the land was poorer, and the tribe kept right on increasing. The Diné, a vigorous, intelligent, highly educable folk, would soon be facing actual starvation.

There is a limit to the amount of land that might be claimed for the Navajo. The other possibility is to make the reservation produce more. The Soil Conservation Service, working with the Navajo Civilian Conservation Corps, has done effective work. Waterworks have been undertaken on a larger scale than ever before, and hitherto unproductive land brought under cultivation. This work has brought wages, without which many Navajos would have suffered acutely. The rest of the job is being done by the Indian Service. Flocks and herds have been both reduced and bred up. Farming has been encouraged. And every effort is made to educate the Navajo to assist in this program, to appreciate it, and to make it work.

The original Navajo sheep was long-legged, bare-bellied, and light on the wool. Often they sheared only two and a half or three pounds, as against New Mexico's average today of seven pounds. Every agent experimented — with Cotswold or Rambouillet, even with Australian breeds — but there was no consistent policy. Worse, there was no effort to rid the range of non-bearing ewes, of scrubby stock, even of the worthless horses which represented wealth to the Navajo, but which ate as much as five sheep apiece.

A government experimental station at Fort Wingate is trying to evolve a sheep suited to the reservation. It should not want too much to eat and little to drink; be able to travel far without losing too much weight; bear wool not too greasy for the Navajo woman's method of handling it, and with a fiber uniform and dense enough for the commercial market. This beast should also cut up into fairly edible mutton. The young enthusiasts at the experimental station say they will have that phenomenon in another twenty years — if they are not thrown out before then.

Day-schools, allowing children to live with their parents, were first advocated by Francis Leupp. Appointed agent by Theodore Roosevelt, he was a newspaper man and a member of the Indian Rights Association — the first socially-minded reformer in the Service. This administration has realized Leupp's dream by opening forty-seven day-schools. Navajo women see to the washing and feeding of pupils, who are given a hot, square meal at noon. Girls are taught elementary domestic science and baby care. Boys are taught gardening, simple carpentry, and animal husbandry. And older people are encouraged to meet at the schoolhouse to use the sewing-machines and wash-tubs.

Three of the old boarding-schools have been turned into craft-schools, where Indians are teaching their youngsters the old arts. Ambrose, at Santa Fe, and Chester Yellow-hair, at Albuquerque, are turning out silver pieces as heavy and as fine as the old ones. And modern Navajo rugs are finer than any since the best old Chiefs' blankets. Government agencies are also creating a market for this work — not as curios, but as fine examples of the silversmith's and the weaver's art.

Navajos, loosely united in clans and under natural leaders, had no tribal organization until oil was discovered on their reservation in 1923. A meeting called then to discuss the disposal of the new wealth has resulted in the permanent Navajo Tribal Council — an effort to induct the Navajo into representative government. Its deliberations are an unforgettable sight, with bustling, harried government men and astute and stately medicine men trying to speak to each other through young Indians, adrift between two worlds. They get some business done, but slowly, far too slowly, for a fast-changing white man's government.

This is a very casual sketch of the present policy of the Indian Service: to improve the Navajo's land, to help him to make a better living from it, and to meet the white man in all the many ways he must. Naturally it is beset by criticism on all sides.

To the missionary, the proposal that the Navajo be encouraged to perform his ancient rites is naturally anathema. His influence is great among the Navajos, many of whom are Christians — the present president of the council is a missionary himself — and among whites who believe hair-raising tales of immoral doings at the great sings. It is not permissible to mention immoral doings at Christian camp-meetings.

The Indian medicine man is distrustful too; he can see the end of his ministrations and of his influence. His fear of tampering with nature is easily transmitted to his people, especially during a long drought, when piñon-gatherers are frozen in an unseasonable snow, or when bad washouts occur.

Doctors recognize that a medicine man can set a bone deftly, ease a sprain by massage, and make proper use of many medicinal plants. Those who know them best agree that most shamans are disinterested men, often truly spiritual characters, who will respond to honest offers of co-operation. Not long since, medicine men were invited to see a new hospital on the reservation. White physicians gravely showed them about, explaining the equipment as one group of specialists to another. The medical director, a woman of grace and perspicacity, then spoke. The white man's methods of healing, she pointed out, were different from those of the Indian shaman. Each might do what the other could not. She begged the medicine men to let the white doctors and nurses do what they could, while they agreed not to oppose the ceremonial sings and herbal medication. The medicine men responded by holding a dedication ceremony in the hospital's white and shining halls.

Besides medicine men, many older Navajos oppose change. They were used to boarding-schools, where their children were both clothed and fed. Jacob Morgan, president of the Navajo Council, expresses their point of view with a vigor worthy of a " first American " cussing out the government. " Disgusting experiments," he calls this letting children move about a schoolroom, make gardens, and keep lambs. He wants his children to sit at desks and learn out of books as he did.

He tells pitiful tales of women whose flocks were reduced below the subsistence level, and who could not send their children to school for lack of clothes or a horse.

Stock reduction is the great cause of complaint, and undoubtedly it has caused much real distress as well as misunderstanding. Orders to kill off sheep have sometimes been promulgated harshly and carried out regardlessly, even brutally. President Morgan, who admits that flocks should be reduced and horses practically eliminated, says the Navajo never opposes any good thing he understands.

Herein lies the crux of the problem. Indians do not think as white men do. Even those who speak English may fail to catch the real connotation of a word. And when a Navajo interprets what an expert from Washington says, not all the gods of medicine men and missionaries could guess what the Navajo thinks. This failure to understand has led many whites to say that Navajos must be treated like children. But that is only to prove oneself childish. The Navajo's mind is quite the equal of the white man's, and different only in content, in habit, and way of thought. If he often does not understand, neither do we.

White critics are, of course, numerous and vociferous. They fall into several groups. Those who follow the missionaries and the old-style school-teachers and want Indians trained just like whites often express indignation at plans to "remodel" the reservation, when God clearly meant it to wash away, and they rave against "forcing Indians to be pagans." Many tourists want all Indians kept primitive and picturesque, though dirty, diseased, and underfed. These sentimentalists, bounding over the reservation in a motor car, shudder away from the sight of a cement dam, a Navajo wielding a hoe or driving a truck. The shrillest of them advocate

" letting the Indian alone," but they submit no detailed plan for letting alone forty-five thousand people in the midst of the United States.

Many Navajos say they want only rain. Enough rain, they like to believe, would restore the life they love, with its periodic moves from the winter hogan, sweet with cedar smoke, to the summer hogan under a juniper tree, where the woman at her loom can watch the children with the sheep; loping rides across the tender gold of drying grass, singing the riding song, going to the sing. And mystery of masked gods in the dark circle of branches, where the power of the whole tribe unites. Only rain — but it will never rain enough to support the entire tribe, unless intelligence can supplement rainfall. Dams and windmills, farming as well as herding, betterment of flocks, increase of income from crafts, and wages. Such things have always been done. The speeding up of land deterioration and population growth make quicker, stronger measures imperative if the Navajo land is to be saved. Navajos and whites must try to understand each other, in spite of the spume of controversy which dims the air. Change is the only certainty. Change, and the ability of the Navajo to learn and to adapt himself.

The road

from Gallup to Albuquerque is not far from the oldest route into New Mexico. The modern highway is straighter than the old trail, because a slower rate of travel demanded water at frequent intervals. Before the days of motoring, all travelers followed the Indian trails. From Zuñi they crossed to Inscription Rock, where there was always water, and across by Acoma, feeling so secure on its sheer rock, to the Rio Puerco and the Rio Grande.

Hernando de Alvarado was the first white man to rest his desert-weary eyes on that valley's fresh and lovely green. He struck it somewhere between our present Albuquerque and Bernalillo. Coronado, following his lieutenant, was led south of Acoma — perhaps that old trick of trying to lose the invader — and came in near our Isleta. There was another way which Espejo found going west, over which traders and the Army traveled for centuries; that went north of our highway to the pueblo of Jemez, and down the Jemez River to the Rio Grande.

But however one comes, even the most hardened or most comfortable traveler must rejoice at first sight of that leafy valley. Below the blue ridge of the mountains it makes a long streak of the green that spells water. East and west that leafy belt ends as abruptly as a line drawn by magic. So far growth may go and no farther. But within that charmed line three races have lived and still live together. And there Albuquerque, tiny metropolis of an enormous and sparsely populated state, is the arch-type of the American town — with a few differences.

XIII

ALBUQUERQUE, "HEART OF THE WELL COUNTRY"

LBUQUERQUE HAS NEVER STRUCK A BONANZA NOR known a boom. Little gold has been discovered in its hills, no oil nor artesian water in its subsoil. The fertile Rio Grande Valley probably produces less nowadays than it did before the building of the modern town; certainly its farmers do not raise enough to feed the city, which ships in tons of food a day. Cut off from the rest of the country, Albuquerque literally would not have enough to eat.

Yet the town has grown steadily since its second founding in 1881, when the Santa Fe Railroad reached it and built its big shops a mile east of the villa de Albuquerque. As a result, there is Old Albuquerque, of flat-roofed adobes around the mission church of San Felipe de Neri, and New Town, a typical town of its size, which has expanded in all directions. It is now the state's metropolis. The census-takers gave it a population of twenty-six thousand in 1930, but civic pride insists the count was highly prejudicial and now claims at least fifty thousand. Whatever the actual number of inhabitants, as many more certainly trade in the town. It is more significant that Albuquerque has never had a serious setback in growth or slump in business.

Even the debacle of 1929 touched Albuquerque late and comparatively lightly and passed while the rest of the country was still in the doldrums. Its population has grown since 1930, new businesses have moved in, and if some have moved out again or blown up, the town's name recurs with comforting monotony as a bright spot on all business maps of the country. The reasons for this equability are various and all inherent in the town's situation. As the center of the state, it got most of the new federal agencies created by the depression. Not primarily a tourist town, most tourists pass through Albuquerque and leave a little cash. When bad times forced the rich to economize by going west instead of to Europe, that region was pleased to discover a breed that spent more on a reduced budget than ordinary travelers did in good times. And though Albuquerque had lay-offs in shops and mills, most unemployed could " go home and eat beans." Few families are so completely urbanized as not to have a little ranch somewhere, and New Mexicans care for their own as long as they can.

It used to be said that Albuquerque had two businesses: the Santa Fe Railroad and tuberculosis. It now boasts a transcontinental airline as well as the railroad, lumber and flour mills; and its trade area meets that of El Paso half-way down the Rio Grande, that of Amarillo almost at the eastern state line, that of Denver at the northern, that of Phoenix well within the border of Arizona. Its wholesale business amounts to nearly a million dollars a year, but its livestock business lags at only three hundred thousand, and farming, in spite of the promise of the Middle Rio Grande Conservancy development, does not appear at all in a list of figures published by an Albuquerque bank in 1938. Retail, restaurants, and building run over a million dollars a year. The Santa Fe, with an annual payroll of well over two million dollars, is exceeded only by the federal government, which brings Albuquerque an income of $3,150,000 a year. But it is still true that for a steady, dependable income nothing quite equals TB.

The Civic Council estimates that between three hundred and fifty and five hundred health-seekers come to Albuquerque every year. This figure may be low, because a specialist says he examines at least two hundred new cases annually, and he is one of five " chest men." Few people stay less than a year and a half. A thousand spend $1,000,416. Hundreds of people who accompany these patients or who stay on because of fear of a harsher climate are thought to bring in another million dollars or so. It is easy to calculate a total of more than the federal payroll and to declare TB the town's leading industry.

Every Southwestern town advertises climate, but generally without stating what it is good for. Sunshine and dry air are recommended for arthritis in Phoenix, for sinus troubles in Tucson, for weak throats in El Paso, as a refuge from northern winters in San Antonio, for retarded children wherever there is a private school; for whatever ails you, if you will only not mention its dread name! Every town in the dry country knows those pale, slow-moving folk — lungers, chasers, TB's, or health-seekers — who sit so patiently in the sunshine trying to rein down active minds to the tempo of the lazy burro, determined to think of only one outcome as possible, refusing to consider a family back home, a career stopped by blood in the mouth, or how to get more money if worry delays the cure. From every class, every state, and most countries of the world they have come to the Southwest, bringing contributions to every phase of its life. But because of mistaken fears of contagion most towns mask their bid for the tuberculous. Albuquerque is practically alone in coming out with the forbidden word, thereby almost taking the horror out of it and creating a psychological atmosphere in which cure is expedited.

Albuquerque's altitude is advertised as the perfect mean. Just under five thousand feet above sea level, its winters have not the sharp edge of higher places, its summers make no such heat records as desert towns at lower levels. Its kindly climate has made a life typical of the Rio Abajo, Down the River, as the Spaniards called it.

The villa de Alburquerque was founded in 1706 and named for the then Viceroy of New Spain, the Duke of Alburquerque. It was only a bit larger than other villages which dotted the valley from the Indian lands of Sandia and Santa Ana on the north to the Isleta lands on the south. Corrales, Alameda, Los Griegos and Duranes, Atrisco and Pajarito all had their churches, their wealthy families. The rich, alluvial valley produced good living where the mother ditches lazed along under willows and goldenrod. Everybody lived well and the rich families lived splendidly in thirty-roomed houses with several patios, private chapels, flower gardens, and orchards. Because the yard-thick house walls were of adobe, they disintegrated as the families lost their lands, and sank back into the earth of which they were made. Few of those great houses remain, though the old people of the Perea, the Armijo, and the Chávez families can describe them in complete detail. Life was easy in the Rio Abajo, where summer is hot growing weather by day and balmy for sitting out at night. Even winter is generous with warmth and no sun is more brilliant than that of January. Old-timers still cling to the lowlands along

KIT CARSON DEFEATED THE NAVAJOS IN
CANYON DE CHELLY, ARIZONA

[photo, Laura Gilpin]

the river, with cottonwoods for shelter from wind and sun and a long view of the Sandias purpling at twilight across the eastern mesa. But newcomers have always built up on the mesa toward the mountains. Time was when all the fine houses were in the lowlands and houses in the highlands were shacks. Now people build on the sand-hills and make them bloom like the valley, except for the few who like the lush valley with its bosques of cottonwoods and Russian olive. Newcomers are steadily destroying the town's character by planting Chinese elms in place of the native cottonwood, which is beautiful all the year. Its summer dome of dense green is even lovelier when its bare branches are a filagree of silver with copper leaves adhering. In spring new growth pushes off the rattling copper, pink tassels depend, and branches sway under a triumphant chorus of migrating blackbirds. And nothing better expresses the whole golden clarity of our Southwest than the cottonwood's vibrant autumn yellow against a turquoise sky. Cotton bearers have given the species a bad name, but it is easy to determine the non-bearing male tree.

The Southwest has been sought by the ailing since seventeenth-century Franciscan missionaries noted the curative virtues of sun and dryness. Their recommendations had gone far, for in 1776, when his lovely young wife had failed to recover in Cuba from an affection of the lungs, Don Pedro Otero of Valencia, Spain, took her on to Nuevo Mexico. That far-away province must have had quite a reputation for salubrity to tempt a man to risk such a journey with a frail woman. She stood it well — three months in a swaying ambulance — and in a town named Valencia for their home in Spain, she bore six children. From then until now a Manuel or a Miguel Antonio has always figured prominently in New Mexico; never have they omitted the name of the family's holy patron, San

Antonio, under whose protection the young wife made her miraculous recovery.

Early in the next century our old friend Zebulon Montgomery Pike spent a happy evening in Albuquerque with Father Ambrosio Guerra and " his adopted children of the female sex. . . . Half a dozen of these beautiful girls, who, like Hebe at the feast of the gods, converted our wine into nectar and with their ambrosial breath shed incense on our cups."

Perhaps the lieutenant's experience should rank as prevention rather than cure, but it suggests some of the potentialities of Albuquerque at any period.

In the 1830's Josiah Gregg, ill from a complication of disorders which his doctors could not cope with, was advised to try the Santa Fe Trail. Three months of sleeping on the ground and living on a diet of saltless meat and raw buffalo liver seasoned with gall cured Mr. Gregg's dyspepsia entirely. Many old-timers' tales, both printed and unwritten, describe pitiful, weak wretches scarcely able to sit a horse or obliged to lie in a jolting prairie schooner who lived and toughened into hardy citizens " you couldn't kill with a shotgun."

After the railroad made travel comfortable, Eastern doctors who knew no cure for " consumption " sent all their patients west. Many tragedies resulted from a too late arrival. Survivors boasted of coming on a stretcher, " and look at me now "; and children born in Albuquerque thought it was a joke to say: " When I came here I was so weak I couldn't raise my head from the pillow." There were no specialists, no sanatoriums, no careful regimens; and every lunger conducted his own cure. Whisky in plentiful and frequent doses was popular and many ex-lungers lived to old age in a state of ruddy preservation, exultant victors over the malignant germ. Some were poor, but sunshine and air that would breathe deep and heal morbid tissues were free. If one could get enough to eat, one could take the sunshine with one's kind on benches in front of drugstores or dangling one's feet from high board walks that sheltered pigs and burros underneath. One group used to meet on a knoll at the edge of the mesa " where they could hear the solitude roll in." " Every time a man coughed up a lung," they tossed another stone onto a pile. It grew into quite a cairn, that pile. Such groups laid wagers on how long each would endure and took up collections to buy coffins when necessary, but refused to turn back from future health long enough to grow sad over present death. Humor was their defense and their salvation. Most consumptives found their kind and made daily calls in friendly homes where an egg-nog, a glass of buttermilk, or a raw egg in sherry appeared as a matter of course. Many marriages resulted from such calls, many people prominent in the Southwest today are their children.

The more venturesome left the town's companionship to hunt health alone. Such a one was George Ellis, who bought a burro and loaded him with two kegs for water, some blankets, bacon, and flour. Then he set out, walking slowly. Nights he slept with nothing to impede the sight of planets wheeling against a mist of stars in a near blue sky. Nobody set a gait too fast for him. If for one day he did not move at all, nobody took note either to urge or to pity. If he spat blood, nobody knew. The burro was a companion, and of all beasts surely none is so well designed to make even the most languid man feel brisk and full of vim. In time Mr. Ellis got himself across the mesa's ten tawny miles and up on the slopes of the Sandias into scrub cedar and piñon. Lying on warm, dry earth one sees many wonders, I am told. Desert poppies merge into drifts like snow. Lupin and verbena make such purple banks as poets attribute to violets alone, and Michaelmas daisies and scarlet paintbrush form soft tapestries against the warm gray of chamiso tipped with sunny yellow. Sage, piñon, and cedar emit the very aroma of health. And bluebirds gabble and flash sky-blue right into your eyes. It would not be too lonely a life for a man who could make new friends. For cowboys drifted small bunches of cattle along the draws where the grama grass was good. Shepherd boys sat wiggling bare toes and watching dusty flocks. And in an occasional house one could rest a day or two and eat well on chile and beans, flaky cheese, and wild things cooked up into savory messes; and improve one's Spanish. A man could sit comfortably on a sun-warmed hillock and pot leaping jack rabbits or scurrying quail in the hills, or wait for turkey or deer under the peaks. And in mountain hamlets like Chilili or Escobosa, San Antonio or Las Placitas, he could buy more supplies and get news of a distant world.

Nobody remembers now where Mr. Ellis went or how long he roamed. But he brought up at last in a canyon where crystal-clear water cascades in glittering falls from one pale limestone pool to another. There he chopped down pines and whittled out pegs to put a house together and shingles to roof it. He married him a lady and raised a family of six husky sons and daughters. They enlarged the house as they needed it and made a garden of native wild flowers, which ran into dozens of species: columbine and mariposa and tiger lilies, purple and white violets, lavender iris, pink roses and yellow lady-slippers, climbing clematis and woodbine. Mr. Ellis, the weakling who could scarcely keep up with his burro, lived to be a hale and hearty eighty years of age. Nothing remarkable about that cure, except the burro, and the imagination.

Albuquerque's first effort to hospitalize her ill and indigent was made back in the eighties by Sister Blandina Segale, a Sister of Charity, who also established the town's first school for girls. Sister Blandina in her old age wrote *At the End of the Santa Fe Trail*, a most exciting and eloquent first-hand chronicle. At twenty-two she had been started off from Cincinnati to Trinidad alone. Because it was so unusual for a nun to travel unaccompanied, she was treated as an impostor in a convent where she sought hospitality in St. Louis; always she was afraid of cowboys, of Indians, of bandits, and had to reassure herself by saying, over and over: " Angels guard your every step." Nothing daunted her really. And nobody fooled her. She understood at once the " land-grabbers," the peculators in the Indian Service, the stupidly pretentious. And when occasion demanded, she expressed her mind in phrases that belied her name.

In Santa Fe she built a hospital, raising money for it almost stone by stone and herself directing the carpenters and masons. Her right-hand men were a Jewish merchant and a Missouri Protestant, for Sister Blandina's was the faith that could cross barriers as well as move mountains. Whatever she wanted she got, and New Mexico's hardest-boiled politicians soon learned that it saved time to give it to her as soon as she opened the subject. When she had St. Vincent's Hospital in Santa Fe well organized, Sister Blandina was quite naturally moved to Albuquerque, where everything was still to be done. There Sister Blandina saw the need for a hospital, and with the aid of a Jewish doctor and a professed atheist, whose professions she never believed (" behind his eyes I saw the golden heart "), she built it. She is not too saintly to relate that when a Protestant hospital refused to take a man not properly introduced, she escorted him personally to St. Vincent's in Santa Fe, only to learn later that he had money and was greatly amused by her efficiency. Warm humanity, laced with humor and lighted with a working faith, make this nun's story such joyous reading. Sister Blandina's life exemplifies the wonders of common sense as well as the glories of religion.

After her day it was not until the turn of the century that real hospitals were built with tent houses for the tuberculous. That word had replaced " consumptives." Then a physician, himself a health-seeker, opened a sanatorium for the exclusive treatment of tuberculosis, the first of the eight which now surround the town. They made great changes. Fewer obvious sufferers walked the streets, and the hideous evil of unrestrained expectoration was overcome as they learned to take care of themselves and to consider others. And " chasing the cure " among others so engaged must be much less forlorn than making it alone. The " sans " developed a society apart from the town, which drew together active chasers and their families and arrested cases living in bought or rented houses.

Life in the san follows a regular routine. At mid-morning bath-robed patients are settled by nurses in " chasing chairs " in the sunshine with umbrellas and blankets, books, knitting, or writing materials. Some take lunch right there; those who can, go to the dining-room. From lunch till three o'clock is the inviolable rest hour, after which lounges and game-rooms are filled; and " ambulant cases " visit " bed cases." Many people live so for years. And a man or woman who has lain for six or eight years facing as stern a reality as tuberculosis has developed a courage to endure and an ability to laugh which is incomprehensible to one who has not done so.

The typical TB appears hopeful and gay. Whatever he may hide, he has certainly brought the ordinary vicissitudes of life into such perspective that he is amused at what the less disciplined find tragic. There is no lack of drama in san life. Doctors can, if they will, tell endless tales — tragic or comic, pitiful or magnificent — brought to high intensity in lives so enclosed.

Neither Kipling nor Maugham found hotter forcing-grounds of sexual complications in their romantic lands of the East. Most TB's are young; the disease strikes those of high-school or college age. Most are of more than average intelligence and sensitiveness. Many are beautiful; none lose by the disease's slimming of the figure and flushing of transparent skin with every afternoon's rise in temperature. Nor by the possibilities of negligee and lounging garments. Sanatoriums are alive with jokes, rocking with romance, hot with scandal, all compressed within a small space and a short time. Occasionally one disappears. Gone east, an arrested case. Gone west, in a box. Some who go home too soon come back to chase again, a longer and less hopeful pull. Some leave because the money runs out. Some go into careful half-time work in town and gradually transfer from the doctors' books to the lists of business or professional people. In all cases the ranks close quickly and the san life goes on.

Few take their own lives. A chest man told me this story of one who did:

" The fellow was about twenty-four, and he and his mother had sold all they had to come west. I knew it was hopeless, and so did she. He soon guessed it, and one day he asked me right out. I didn't want to be too discouraging, so I told him he might make an arrested case and live well enough for some years. But I didn't fool him; their money was almost gone, you see.

" He said: ' Well, I've got to die, that's all. My mother's got enough to get back home and start again if I go soon. . . .

No, you needn't worry, I have ten grains of morphine I got from Mexico.'

" I suggested that maybe his mother mightn't care for that, but he said: ' Oh, I've told her, she understands me.'

" And when I spoke to the mother, she bore him out. I said that few people who talk about committing suicide ever do it, but she just said: ' You don't know my son.'

" He even set the day, but he never spoke of it, and when the time came I forgot it, until the phone rang at four o'clock in the morning. It was the hospital; he was awake and wanted me at once. You can bet I hustled into my clothes and over there. I found him sitting bolt upright against his pillows and on top of the world.

" ' What's the matter with me, Doc? ' he said. ' I took those ten grains at nine o'clock and went to sleep. I thought I was dead, and here I am awake again and feeling fine. I've got to die.'

" It was curious, but morphine is like that, tricky. There was nothing I could do except sit by, so we talked. Never talked about so many things in my life. He had no religion. We talked about philosophy, about love and death, about people and life. . . . No, he wasn't afraid nor melodramatic. He was a hell of a fine fellow, I tell you! I never saw such courage, and I thought I'd seen things before I met that lad. . . . I didn't wake his mother. No use. Pulse got weaker and skipped a beat now and then, but I knew he was good for hours. I waited till he was sound asleep; then I told the nurse to look in on him every now and then and I went home. . . . Sure, I knew. He lived till eleven. Ten grains of morphine and it took fourteen hours to kill him! . . .

" Yes, I can tell you a more cheerful one. Love and sex and changing morals. This was a mother and daughter, came west

ANTA FE HAS DEVELOPED A NEW ARCHITECTURE
FROM THE OLD-STYLE ADOBE HOUSE

[*photo, Ruth Frank*]

SIMPLE LIVING MAY BE VERY PLEASANT IN THE
NEW MEXICO VALLEYS

[*photo, Ruth Frank*]

on a small allowance and took an apartment. The girl was only about eighteen and her condition wasn't bad; I just examined her regularly. Then one day they called up for an appointment.

"When they came in I said: ' Why, I just examined this kid; she's all right.'

" ' Yes,' said the mother, ' her chest's all right, I guess, but she's pregnant.'

"You see, she was engaged to a fellow who had been out to spend Christmas with her. They just took one little ride on the mesa, and here she was. Well, I didn't think she ought to bear the baby. One baby is risky, but the mother may get by. Second baby, certain breakdown. Third baby, certain death. So I advised an abortion. I explained that it would mean a doctor's fee and hospitalization — about a hundred and fifty dollars. I said they'd better write the father and get it.

" ' Write my husband? ' said the mother. ' Heavens, no, he'd throw her right out, never give her another cent. No, I'll manage it.'

"And she did. The kid got through all right, and the nice end to this story is that the boy came out in the spring and married her. He and the mother showed up as pretty damned decent against that skunk of a puritanical father, didn't they? "

Now and then the sans have reached out to make a notable mark on the town. Twenty years ago it happened through a newspaper. An editorial drew a snarling refutation from one " T. B. Crabb " who dared the editor to publish it. The editor promptly did so, calling on T. B. to make himself known. For months he did not; then he wrote again enclosing two cards, T. B. Crabb and Curtis Lyter. A caller from the paper found a long and emaciated Kentuckian, paper-white and plainly doomed. Forced to leave a prosperous business to chase the cure, Curtis Lyter's active mind was bound to leap the railing of his sleeping-porch. For a while he wrote an occasional comment on personalities or affairs, sometimes vicious, always clever. " Just to get it off my chest," he wrote, " which my doc says ain't so good when he listens through his stethoscope." At last the paper tempted him into writing a daily column. Sarcastic and often bitter, it hit so close, rang so true, penetrated so deep, that all but the immediate victim responded with hearty laughter. Even T. B. Crabb himself, writing with his portable typewriter on his empty chest, could see that his wrath was funny and would laugh in his hoarse whisper as he reread his cleanly typed pages.

During the Harding campaign, T. B. Crabb nominated himself for president and conducted a " sleeping-porch campaign." He pledged himself to put water in the Santa Fe River (which is too often quite dry) and to erect a municipal windshield for Albuquerque (whose spring sandstorms are the health-seeker's greatest torment). He got one vote. Ima Chaser, who alone could match his barks, wrote that she had met T. B. at a Hallowe'en party and, deciding that he must be handsome under the mask, she deserted her party for his sake. Ima Chaser preserved her pseudonymity to the end; probably neither she nor T. B. Crabb attended many parties.

When Curtis Lyter died, his funeral was attended by all the newspaper people in town. On his paper, the editor had come for his wife's health, his assistant for his own, the sports writer's wife was bedridden, the society reporter was a lunger's daughter, the high-school boy who was to become a successful novelist had seen his father die in a hemorrhage.

They sent T. B. Crabb back to Kentucky in a box, but what he so well expressed — that strangely uplifted spirit, gallant without heroics, nonsensical, but realistic — continues to mark the town.

Albuquerque's principal characteristic is a don't-give-a-damn detachment, product of years of chasing. Matters that stir up violent controversy in other towns arouse quiet amusement, or no notice at all, and pass into history.

Such a case was that of the Pioneer Mother. The Daughters of the American Revolution, at once patriotic and business-like, offered statues of our pioneer mother to many towns along the Santa Fe Trail. Santa Fe was, of all places, the most suitable. But Santa Fe's artists fired up as usual, pointed out that the statue was hideous in itself, worth about two dollars in actual cement, and calculated to realize the patriotic Daughters a tidy sum all in all. Santa Fe declined the gift. For a few days the situation looked awkward. Then some Daughter wisely thought of Albuquerque. Albuquerque's mayor, a park-maker, had one under construction just then where he thought a statue of anybody's mother would do very well. "Haul her in," he said in effect, "and set her up." Albuquerque, busy as usual with its affairs, took little note as Daughters and Sons of the American Revolution gathered, Boy Scouts marched, patriotic songs and speeches rang out, a string was pulled, and the Pioneer Mother advanced her ample foot, her hand on her child's shoulder, her sweet and sappy face turned ever toward the West.

Tuberculosis is not unknown in the rest of the country; it is only not mentioned. Every state has a public sanatorium, most of them publish magazines with titles like *The Texas Chaser, The Sanitarium Digest, Quiet Hour Optimism, Herald*

241

of the Well Country. Albuquerque has the only weekly newspaper, *The Health City Sun,* as well as a civic organization devoted to getting TB's to come, to looking after them once they are there. It advertises: " When you decide to come to Albuquerque, send us a wire, collect, giving us the date of your arrival and the number of the train and Pullman. This will enable us to find you and get you located more quickly. We will gladly meet you without charge or obligation." They actually do.

The town has dozens of convalescent homes and houses which " take sick." There the newcomer meets graduates from the sans, and a general attitude of easy acceptance. People stroll along the streets in bath-robes and slippers and stop to chat with others in chasing chairs on the lawns. To have the bugs is no disgrace; it opens the door to friendliness.

" Well," says the laundry man, " how'r you gettin' along? I chased for four years myself. Had this job now for two. Guess I could go home again, but the wife and kids like it here. . . . So long."

Even the coal-heaver stops to wipe a dripping brow and explain how his wife is making it, or why they decided to bring the daughter out before it got too late.

The entire life of the town is geared to accept arrested cases and to work them in. Everybody knows about tuberculosis; almost everybody has had it or seen it close. Business men create part-time work, outdoor jobs like driving delivery trucks and buses go to TB's as a matter of course. Nobody is surprised if a busy man disappears for a few weeks of " throwing rubies," hemorrhaging, while his wife carries on his business. Many women support bedridden husbands by work in laundries and stores, by sewing or peddling. Teaching is perhaps the only occupation that is barred to the tuberculous; for a wise town knows that the only real danger of contagion is for children.

Doctors advise tuberculous women against childbearing for their own sake and for that of the child, who is very liable to contract the disease unless he can be segregated from his mother for his first five years. After that the danger is not so great until puberty. Many patients who break down later have contracted TB during the teen age. Tests in Albuquerque of high-school and university students of twenty years of age show seventy-three per cent of positive tuberculin reactions as against an average of fifty-nine per cent for the United States. Of such cases, the number in which the disease ever becomes active is so low as to be negligible. Thus statistics prove what experience has shown, that adults are in no danger of contagion; in most people an almost perfect immunity has been set up. An adult who breaks down with TB in the Southwest is rarer than the white buffalo.

Consequently Southwesterners have no fear of tuberculosis. The health-seeker does not have to meet a look of dread, is not shunned, refused a home or social life. Socially as in business the dry country considers its TB's. Everybody has a quick eye for one who must walk slowly, sit often and for a long time, be protected from drafts, not allowed to dance, and excused early. " I'm only going out one night a week," is accepted without question. It used to be said of Albuquerque that one came there only because one was " bankrupt in health, wealth, or reputation." Now that it is no longer a shooting offense to ask what a man's name was back east, health is the usual reason for migration. When the Rotary Club was organized, only one member out of twenty gave his birthplace as New Mexico. The others were all in town because of a bug in some one of the family lungs. Nowadays more members of the service clubs are natives of the state, but push any family history back a generation or two and somebody is apt to show up with weak lungs.

This background of disease does not slow down the town as one might expect; it gives instead a sophisticated and cosmopolitan aspect quite out of keeping with its size. Its leaders, men of national and international standing in various lines, would be successful in big cities if it were not for TB. Those who have been ill themselves live full and active lives in sunshine and low humidity. There are no conspicuously rich folk in Albuquerque, except for Ruth Hanna Simms, who married an Albuquerque man from Arkansas and who has slid so gently into the town's life that her ripples never rock the boat, only swing it more easily. Otherwise, rich people stay a year or two, find none of the smart doings they crave, and go on to Tucson, Phoenix, Pasadena, or Colorado Springs. The best situated Albuquerque families live nicely with one maid and two cars, entertain simply but indulge in brisk and well-informed conversation, and annoy the rest of the state by their refusal to turn out for big official affairs. This sort of society is naturally intricately connected with important lives in larger places. Visitors come, attracted by the small town in a balmy and healthy climate which is a city in its manners and habits of thought. And it has sent its dozens of cures back into metropolitan centers. I do not name them because perhaps it is not known back there that a President's adviser, the musical-comedy star, the editor of a magazine of wide circulation, the Wall Streeter, the bank cashier, the manufacturer, the college professor, and many more are ex-lungers from an Albuquerque san. But they know, and when they come back, they say so, with gratitude for a town that made them feel that being sick was just the prelude to getting well.

Albuquerque,

*in spite of its differences, is a town typical of the United
States. Almost nothing of its past is left except its name.
First it rushed over to meet the railroad, and left its old
Mexican plaza to doze by the river. Then, falsely inspired,
it turned back, shook the peaceful old plaza up, and rebuilt
it into something recognizable only because it is largely la-
beled. Albuquerque has no gift for the picturesque. Its best
is in its honest acceptance of what it is — a modern, busy
town, and a good place to live.*

*But Albuquerque represents only one facet of New Mex-
ico's life, the latest. The state has another white man's culture which is more steadfastly rooted in its soil, which has
a longer history, often more picturesque and exciting, and
which may even suggest to us a way to realize the state's
greatest possibilities. There are many villages such as Albuquerque once was, when its flat, adobe houses surrounded
the mission church and the plaza, when church bells marked
the hours, and the most important days were the days of the
saints. Only in those villages does one really know New
Mexico.*

XIV

VILLAGES OF THE SAINTS

ANY CONTOUR MAP OF NEW MEXICO WILL SHOW HOW topography has made the pattern of living. Mountain ranges, tending generally north and south, divide the waters which will reach the Gulf of Mexico through the Rio Grande and the streams which led the pioneers across Texas, and those which the Colorado and the Gila will carry to the Gulf of California. Between the ranges, the valleys. Some are narrow, with ever flowing streams and fertile with humus from the slopes. Some are vast alkali flats, wind-eroded deserts, or stretches of wavering grass. From an airplane, the country shows like a colored map. Valleys are the green of willow and plum thickets, or the heavy green of cottonwoods; the clear verdure of early growth dusted over worked land, or the midsummer lushness of mature crops. Toward the main streams, canyons fan out onto the floors of the great valleys; away from the rivers, they flatten down onto dun-colored plains.

The line between green, irrigated lands and tawny downs marks, too, an almost exact division between Spanish- and English-speaking folk. The Spanish naturally pre-empted the

246

valleys. Wherever Indians were already in possession, Spanish colonial policy protected their rights, but the Spaniard found much unoccupied land he could use. The titled conquerors and lusty Spanish soldiers had no use for spades and plows, but from Oñate's expedition on, many people came to settle and make homes. They were European peasants. The Spanish word is *paisano*, from *pais*, land: people of the land. They knew land and how to work it. Most importantly, they could distinguish between farming-land, grazing-land, and land that would never be good for anything. For they came from semi-arid Mexico and Spain. Wherever they had lived, they had dug deep, still wells or made leaping fountains, and diverted streams into irrigating ditches. Because of experience, perhaps because of a religious or fatalistic acceptance of the ways of nature as the ways of God, they have never tried to force an alien pattern on the earth.

Unlike the Nordic pioneer who settled on isolated farms, the Spanish clustered in towns. They fought Indians only when they had to, to assure safety and security. Security was what the *paisano* wanted, then as now. To make a fortune was farthest from his mind. To develop land, which so often means to exhaust it, and then to move on, was inconceivable to him. He loves his land, and seldom yearns for farther, greener pastures. And, in spite of constant efforts to get him off his ancestral holdings, many of the green valleys are still the homes of the descendants of their first settlers. There, but shutting out a few things, one may still find a life little changed from that of three hundred years ago.

Aside from shutting the eye, one should take time. Drive rapidly through a village, and there is nothing to see. One might not even recognize a town in the scattered houses, each with its fields and orchards, haystack, and tidy garden packed

247

tight with bloom. A windowless house might mean nothing, in spite of a cross leaning against the wall, and the village church and clean-swept plaza seem only a wide place in the road. One must stop to feel the warmth of the sun, and to breathe the scents it coaxes out of gold roses of Castile in spring; sweet grass, booming with bees in summer; dropped fruit and dusty goldenrod in autumn, and drifting piñon smoke in winter. And only by stopping does one meet the people. Our villages are used now to rushing cars and take no note of them. The visitor who pauses is greeted as hospitably as though he had come afoot, or ridden in on a jaded nag. Brake your car, and in a few moments friends will appear. A horseman, asked the way, will dismount and stand with his hat in his hand, the reins over his arm: the act and pose of a nobleman. The home of such a man is like the castle of impoverished nobility. The wife, called from her washing or grinding, greets her guests like a great lady, without the gaucherie of apology. If it is meal-time, the visitor will be asked to stay, and the hostess will excuse herself while the menfolk entertain the guests. One sits in the front room. Nowadays it is furnished with brass or iron bedsteads, each piled with several mattresses and draped with a crocheted or embroidered spread. A grosgrain carpet is overlaid with modern rugs. The adobe walls may be calcimined pink or blue, or stenciled by the daughter just home from the convent. Lithographs of the family adorn the walls — bridal couples, grandparents, with stern expressions and heavy jewelry, boy and girl graduates. There may be a plaster saint, or a chromo of the Virgin of Guadalupe. None of this conforms to the taste of precisely today, but it has the consummate taste of expressing perfectly the family whom it serves: immaculate cleanliness, good handiwork, willingness to learn, a desire to have the best, pride in one's children, reverence for one's elders, piety and hospitality.

The dining-room is probably the kitchen too. A shining stove, a cupboard filled with flowered china, an oilcloth-covered table, and here, as in the other room, wide window-sills packed with flowering geraniums in lard pails, and the unique and unforgettable smell of chile. In summer it will be the fresh aroma of green chile, bursting its toasted skin on the stove; in winter, the warming scent of red chile stewing with meat. The meal, whatever the time of day, is pretty sure to be chile con carne, perhaps eggs, probably thick-crusted bread, solid with nourishment, or, if one insists, tortillas hot from the stove. Beans, the rich, red *frijoles* swimming in their flavored soup, are never omitted. Nor a compote of dried peaches or apricots simmered slowly down with a little sugar and spice. Coffee, strong as lye, murky from the pot that never gets empty, and no hotter than the back of the stove, accompanies everything. Sometimes fresh cream is offered, but more likely most of it went into making flaky cheese, and canned milk is served. The gentleman of the house sits with his guests, talking of politics, of friends in common, of crops, or of the next fiesta. The señora does not sit at table, but that involves no loss of dignity, as she watches her guests, offers another dish, or refills a coffee-cup. If language is a barrier, the children carry on in English, to the admiration of all. Cigarettes follow the meal. Perhaps the lady of the house will smoke, cupping the cigarette in her hand, while blue smoke curls out of slender fingers; often she merely accepts it with a gentle gesture of thanks. As a rule, one may not pay for such a meal, though a present is in order. A present brings another present: a pat of cheese, a jar of jam, a loaf of bread, perhaps a few crisp *biscochitos*, sugared on top. An aristocrat from any land would be at ease in such a place; only crudity could find anything to laugh or sneer at.

These people are aristocrats. No other American family trees go back so far, for the Catholic church was keeping records long before the United States had thought of vital statistics, or been thought of itself. The marriage on, say, May 23, 1678, of Juan García y Sánchez, legitimate son of Felipe García and María Sánchez, both white, and Julia Ortiz y Roybal, legitimate daughter of Jesús Ortiz and Isabel Roybal, both legitimate: the baptismal record of each child follows in due course, naming the godparents. Their marriages, their children, and the deaths of all thread the generations into centuries, connect men and women now living with the men who settled New Mexico in the seventeenth century.

Their villages, named for Spanish dignitaries or Christian saints, are much alike. Flat-roofed adobe houses cluster round the church, thick-walled as a fortress, and with a belfry lookout. Some villages had lookout towers like one in Manzano, not far from Albuquerque — a circular structure with loopholes, and a wide view of the Estancia plains, over which Apaches came raiding as late as the 1880's.

The first settlers brought tools. Oñate's lists include axes, adzes, shovels, knives, hammers, anvils, and nails. Building materials were found at hand. Every man built his own house, assisted by his neighbors in cutting and hauling pine logs for roof-beams and door-jams and in making adobe bricks. Women helped about laying the walls and plastering them with mud, as smoothly as a modern plasterer. On top of the roof-beams they laid split cedar, or small branches of aspen, in herring-bone pattern. On that went brush, and finally mud, tamped well down, and fairly waterproof if kept in good repair. Sometimes they added an outdoor shelter of evergreen branches, or even a roofed porch. A house might start with one room or several, but as families grew, so did houses, putting out wings which might in time come together to make a *patio*, or *placita*, as it is called in New Mexico. Where sandstone was plentiful, houses and fences were built of stone, closely laid without mortar, or put together with mud. Shaggy cedar posts were set close to make fences or sheds for stock. Every house had a storage room, piled with grain, hung with herbs and chile, set with baskets of dried fruits and vegetables. Ever present fear of drought makes for providence.

Life followed the rhythm of the seasons. Before the last snow patches had melted in the fence corners, men were digging silt out of the ditches and repairing flumes or gates. Every man owed so many days' ditch work under the elected *mayordomo*, ditch boss, who also doled out the water so the man living up the stream did not rob his down-stream neighbor. Fields were plowed while silvery cottonwoods shimmered into tender green and bent under the weight of caroling blackbirds. Women planted flowers in the dooryards and helped to scatter grain in the furrows, which ran, not in rigid lines, but curving with the hill slopes. Sheep were brought up from the winter range to secluded spots for the lambing. By Easter, when the red willows were in leaf, and peach and apricot blossoms were drifting, the brown earth began to show green, and first irrigating was in order.

Where water is scarce, land requires steady cultivating, and all summer, between floodings from the brown ditches, both men and women wielded the hoe. As wild fruits and berries ripened, they were gathered and preserved. When the baby lambs were strong enough, and the shearing done, flocks were moved up into the high meadows, where grass was fresh and fine after the valley pasturage was burned off. Rabbit drives rid the fields of pests and provided both food and fun. The only other breaks in work were saints' days in one's own or in neighboring villages. The days of San Juan, San Pedro, Santiago, and San Antonio all come in summer, and many towns bear those names. Many men went off to work other men's land, to sheer other men's sheep, or to ride herd on other men's cattle. So a little coin came in to buy luxuries.

In autumn, when Michaelmas daisies and bee-balm were purple, goldenrod yellow, and alfalfa fragrant with bloom for the last cutting, crops were gathered, and corn hung to dry, or shucked in particolored piles. Wheat was threshed in the Biblical way, under the hoofs of animals driven round and round on a hard earth floor, and tossed to let the wind blow the silvery chaff away from the golden fall of heavy grain. *Ristras* of chile made pungent, scarlet loops along the walls. Women, going down to the bosques along the river for mushrooms, stirred up coveys of almost grown quail, and meadow larks to warble along the fences.

A hundred years ago village men joined their rich neighbors and Indians from the pueblos for the annual buffalo hunts on the Staked Plains. Then, after frost and before the caravans set off for Mexico, was piñon-gathering time. Hills in New Mexico are dotted with the dwarf trees that bear these sweet and tender nuts. It is God's crop. No sense in planting a tree that takes thirty years to mature, and will not be hurried by cultivation. A good piñon crop comes about once in five years, and nothing will alter that. One may laboriously gather the fallen nuts from the ground, but a quicker, easier way is to rob the nests of provident little squirrels and chipmunks.

Crops in, sheep moved back to winter range, preserving done, winter's wood stacked in the portal, all who were going gone down the Turquoise Trail to Chihuahua, life settled in for winter. Time for handiwork and tale-telling. *Matando Apaches*, killing Apaches, is the phrase still used. It's a dull (and rare) old man who can't remember how he, his father, or his grandfather rode out across the plains and met the Indians, and how the Indians ran at last. I can do it myself. They can tell how Kit Carson escorted his little niece, Teresita, Governor Bent's daughter, from Taos to the convent in Santa Fe, and how the Indians rode up, and the child cowered in the bottom of the carriage while Colonel Car-són parleyed with them, and carried her on through. Everybody knows tales of Billy the Kid, or of Geronimo, of how the Isleta Indians paid off Uncle Sam's troops, of how funny an erstwhile United States Senator looked when the Penitentes drew blood from his bared and shivering back.

While one yarned, others worked. Women washed and carded wool, dyed it with mountain mahogany or yellow chamiso, spun it on spindles whittled out of pine wood, and rolled it ready for the weaver. Men wove on big looms brought from Mexico, teaching their sons their fathers' craft, making striped blankets, soft of weave and of color. One who could adz out pine logs and put together a cupboard without nails could also carve and decorate an altar for his church, a saint for his veneration. A few women had learned from the nuns to crochet or embroider, making beautiful spreads from coarse cotton stuff. And no village was ever too remote or tiny to produce one who could vary the tale-telling with ballads.

Ballad-makers often journeyed from town to town to compete at the *bailes*, where they also made extemporaneous couplets to mock the couples in the dance. Every family or village festival called for feasting or drinking. The Spanish word, with classic restraint, is *traguito*, "little swallow"; but enough little swallows can make quite a summer.

There was naturally a dark side to this life of peace and sunniness. Not only the sorrows and tragedies of ordinary life, but darkness peculiar to the people and the times. In the shadow of the church, the *morada;* in the shadow of the saint, the witch.

Brothers of Light, Penitentes, founded in Spain, but now discouraged by the church, practice their flagellations in many New Mexico and Colorado towns. It is said that no Penitente was ever convicted of a major crime. It is also denied. Penitentes are a secret fraternity; most men will deny membership. A medieval expression of the universal need for atonement, *Los Hermanos de Luz* indicate as nothing else does how far New Mexico villages are from our modern concepts. Neither priestly disapproval, public education, nor the intrusion of an industrial civilization has yet affected them much. I knew one Hermano Mayor who had served through the World War, and who directed the Penitente ceremonies in his O.D. uniform.

Equally persistent are the witches. Hooting owls still foretell disaster, and any old woman may be brewing up evil over her fire at night, and flying off on her broomstick to meet the devil. Crescenciana used to tell me that any old hag we met with her blouse stuck full of pins was a *bruja*. Each pin denoted a victim. Brujas may cause illness, crop failure, loss of love, and general bad luck. The witch can lift her own spell, if one can threaten her into it; and there are beneficent healers, *curanderos*, who can prevail against the wickedest witch. One seated his patient in a chair and set under it a broken egg in a saucer. He then performed his rites, causing the evil to strike down so hotly that it cooked the egg. A roomful of Juans and Juanas at midnight with liquor and no air is potent too. Not a few curanderos can remove a pain in the form of a lizard, a stone, or a ball of hair. They prescribe potions, often showing real knowledge of native herbs.

A bewitched woman had been relieved by a curandera. Then her husband, quite well before, began to shiver at night, feel pain in his abdomen, and show all his wife's former symptoms. He concluded, quite naturally, that the curandera had transferred the evil from his spouse to him. So one night as his wife lay asleep beside him, he rose up and killed her. All this was brought out in court, where the man pled the witch's spell in extenuation of his crime.

So were the villages of the saints a hundred years ago. In all essentials they have not altered greatly. Witches are still apprehended. A saint may be turned to the corner and admonished: "That wall is all you'll see until she gets back safely," or whatever the prayer may be. Family and clan are strong, work and fiesta alternate, and the church has not lost its power. Material things have changed more than the intangibles. Tools are better, there is more sawn timber, and fewer hand-hewn beams; manufactured goods abound in clothes and household effects, in motors on the farm and on the roads — even in plaster saints instead of those carved by hand. A whole generation has been to school now and speaks English in preference to Spanish, even when the softer accent still lingers. Education is destroying the power of the witches, and the public health department is finding an eager response even among people who do not yet speak English.

New Mexico, which has brought up the tail end of so many processions of progress, takes proud leadership in public health with the model law for rural communities. Only seven states which have copied our law and New Mexico have complete public health coverage. Every district has a public health doctor to fight epidemics and communicable diseases by clinics and demonstrations as well as by direct action. His right-hand man is the sanitarian who watches milk, water, and meat, and who thinks the most beautiful structure in the world is a sanitary privy. One costs only seventeen dollars, but as that price is prohibitive for many people, public health officers pray for an angel to establish a revolving fund for privies. WPA has helped; one privy proudly bore the sign: "WPA Project."

New Mexico has seventy-three public health nurses who supervise almost a thousand midwives, both men and women. Most babies are still delivered by a revered old woman, slow on her feet, half-blind, and too old to learn. Many are born in dirt-floored rooms with no screens, no ice, no clock, and only ditch water which must settle before it is boiled. Nevertheless infant mortality is declining, standards of midwifery are improving, public-school girls are training for the work, and the Archbishop plans to introduce an order of nun midwives. The church has issued a catechism in Spanish, whose first question is answered: " God gave us life," and the last: " The doctor can give injections to prevent diphtheria, smallpox, whooping cough, and typhoid fever. Ask the doctor to protect your children."

Our public health officers say that New Mexico's traditional diet is not bad at all. Frijoles have the highest protein content of any bean, and chile is chuck-full of vitamin B. Two cups of beans, a cup of cooked tomatoes, tortillas (of corn, not insubstantial wheat), and one cup of milk are an adequate and balanced day's ration. Most children need more milk than they get; but even without it our youngsters have better teeth and bony structure and look rosier than children of an equal income class in the United States as a whole.

Happily, much improvement in health and in ease of living is not incompatible with the old virtues of thrift and play. The threat to the village life has been from without, and it still is.

After the American occupation, increasing population bred grim determination to acquire land, not only in the man from the States but in the cleverest men of Spanish blood who hitched their wagons to the rising star. Generally the villager, content with life on his little ranch, did not wish to sell it. Guile was required, legal skill, patience, and the help of men in the confidence of their people. None of these was lacking. Various methods devised some seventy years ago are still effective.

Landownership in the entire Southwest is complicated because so many titles go back to the Spanish King, who then graciously bestowed great estates on individuals, families, or communities. Grants to individuals were generally in recognition of military or other services to the crown. Village grants were offered to tempt settlers into dangerous places. The Sebolleta Grant lured twenty families from Belen out toward the Navajo country, where they fought for generations to hold their little walled town. This was only one of dozens of towns which held the savages back. Tomé was decimated by the Apaches. Abiquiu's whole history was marked by Comanche raids.

Mexico, during her brief rule in New Mexico, also made land grants, hoping to buffer her frontier against the States. Under both Spain and Mexico the ceremony of taking possession was touching. One alcalde's report reads:

" I have placed him in possession in the name of the King, whom God preserve, and I took him by the hand and conducted him over the whole tract, shouting and plucking up grass and casting stones in the name of the King until I shed tears."

This formality did not extend to surveying. Land was so abundant in those days that accurate description was deemed unnecessary. An apple tree might be named as a marker, a ditch, or "the cross on the grave of the late Martín." The pueblo of Sandía lost valuable land because "the mountains" was held to refer to the foot and not the crest of the range. In other cases the same word has been ruled to mean the crest. So much depends upon your lawyer! "Mr. Baca's house" was named as the southern boundary of the Elena Gallegos Grant, which runs east and west for twenty miles. This gave Mr. Baca probably the longest house on record, happily with a southern exposure. One of the smaller grants in the Rio Grande Valley had the river as its eastern boundary; that erratic stream now runs west of the grant's entire length. The prize case, perhaps, is that of the town of Bernalillo. When the villagers purchased that site from the Indians the agreement left "the burned meadow" free for the common use of all. That was about 1820. As all meadows were burned annually it took a pretty piece of reasoning to establish the holdings of a lumber company a century later. It was done, of course. The New Mexico legal fraternity performs such feats daily. Technically such cloudy titles are cleared by sale under tax lien, thus wiping out the interests of claimants who cannot be accurately determined anyhow.

Cases like these, the delight of antiquarians and the source of lucrative practice for lawyers, soon proved too much for the regular courts. Judges trained in Massachusetts or in Tennessee and convinced that God Himself considered English the only sensible language were soon swamped by Spanish land measures, unfamiliar customs, and confusion of tongues. They demanded relief, so Congress established the Court of Private Land Claims in 1891.

Its records contain material for generations of writers yet unborn. They range from the untold tragedy of a woman who lost her house because she marked a cross on a paper she could not read, to affairs as grandiose as the dispute over the Maxwell Land Grant, which involved a British and a Dutch company, dispossessed hundreds of settlers, gave the winners millions of acres, and precipitated the " Squatters War."

The technique by which these transfers of land have been made is simple and entirely legal. And it may be duplicated in a series of counties. Under Spanish law, when a man died his children inherited equally, always with a water frontage. Consequently a grant might in time have a hundred owners, each possessing a strip of land running back from the river or " mother ditch " to the hills. Grazing-land was held communally.

Then a far-sighted gentleman would begin to buy little parcels of land, always specifying his right to share in the common grazing-lands. Some men so achieved the use of millions of acres. They let the villages alone, but they were preparing for the future. In time some plausible Spanish-speaking citizen would get around among the villagers and advise them to petition the courts for a division of their grant. Fear that the powerful new owner might claim it all gave the idea merit. A lawyer would then be secured, who would accept a percentage of the grant as his fee. New Mexico still carries on its statute books a law approving this method. The lawyer would beg the court for a division of his clients' holdings; a commission, appointed by the court, would decree that the grant should be sold at auction, and the money divided. The bidder, curiously, often turned out to be the busy buyer of small plots, or his lawyer. The seller would, of course, have his share of the purchase price — a few hundred or even thousands of dollars. Often he retained a few acres, and the new owner was not too captious about the cutting of firewood and the grazing of a few sheep. The new owner also paid wages for sheep-herding or wood-cutting, just as the old patrons had done, and between herding jobs a laborer could work in the Colorado sugar-beet fields, or in the mines.

The real pinch was felt when big owners began to run larger herds and flocks, and to enforce restrictions. By 1925, hundreds of small owners had lost the privileges which had made life possible for them. Others, who had held on so long, were losing their farms for taxes.

Buying up tax titles is also recommended for acquiring land. Often many owners of a grant are unable to pay taxes on their commonly held grazing-lands, assessed perhaps at a dollar and a half an acre. The state takes over the land for delinquent taxes and resells the whole grant for thirty-five or forty cents an acre. Having influence, the new owner then gets the assessed valuation reduced to fifty cents an acre. Seldom does he pay taxes for long, even on that basis. For he may promote a resettlement scheme and sell the holdings to the federal government for two dollars an acre.

These activities are admired as " developing the land." Land, according to the prevalent ethic, must be developed, no matter what becomes of the people. The arch example of the effect of such procedures is in the middle Rio Grande Valley, where an elaborate job of engineering and of financing resulted in a dam on the tributary Chama River, and a network of drainage canals covering the valley for a hundred miles. There was also a network of debt, which has resulted in the loss of hundreds of small farms.

It is true that some sort of large-scale reclamation program was imperative. Years of abuse of the watershed were causing rapid deterioration of the Rio Grande Valley. But unfortunately the Middle Rio Grande Conservancy project was designed to make the land commercially profitable, to replace small farmers with large businesses operating under a system of debt and credit. Many students believe that the land can never produce enough to make such methods profitable. What they surely do is to force debt on people who do not need it, and get along better without it. As they have lost their grazing-lands and their jobs in town, many formerly sturdy and self-respecting people have been forced to seek relief. Even those who still keep a plot of ground and raise their chile and beans face real need for cash. However exciting the engineering feats may seem, the failure to consider the human problem has had unfortunate results for all who live along the Rio Grande.

Developing land, however advantageous for the developer, may lack something from a larger point of view. I should like to live long enough to see the money, skill, patience, and foresight which are spent on land applied to the development of a New Mexico village. Not to change it, nor to preserve it as a museum piece, but to relieve it of economic pressure from without so the people could work out their own way. Perhaps because of his love of land, his disinclination to leave his native place, and his ability to enrich an austere life with simple pleasures, the Latin seems to have a basic stability which the Nordic in similar situations lacks. Psychologists say that a man needs to work with his hands, to feel security, to know faith, to realize dignity as a member of a group, to find some outlet for his creative urge. The New Mexico village, freed of the worst of its man-made handicaps, might offer a chance for the realization of this ideal.

A tentative start toward village development has actually been made. In Nambé, twenty miles north of Santa Fe, Florence and Cyrus McCormick have supplemented the county school funds to make possible a five-year experiment. There the University of New Mexico, aided by county, state, and federal agencies and, most importantly, " the Community of Nambé," is trying to help the people to live more fully and more wisely in their own valley. Unhappily, their economic dilemma is not being considered; but all that the school can do is most intelligently being done. Once the initial distrust was overcome, parents have proved eagerly interested. Mothers attend clinics and swap canning lore with the teachers. Fathers make cribs and tables in the workshop. Both admire the boys' gardens, where they experiment with erosion control, and the cultivation of vegetables formerly unknown. Babies in the day nursery wake out of naps to big cups of milk from the McCormick cows, and to sunny sand-piles, and games in English. Children of all ages are watched and weighed, and those who fall below standard are fed up. The next generation in Nambé will approach life with sturdier bodies and less language handicap, and with a working knowledge of soils and plants, of household arts and baby care. If only it could go on in every village and forever!

The federal government, too, is doing interesting work through many agencies. I visited a string of villages along the Pecos River which are, remarkably, free from debt, barring a few mortgages on the upland pastures. Government men hope by increasing production to prevent the end that debt would have portended a few years ago. Working through the mayordomos, they have replotted ditches, advised about fertilizing and rotation of diversity of crops.

I noted a ragged dam, a pile of brush and stones in the stream, looking as though it might go out in the next freshet. " Why don't you fix that up? " I asked, trying to seem intelligent.

" Oh, no," replied the engineer, " that dam has been there for twenty years, and if it does wash out a few men can roll up their pants and wade in to fix it without any expense at all. A cement dam would mean debt the village could not stand; and we are as proud as they are of their debt-free condition."

Later I talked with an old villager alone. Summoned from his field, he wiped his face and puffed as he remarked that farmers work on Saturday too. His sons worked with him, he said, though the youngest had gone off to town to try that. " He'll be back. Youngsters have to have their fling, but the old ways are best."

I asked what he thought of this government work. " It's all right," he said. " That young man knows what he is doing. We'll do what he says as long as they don't ask us to accept a debt. We don't want any conservancy! "

For such people, basic needs can be met by the economy of the typical village, and a few months of outside work a year by men and some women can bring in enough cash to assure greater security, a few luxuries, and understanding of the outside world which will enable those who wish, to leave the village without too great a wrench. There are always youngsters who must go, and they should. The majority of the population, as everywhere, is happier in the limited circle of the family neighbors and the saints.

New Mexico's villages

have long had the gift of quiet, unobtrusive living. Nobody noticed them, except during a political campaign, when interpreters ran through the land. Now they are known as the Italian hill towns are known, or the villages of Provence or of old Spain.

Chimayó is a shrine for æsthetes, as well as for believers in the potency of its healing Sanctuary. Cundiyó, like Ronda, inspires poets, and Carcassonne sings no better in nostalgic verse than "The Santa Clara Valley, Far Away." Modest old towns have been recorded in pigments, as well as in words; they are the basis of a cult. Their ways are respected, their crafts are encouraged, their language is taught, their simple pleasures are imitated by sophisticated folk from distant places. And the greatest of them all, their capital, has become one of the best-known and most admired towns on the continent. Not to know Santa Fe is to admit oneself ignorant indeed.

And Santa Fe, after changing doctrines of three centuries and a little more, has come at last to accept an honored place as the supreme village, the ancient adobe capital, the town which actually does not wish to grow, which claims the distinction of changelessness.

XV

SANTA FE IS ALWAYS SANTA FE

ANTA FE HAS BEEN ADVERTISED, AT VARIOUS TIMES, AS
the City Different, the Crossroads of the Centuries, the Royal
City, the ancient Capital, and the Athens of America. It has
run through more mutations than most, and without, apparently, altering its essential quality. For three centuries Santa
Fe has always been aware of itself as something special; not
conceited, exactly, just sure of its pre-eminence. Times and
tastes have changed. Hot causes have grown cold, ardent
advocates have grown old and been succeeded by younger
apostles of new ideas that affright their elders. But faith
in Santa Fe never fails. Always battling for something, often
racked by bitter internal squabbles, the town unfailingly maintains a solid front against outside criticism. And, best of all,
Santa Fe is always amused at its own antics, always bur-
lesques its own show. No wonder the whole world goes to
Santa Fe. And no wonder everybody has something to say
about it. Sunshine warming cool, rarefied air tempts one to
sit in the plaza, or in a quiet garden, and write letters home.
So we have a long series of impressions of the ancient capital.

One of the first Spaniards to report on it was Alonzo de Benavides, who wrote in 1630: ". . . the villa of Santa Fe, where reside the governors and the Spaniards who must number as many as two hundred and fifty, though only some fifty of them can arm themselves for lack of weapons. . . . They must have in service seven hundred souls, so that between Spaniards, half-breeds, and Indians there must be a thousand souls. And it is a folk so punctual in obedience to its governors that into whatsoever fracas comes up they sally with their weapons and horses at their own cost, and do valorous deeds. There lacks only the principal [thing] which was the church. The one they had was a poor hut, for the religious attended first to building the churches for the Indians they were converting, and with whom they were ministering and living. And so, as soon as I came in as Custodian (1622) I commenced to build the church and monastery, and to the honor and glory of God Our Lord it would shine in whatever place. There already the religious teach Spaniards and Indians to read and write, to play and sing, and all the trades of civilization. Though cold, the spot is the most fertile in New Mexico."

Of Santa Fe, the Spanish provincial capital, few contemporary accounts have been translated into English, but Harvey Fergusson, in *Rio Grande,* makes comprehensible and dramatic that " holy war on both sides," which we call the Pueblo Rebellion. In 1680 the Pueblos took Santa Fe, and with *tombé* and dance restored the true gods. Twelve years later De Vargas recaptured the town and set up his true faith again. Paul Horgan, in *From the Royal City,* describes the huge De Vargas, " built for armor," shooting Indians and making the cruciform gesture — equally for the love of God. Other sketches in the same book vivify colonial life in the old Palace:

a fiercely proud Spanish noblewoman's scorn of her son's amour with the Indian serving maid; a struggle between the ignorant Franciscan monk, scarred and soiled by his daily task, and the haughty Jesuit, newly come from the intellectual courts of Europe; and the excitement of the arrival of a wagon train from the " States."

Of the American occupation there are fascinating contemporary accounts. When Texas declared its independence of Mexico, it claimed everything east of the Rio Grande, and in 1841 sent out an expedition to hold it. With the Texans marched George W. Kendall, who told the story well in *Narrative of the Texas-Santa Fe Expedition,* a tragic tale of diseased and weakened Texans, and their capture by Governor Armijo of New Mexico, and of the cruel treatment they received as prisoners. Santa Fe was not a charming town through bars.

The United States did better than Texas. It not only took Santa Fe without firing a shot, but sent down a young lady who wrote most engagingly about the royal city. Susan Shelby Magoffin's diary, written in 1846, was not published until 1926, as *Down the Santa Fe Trail and into Mexico.* Young as she was, she understood that her brother-in-law, James Magoffin, was in Santa Fe to seduce Governor Armijo from his allegiance. Lesser officers he wooed with promises of dignities under the new government, and he convinced the people that the bluecoats could protect them from the Indians better than Mexico had ever done. So the Mexicans offered no real resistance, Governor Armijo fled to Chihuahua, and General Kearny consummated his bloodless conquest by running up the Stars and Stripes over the old Palace on August 18, 1846.

Susan Magoffin had no difficulty in gossiping with the ladies who called on her even before she learned their language.

The peddlers who brought her fruit and sweets loved her at once, and she appreciated their gentle courtesy. Altogether the first *gringa* who reported on Santa Fe was *muy simpática*. But to know her fully one must read also of the horrors she braved between Las Vegas and Santa Fe. She was traveling, remember, with her husband and her physician. " It is truly shocking to my modesty to pass such places with gentlemen. The women slap about with their arms and necks bare, perhaps their bosoms exposed (and they are none of the prettiest or whitest); if they are about to cross the little creek that is near all the villages, regardless of those about them, they pull their dresses, which in the first place but little more than cover their calves, up above their knees and paddle through the water like ducks, sloshing and spattering everything about them. Some of them wear leather shoes, from the States, but most have buckskin mockersins, Indian style.

" And it is repulsive to see children running about perfectly naked, or if they have on a chimese, it is in such ribbands it had better be off at once. I am constrained to keep my veil drawn closely over my face all the time to protect my blushes."

Susan was only eighteen years old, and perhaps she expected too much of a foreign capital, for thus she describes Santa Fe:

" On one square may be a dwelling house, a church or something of the kind, and immediately opposite to it, occupying the whole square, is a corn-field, fine ornament to a *city*, that. A river runs through the place. . . . The plaza or square is very large — on one side is the governmental house with a wide portal in front, opposite is a large church . . . 'tis not finished — and dwelling houses — the two remaining sides are fronted by stores and dwellings with portals, a shed the width of our pavement; it makes a fine walk — and in rainy weather there is no use for an umbrella."

Mrs. Magoffin's own " reception room, parlour, dining-room, and in short room of all work," she describes as " a long room with dirt floor (as they all have), plank ceiling, and nicely white-washed sides. Around one-half to the height of six feet is what may be called a schreen, for it protects ones back from the white-wash, if he should chance to lean against it; it is made of calico, bound at each edge, and looks quite fixy; the seats, which are mostly cushioned benches, are placed against it — the floor too . . . is covered with a kind of Mexican carpeting, made of wool and coloured black and white only." All this very closely describes the favored type of house and furnishing in Santa Fe today. Only now it is not the best you can get on a remote outpost; it is Spanish-colonial arts and crafts.

General Kearny and all his officers put themselves at Mistress Susan's orders, and escorted her to a fandango. She reports: " Another Spanish beauty, I saw this evening with her face painted, a custom they have among them when they wish to look *fair and beautiful* at a ' Fandango,' of covering their faces with paint or flour paste and letting it remain till it in a measure bleaches them. There I saw one of them had paste — and with it more the appearance of one from the tombs than otherwise. Another had hers fixed off with red paint, which I at first thought was blood. . . .

" First the ball-room, the walls of which were hung and fancifully decorated with the ' stripes and stars,' was opened to my view — there were before me numerous objects of the biped species, dressed in the seven rainbow colours variously contrasted, and in fashions adapted to the rein of Henry VIII, or of the great Queen Elizabeth, my memory cannot exactly tell me which; they were enveloped, on the first view in a cloud of smoke, and while some were circling in a mazy dance, others were seated around the room next the wall enjoying the scene before them, and quietly puffing, both males and females their little *cigarritas*, a delicate cigar made with a very little tobacco rolled in a corn shuck or bit of paper. . . . El Señor Vicario was there to grace the gay halls with his priestly robes — he is a man rather short of statue, but that is made up in width, which not a little care for the stomach lends an assisting hand in completing the man. There was Doña Tules, the principal monte bankkeeper in Santa Fe, a stately dame of a certain age, the possessor of a portion of that shrewd sense and fascinating manner necessary to allure the wayward inexperienced youth to the hall of final ruin. . . . There in that corner sits a dark-eyed Señora with a human foot-stool: in other words a servant under her feet — a custom, I am told, when they attend a place of the kind to take a servant along and while sitting to use them as an article of furniture.

" The music consists of a gingling guitar, and violin with the occasional effort to chime in an almost unearthly voice. *Las Señoras y las Señoritas* were dressed in silks, satins, ginghams, and lawns, embroidered crape shawls, fine *rabozos* — and decked with various showy ornaments, such as huge necklaces, countless rings, combs, bows or ribbands, red and other colored handkerchiefs, and other fine *fancy* articles. This is a short sketch of a Mexican ball."

The Doña Tules who was " alluring inexperienced youth " was Gertrudes Barela. Born in Taos, she was mistress of a gambling hall so exclusive that men might go only on invitation. Governor Armijo was her biggest catch until Colonel David D. Mitchell, of the U. S. Army, needed quick cash to supply his troops. Knowing that Doña Tules always had

money, he tried to borrow, but the lady proved obdurate until
Colonel Mitchell, willing to do anything in line of duty, escorted her to a ball and walked the length of the ball-room
with her on his arm. I wonder if this was Susan Magoffin's
fandango. She does not mention Colonel Mitchell. Perhaps
other officers had other reasons for taking Doña Tules to
the parties. At any rate, Colonel Mitchell's troops marched,
properly equipped.

In 1846, to protect the soldiers from the lures of lesser,
cheaper Doña Tuleses, the commanding officer had laid out a
fort, star-shaped to keep them digging and building for a long
time; and they erected officers' homes, which, though of adobe,
had pillared piazzas and wooden trim. Even the old Palace
was bedecked with scrolls and railings. By the eighties, brick
was being shipped in for the Catron and Staab houses, and
for the Andrews home on Palace Avenue, which someone with
utter lack of historical sense has recently plastered over to
look like adobe. The one-storied houses around the plaza were
replaced by frame or brick blocks, and their portales, so
grateful a shelter from the midday sun, were taken off. Even
after the American occupation and the establishment of
Protestant missions, Santa Fe's clergy lent tone to her social
life, as Bishop Lamy's French cathedral ennobled its adobe
flatness. Many Europeans, attracted by Indian life or old
manuscripts, lingered on to enjoy the society of foreign priests
who knew good food and good wines as well as cultivated
talk.

W. W. H. Davis, author of *El Gringo*, attended a supper
honoring Bishop Lamy on his departure for Rome: " It was
such a supper as I had not expected to see in New Mexico, and
the tables would have compared favourably with a similar
entertainment in the States. . . . While we were discussing

the viands the scholars served in a little harmony in the shape
of vocal and instrumental music. . . . After the boys had
retired, other sentiments were pledged in ruby wine, accompanied by a few songs, when the company separated at an
early hour, each person being able to walk home without the
friendly assistance of his neighbor."

For forty years after the American occupation, the adobe
royal city was an Army post — social, gossipy, and as brilliant as it could manage. Bugle calls marked off the hours
of the day. And Sunday evenings, when the band played in
the plaza, everybody went strolling there, or sat comfortably
in victorias to watch others make the flirtatious circle. The
officers' best horsemanship was taxed to rival the curvetings
of Mexican caballeros, whose excellent mounts wore trappings
of fine leather and hand-wrought silver.

In 1862 the Confederates, hoping to reach California, met
a Northern force at Valverde, near Socorro. The skirmish
resulted in a draw rather than a victory, but General Sibley
led his Texans on. In both Albuquerque and Santa Fe he
raised the Stars and Bars over forts where he had served as
an officer of the United States. But at Glorieta Pass, fifteen
miles east of Santa Fe, a Union force turned the Confederates
back. Small as it was, this victory at Glorieta Pass must rank
as one of the decisive battles of the war, for it held the Southwest for the North.

From that invasion comes much of the traditional New
Mexican attitude toward Texans. Old people, in my own
youth, used to recount what they remembered of the terrible
Tejanos. Huge men they were, red and hairy, uttering incomprehensible noises instead of words, frightening babies,
stealing cattle, breaching wine and brandy casks, and, when
drunk, even desecrating chapels. My grandfather claimed

that the unequaled size of our cottonwood tree was due to the fertilization the Tejanos gave it when they butchered in the patio where it grew. Quite naturally, to simple Mexican people, " Tejano " was a name of loathing and of fright.

Santa Fe, knowing little of North and South, and picking the least decisive battle, erected a monument, which is the only one in the United States to dare an unmentionable word:

*To the Heroes
of the Federal Army Who Fell
at the Battle of Valverde
Fought with the Rebels
February 21, 1862*

In the seventies Susan E. Wallace was mistress of the Palace, while her husband, as Governor, tried to avert Billy the Kid's Lincoln County War, and, as author, polished off *Ben-Hur*. In contrast with the girlish Susan Magoffin, Mrs. Wallace was a cultivated woman. She recognized the Spanish and Indian heritage of the people who served her. She knew a New Mexico adobe house for an adaptation of Spanish and Moorish architecture. She found in an Indian pueblo much to remind her of Montezuma and Quetzalcoatl. She got about, in that vehicle so tellingly called a buckboard, as few women do now over paved roads and in motor cars. She saw the Jornada del Muerto, Zuñi, and Inscription Rock. She went down into mines, and paid too much for turquoise. She was a realist, but one who saw the graces as well as the disgraces. She found Santa Fe dirty, swarming with hungry dogs, and the women ugly and swarthy, except the few Castilians. But she commented on the beautiful manners in the poorest *jacal*. And she said that Santa Fe was " what the ancient Pueblos called it, ' the dancing ground of the sun.' " " A morning," she wrote, " such as breaks nowhere except over the hills of Paradise and New Mexico."

Mrs. Wallace's greatest service to her adopted territory was that she rescued priceless documents. One day, when she was bored, she pushed open a heavy iron-bound door and came upon a mass of musty old documents, dumped into boxes, or spilling onto the floor. She learned how one governor from the States had burned old Spanish records, how another had hired men to haul them away. She salvaged what was left, and she read many. She quotes a love-letter, living and beautiful still, written in 1692 by a Rosa in Castile to Don Eusebio de Cubero, an officer with De Vargas. And she complained, as everyone of her sort has since, that " the foreign charm which was the dower of the historic city is dying fast."

Governor L. Bradford Prince and his lady carried that cultivated tradition into the nineties. While the Governor wrote *New Mexico History* and *Spanish Missions,* and collected Indian and Spanish antiquities, " Governor Mary " entertained with lofty lavishness in the Palace. And it was entertaining — engraved invitations and menu cards, eight-course dinners with the proper wines, and imported delicacies. Every enterprising gentleman had an express frank then, and oysters, frogs' legs, sweetbreads, and tropical fruits and flowers were not too exotic for Santa Fe. Uniformed Negro servants served officers in blue and gold lace, and guests of honor were distinguished folk from everywhere. A lady who remembers those functions, said: " It was worth your while then to dress in satin with a four-foot train, sixteen-button gloves, and jewels. We had a real Society; none of this sitting on the floor to eat *frijoles* out of an Indian pot."

Many of the dinners had political undercurrents, for Santa

A QUICK STORM OVER A MOUNTAIN VILLAGE
[*photo, Ruth Frank*]

TORMY DAYS AND WINTER NIGHTS OLD PEOPLE SPIN,
WEAVE, AND TELL TALES
[*photo, Ruth Frank*]

Fe was always the capital. During the biennial sessions of the legislature, ladies from all over the territory spent weeks in Santa Fe; the Palace Hotel was as gay as Saratoga, every large house had guests, and *politicos* who were sure of re-election engaged houses from term to term.

The last upsurge of Latin exuberance colored the gubernatorial term of Miguel Antonio Otero, scion of a Spanish family prominent in New Mexico's public life since 1776. " Governor Gilly " and his pretty Southern wife entertained lavishly, and the War Department provided a military band of forty pieces for Sunday concerts and visits of state. When President Roosevelt came, in 1903, the Governor and his band escorted him around the plaza, where a little girl, perched in a tree, dropped a shower of flowers into the open victoria. Colonel Teddy was a prime favorite in New Mexico, for half of his Rough Riders were New Mexicans, and he delighted to greet them.

But less frivolous days were ahead; Santa Fe embarked on its first crusade. In 1905 the University of New Mexico had remodeled its big brick building into a clumsy similitude of an Indian pueblo, and the new Harvey House at Lamy was built around a patio. Santa Fe, without a moment's hesitation, adopted both styles as " Santa Fe Architecture." The pueblo pleased them most, and the New Museum borrowed features of the pueblo missions, especially the twin towers of Acoma. At once, garages, movie houses, hotels, and business blocks reared two towers, until Gus Baumann caricatured dog-houses and privies so adorned. Nothing was four-square or in alignment. Carpenters, to hold their jobs, had to make new-cut pine look as though it had been worm-eaten for centuries, and every cement wall sagged off into fat angles.

By this time Santa Fe was no longer dependent upon home-grown culture. New Mexico had been discovered by a hitherto unknown race, who used unfamiliar words with accents very strange. They spoke of Amerindian culture, of colonial arts, of racial rhythms, and of such color that even a native began to see red, white, and blue in a muddy ditch. Some painted pictures, some wrote books and poems, and they all went nuts about something: ruins or Indian dances, old Mexican plays, or tin sconces. Their women appeared in men's pants and cowboy hats; their men wore velvet blouses and Navajo jewelry. They took over adobe huts and filled them with battered furniture, noseless wooden *santos,* torn Navajo blankets, copper kettles with holes in them, and Indian ceremonial garments acquired by all sorts of trickery.

" Do you suppose it's our altitude? " the lawyer asked the doctor over their daily whisky and soda.

" On the contrary," replied his crony. " It's the latitude they bring along."

They brought laughter, too. " The Historical Parade," which had been a labored feature of every fiesta, with a stern De Vargas in Canton flannel and a tin hat, was burlesqued in the " Hysterical Parade," which parodied the whole year's pretentiousness. Visiting dignitaries, tickled to see themselves in such clever skits, made a practice of returning every year. The whole town took on a prankish temper, which, like the Pueblo Koshare, pranced along beside every solemn procession to mock it. The arch-jester, and Santa Fe's most jealous and ardent lover, was Dana Johnson, editor of the *Santa Fe New Mexican.* The flickering humor of his column, " Solos by the Second Fiddle," made everybody laugh, even him whose flanks were flicked; and his witty advocacy of every good cause put his paper on New York's news-stands.

The town, providentially, kept on dragging its past. Up

the canyon and down in Agua Fria, people lived as always in little adobe houses, with tiny gardens, a burro, and dogs. Bells called them to mass, old women walked sedately draped in black shawls, religious processions were long and devout. Ladies of all the churches met in society or sodality to sew for charity, and to whisper of the scandalous doings of the artists. They also met as the Woman's Board of Trade, which boasts of being the first woman's club devoted to civic — and not self — improvement. They put greenery in the cemetery and in the plaza, books in the library, and the fear of the more deadly sex into the hearts of the city council. Santa Fe women get what they want. And generally what they want has greatly benefited the town.

They found allies in the very artists who filled them with such delighted shock. Santa Fe had proved a refuge for many sensitive people with serious work to do. A small town with its full share of malicious gossip, its background is filled with rich mists of Indian and Spanish associations. The artist's conscious need for beauty is fed by the human as well as the natural aspects of the country. Living was cheap, and he made it very simple. Painters' smocks and overalls are quite as correct as dinner-coats and formal dresses. But as artists broke down the town's old inhibitions, they generously repaid their debt by contributing to every phase of its life. As the unstudied charm of an adobe village was inevitably lost, their taste has trained and bullied its citizens into keeping the town harmonious with its varied history. Every step has been contested by people who never cease trying to flatten the City Different down into dullness. Just now they persist in routing all traffic through the tiny plaza, thereby destroying the sunny welcome of the little square, irritating those who would like to stop, and confusing those who would like to rush straight through. But the lovers of the Ancient Capital may prevail again. They have saved its narrow streets, its high adobe walls and hidden gardens, its *acequias* running clear mountain water, its trees, and a respect for its Spanish-speaking folk. And they have done many practical jobs.

When the Palace Hotel caught fire, the fire department's ladders had been lent to the painters, the hose leaked, and before anything could be done, the mammoth frame caravansary, tinder dry, was a glorious flaming spectacle that collapsed in cinders. Then Ashley Pond, a rich young man who liked to start things, organized a new fire department. In his bedroom he installed a pole, down which to slide to his garage, kept his pants stuffed into his boots, his helmet in his car, and his wife trained to leap to the telephone at its first tinkle. On alarm, operators ring all the firemen with one plug, and in a moment the town shrieks with sirens. Office workers, with pencils behind their ears, doctors in gowns, painters in smocks, and workmen in overalls leap aboard trucks and cars, as they tear through stopped traffic. With no uniforms, they have excellent equipment, and they fight fire so well that insurance rates are as low in Santa Fe as anywhere. No dinner party is sacred when the alarm goes. Tuxedos and tails, even fancy dress, cling to the flying truck, climb ladders to blazing roofs, or dash into smoking cellars. All a fireman gets is dry cleaning, and glory.

When the Woman's Board of Trade needed money for the plaza, the Santa Fe Players appeared to earn it. They wrote and staged plays, found hidden talent in stores and kitchens, broke down much silly snobbery, and gave everybody a good time.

Meanwhile Santa Fe, without planning or advertising it, had become the City Articulate, and its writers suddenly flooded the smart, liberal, and artistic reviews, the dailies, and even the *Congressional Record* with propaganda. Santa Fe had decided to save the Indians, and did, by defeating the injudicious Bursum Bill of 1921.

By the time this was accomplished, Indians were in town all the time. Little boys danced for the tourists, venders of turquoise and pottery commuted regularly from Santo Domingo and San Ildefonso, prices soared, and cheap and slovenly work prevailed. Everything had to be encouraged, combated, and finally suppressed. Only suppression proved impossible. The Santa Fe and Fred Harvey, through the Indian Detour, operated scheduled and chaperoned trips from Santa Fe to the pueblos, offering artists and Indians as equal attractions.

" So," said Alice Corbin, surfeited with the whole thing, " we've saved the Indians for Fred Harvey."

An Indian association had followed as a matter of course, with social and financial lists well represented. Santa Fe raised funds by selling summer visitors tickets to the " Poets' Round-up," staged in somebody's garden. There each bard, " dressed Western " and ruffling his favorite manuscript, steps out on the call: " Comin' out of the chute! " reads, and retires. Afterward they stand shyly by to autograph books if any buyers appear. In time the entertainment became so lengthy with a plethora of poets that " Writers' Editions " took it over and made the poets vote on each other's qualifications, thus sharply reducing the number of readings.

By 1932, summer visitors, like Indians, threatened to become a disaster as well as an asset; and the ever alert Santa Feans had to save the town from a second Texas Invasion. These Tejanos, mounted on rubber, not horse-flesh, and seeking culture, not conquest, were welcome and profitable summer visitors. Then word got around that the Southwestern Federation of Women's Clubs had been offered land for the "Culture Center of the Southwest." Santa Fe took fright at once, and forty or fifty Santa Feans responded to the danger call.

Mary Austin, enthroned on the bootblack stand in the Chamber of Commerce, related the ruination of Carmel, and darkly foretold that a culture colony would destroy the happy casualness of Santa Fe. The meeting, composed of business people and club women, as well as writers and painters, agreed that visitors in ones and twos were welcome. But against culture-seekers in bands they were adamant! As the Old Santa Fe Association, they joined hands with *La Union Protective*, better known as the "Protective Onion," whose grandfathers certainly remembered the Tejanos of '63. Arkansas, Oklahoma, Arizona, and New Mexico were included in the scheme, but Texas stood out. Daily it was reiterated that no slight to anybody was meant; but the nation's press editorialized on little Santa Fe's fight against "the Texas Invasion," and laughter ran from coast to coast.

Historical note: Frank Dobie, in *The Flavor of Texas*, quotes Bigfoot Wallace, who once was spreading himself for the ladies:

"Among other whoppers," he said, "I told her there was a vermint in Texas called the Santa Fe, that it was still worse than the tarantula, for the best brass band in the country couldn't cure their sting; that the creature had a hundred legs and a sting on every one of them, besides two large stings on its forked tail, and fangs as big as a rattlesnake's."

Deed to the proffered land never passed, and Santa Fe was saved from organized culture. But the quaint and quiet little capital has not been protected from other invaders. Luxurious

hotels and good bars; wealthy homes well stocked and hospitable; artists and writers to talk about; and a reputation for
easy manners and morals have drawn to Santa Fe that tribe
which roams the world looking for what it has not, talking
about what it does not know, seeking emancipation from what
it can never escape. Within twenty minutes of the arrival of
the bus from Lamy, a new flock of white-faces appears in stiff
levis, new sombreros, and bright shirts and neckerchiefs. They
choose their bar and dispatch their letters of introduction. To
them, Santa Fe is a way-station between the Lido and Hollywood, Taxco and the Ritz Roof — a slightly different back-
drop for their own amours.

But the City of the Holy Faith is too old and too secure to
be affected by trivial passers-by, who can never share its spirit.
Snow masks and melts away from red or golden hillsides, and
bluebirds flash from pine to juniper tree. The vague profile
of the Conquistador and his horse on Santa Fe Peak shows
bright green when the aspens are in leaf, red gold in September. Willows burgeon and turn red along the ditches, and
Santa Fe gardeners set off their pink hollyhocks and blue lark-
spur with the gray of chamiso and Russian olive. Creative
people find it a congenial place to work. They have made it
truly the Crossroads of the Centuries. Since Cæsar's invasion
of Gaul, the white man has conquered and brushed aside the
primitive. In Santa Fe he is trying to learn from him. This
effort, and the artist's sensitiveness to real human values, save
the town from snobbery. Rich and important people may
come, may help; they are not allowed to dominate.

All the old organizations wag along, including the standard
national ones. Younger leaders are concerned with social
problems, such as that word did not connote in Grandmother's
day. They have revived the old Indian market in the portal

of the Old Palace; they help village craftsmen to sell their handiwork. They study the plight of the Agua Fria folk, whose little farms no longer produce, now that the Santa Fe River has to water so many lawns. A Maternal Health Center precipitated a minor row, but was tolerated when the offensive phrase " birth control " was dropped. So Santa Fe, always the beloved town, has come from a Spanish frontier presidio by way of an international trading center, through military pomp, social airs, political intrigue, to cultural preoccupations — leaving much behind, bringing much along, and finally arriving at a real desire to make the Royal City a better place for everybody to live in. And through it all, Santa Fe, bless it, is always Santa Fe.

The New Mexico Pueblos

have, of all Indians, been subjected to the most intrusive curiosity. Their villages are so easy to get to, and they look so like toy towns, that it is hard to remember that they are ancient theocratic city states. Their costumes are so like fancy dress and their work seems such play, as they sit on the floor molding clay pots, polishing stones, or stringing beads, that it is easy to forget that they are mature men and women, heirs of long-tried tradition and of highly stylized arts. Above all, their children appear so doll-like with round, brown faces, bright jet eyes, and straight black hair that one must make an effort to recall that they go to school every day and learn what our youngsters do. It is especially hard for tourists unaccustomed to brown faces to realize that these people understand English, are sensitive to criticism, and have a legal right to refuse to receive visitors if they wish.

As a rule the Pueblos are polite to visitors and ready to do business. But they deal with us only at the periphery of their real life. The pueblo, earth-colored, sunlit, and tree-less among its cultivated fields, is a magnetic center which exerts a strong and steady pull against the changing outer world. The Pueblo Indian, wherever he goes, seldom alto-gether loses his connection with the deep and vital magic that centers in his kiva.

XVI

THE PEOPLE OF THE PUEBLOS

THE PUEBLO INDIAN IS, IN ONE REGARD, THE MOST FORtunate of all Americans, for he is the heir of an entailed estate, inalienably his. His position is even happier than that of the British nobleman in that he pays no taxes. Naturally he has the calmness and assurance of a landed proprietor. He may be poor, and he often is. He has lost much land, and he has been robbed of water by white farmers above him on his streams. But in spite of all these deprivations the Pueblo is, always has been, and so far as we can see always will be owner of the land he uses. No wonder he moves with an air of confidence among a nation of nervous and insecure white folks. Perhaps the Indian has a natural serenity that the white can never attain. Most of us believe we could be calmer under stress if we, too, were assured of permanent ownership of land enough to support us.

The Pueblo owes his happy situation to Spain, though he suffered many vicissitudes before he became a landowner. After Coronado's conquest and Oñate's settlement, Spain followed usage common throughout her colonies and bestowed the conquered territories upon soldiers and colonists. By the end of the seventeenth century New Mexico was occupied by about twenty-eight hundred whites, living on small ranches, larger haciendas, or among the Indians in their villages. There were about thirty missions in the pueblos. There the Indians were in charge of the missionaries who directed them in agriculture, taught them doctrine, supervised their morals by forbidding their old customs, and collected the tithes. Soldiers lived in the pueblos to protect the priests, and doubtless many soldiers' families lived in houses near if not actually a part of the pueblo's communal block of rooms. Even as long ago as the seventeenth century must have begun the gradual amalgamation which has changed certain purely Indian villages into villages which now show no dominant Indian features at all.

It was not a happy situation, and the " reduced " Indians several times stirred restively under the blanket of Christianity which had been laid on them. But they had no tradition of union; each pueblo was a separate city state detached even from pueblos related to it by language and presumably by blood. Abortive revolts were put down by the prosecution of their leaders for witchcraft. The Spaniards felt secure.

Among those witches was Popé of San Juan, whose fury carried him to such lengths that he actually organized the governors of twenty-nine pueblos and led the revolt of 1680. He even enlisted distant Zuñi and the Hopi villages. But it was the Pueblo's one outburst, his only real effort to fight the white man in the white man's way. Popé was such a Pueblo as has not been recorded before or since. And even his genius for large-scale planning faltered and failed as soon as the one hideous outbreak was over. When the Spaniards were gone, the Pueblos lapsed back into their old ways, and twelve years later were an easy conquest for the next invader.

That was Governor and Captain-General Diego de Vargas who fought brilliantly when he had to, but was more notable as a wily schemer who in a few years had all the pueblos back in bondage. De Vargas boasted that he captured Acoma without bloodshed, whereas Oñate had fought a fierce and sanguinary battle there. But De Vargas himself wrote: " I have been obliged to raze whole villages to the ground to punish their obstinacy." Some he obliged to leave their old sites. San Felipe was moved down from its well-fortified crag to a handier and less defensible position. Jémez was forced out of the canyon it had been so strategically built to command.

In Hopiland the Indians forced the change. Led by their shamans, the fighting men of Oraibi swarmed over to Awatobi, where the Indians were said to be practicing forbidden Christian rites in the great mission church. Trapping them in the kiva, the infuriated pagans fired it and poured chile in on the roaring flames. So the church had its Indian martyrs who had died for the faith. But their blood seeded no new converts; it practically eradicated Christianity from Hopiland for two hundred years. In Zuñi likewise the mission was destroyed and not rebuilt until the twentieth century.

In spite of a few exceptions, the Pueblos were subdued. They were not defeated, nor have they been defeated yet. Forced to abandon their villages, they built new ones in the old way, and continued their old customs. Even when they gratified the padres with their piety in hauling heavy beams and stones for churches, they built kivas alongside them. The old practices were not much interrupted by the mission bell, and more prayer sticks than crosses were planted. The Pueblos simply gave up overt belligerency for inner, pacific resistance — a much stronger method because it was entirely in harmony with their character. Pueblos are a peaceful people, they fight

only when they have to. But they are obdurate, and tireless
in their obduracy.

The Pueblo's mental make-up has helped him to maintain
his inner life inviolate. He thinks and acts, seems conscious
of himself only as one of a group. He has no conception of
individualism — no personal ambition, no exhibitionism; no
handle, really, which the white man could grasp to pull the
Pueblo out of his charmed circle. For everything in the
Pueblo's character, habit, and belief turns him in, not out. His
morality is based on the good of the group; sin is an offense
against the common good; his religion has come down from his
ancestors; he is taught reverence for his elders, who are the
keepers and the teachers of ancient lore. He is conservative;
and, like all conservatives, he is afraid of change and afraid of
ridicule. The most potent weapon of censorship and of cor-
rection in Pueblo life seems to be ridicule. He also has a gift
for secretiveness which amounts to a genius. No Pueblo ever
tells anything he does not wish to tell. He does not refuse to
answer questions, but the deviousness of his replies produces
a smoke screen of error more impenetrable than any stone wall.
Smiling behind such defenses, the Pueblo has maintained his
culture through four centuries of concerted efforts to convert
him from his religious beliefs and to give him a sense of shame
and inferiority — a stubborn persistence which is a cause of
continuing annoyance or admiration to white people, according to whether they wish to change the Indian or to study and
know him as he is.

But remarkable as the changelessness of Pueblo culture
is, closer study reveals that insidious modifications are always
going on, and always have been. Elsie Clews Parsons in her
wonderfully detailed and scholarly *Pueblo Indian Religion*
cites hundreds of examples of how Indians have influenced

one another. Tribes, clans, and individuals have shifted about, taking their customs and their ceremonies with them. They have learned, stolen, even bought each other's rites and "medicine." Students have traced relationships with plains Indians and with Indians far down in Mexico. Ethnologically D. H. Lawrence was quite right when he included descriptions of New Mexico and Arizona Indian dances in his *Mornings in Mexico*, and when he described a New Mexico pueblo as the hidden place to which *The Woman Who Rode Away* was taken. Archæological remains show that this interchange was going on long before white men recorded their history; it has been even truer since; and modern life has accelerated those cultural exchanges as it has everything else.

After the great revolt a group of Tewas took refuge in Hopiland, where their descendants in the village of Hano still use the Tewa tongue. Laguna was settled by people from Acoma with later infiltrations from other villages. When the last seventeen survivors decided to abandon the pueblo of Pecos, they went to join their kinfolk at Jémez. That village already had been greatly affected by the Navajo. During the period of De Vargas's reconquest many Jémez had gone to live among the Navajos, bringing back Navajo ways and doubtless half-Navajo children. Taos has been similarly affected by the Utes and Comanches who came in to trade their buffalo hides for grain, or to raid and plunder. Recently Taos Indians have journeyed over into Oklahoma and brought back the peyote cult, which has caused great political upheavals.

The Spanish influence has varied from enforced changes — the pueblo governor is an officer insisted upon by Spain — to many entirely unconscious borrowings, and to the complete transference of certain villages from the Indian's to the white man's world. Cuyumungúe, Alameda, Galisteo, were listed as

Indian in 1680. They now repudiate any Indian connection. Others are just on the turn. In Nambé a few Indians still keep the kiva alive, but it will soon be gone as it has recently disappeared in neighboring Pojoaque.

The portrait of the modern Pueblo can be painted only in cross-hatching — his native traits and customs intermingling with many foreign additions. Even the oldest chronicles, along with purely Indian features, record the beginnings of alien influences.

Coronado reported: " They do not have chiefs as in New Spain, but are ruled by a council of the oldest men. They have priests who . . . go up the highest roof of the village and preach from there, like public criers in the morning while the sun is rising . . . there is no drunkenness, no sodomy nor sacrifices, nor do they eat human flesh nor steal, but they are generally at work."

This is all true today. But Coronado's successor, Espejo, noted in 1582 that in exchange for " maize, tortillas, turkeys, and pinole," he gave them sleigh bells and small iron articles. So early the Pueblo was replacing the deer hoofs and shells, which were the traditional rattle in his ceremonial dress, with the white man's iron. At Zia, Espejo found the men wearing " a small cloth for covering their privy parts and other cloaks, shawls, and leather shoes in the shape of boots." Not far from the dance costume of today. The woman's dress was " a blanket over the shoulders tied with a sash at the waist, their hair cut in front, and the rest plaited so that it forms braids, and above a blanket of turkey feathers. It is an ugly dress indeed." Except for the turkey-feather robe he describes the dress the Pueblo woman wore until very lately; she still wears it in the dances. And we disagree with Espejo; it is not ugly.

The church, of course, was the Spaniard's greatest instrument of change. But it still remains a wonder how little Catholic are the Pueblos, baptized these four hundred years. And how much they have managed to affect their conquerors. On the lower levels of superstition Indians and Spaniards exchanged devils and witches, evil spells and exorcisms. France Scholes, writing for the *New Mexico Historical Review,* says that betrayed wives commonly sought Indian shamans to recall errant husbands or to hex the hated rival. Even today, in as modern a town as Albuquerque, a woman who works hard for her living was found paying good money to an Indian witch from Santo Domingo.

On a higher plane, the church has found enough tolerance to permit the Indian to honor the saint by a pagan dance, even to dance before the altar on Christmas Eve. And the Indian accepts the white man's magic as another way to propitiate the gods, and God and the saints as worthy additions to his pantheon. Madre María de Jesús, a sixteenth-century nun who never left Spain, was seen and adored by Indians in New Mexico, who marveled at her white skin and blue robes. And the Zuñi Indians, still the most pagan of all, dance annually for their " doll," a Christian image so dressed up that even its sex is in doubt.

Dr. Parsons suggests that Indians do not like the Jesus story, especially the Crucifixion, because the notion of individual sin and redemption is offensive to them. She quotes Benavides's account of an Indian " wizard " who howled with irritation at certain Christian observances. " You Christians are so crazy that you go about all together flogging yourselves like crazy people in the streets, shedding your blood. And thus you must wish that this pueblo be crazy also." The modern Pueblo finds the Penitente flagellations just as crazy today.

That the Pueblo has been able to select what he liked from

TAOS, THE NORTHERNMOST PUEBLO, WAS THERE
WHEN THE SPANIARDS CAME IN 1540

[*photo, Ruth Frank*]

the white man's religion and refuse the rest must be largely due to the fact that he lived apart in his own town. There, by making certain gestures in public on specified days, he could live much as he pleased. From the time of the reconquest he occupied the privileged position of a landholder whose pueblo was his castle. The first record of a land grant to Pueblo Indians was dated 1689, when the Governor in exile at El Paso was authorized to grant land to the pueblos — perhaps as bribes. Eleven pueblos in New Mexico had documents dated 1689 and signed by Governor Petriz Cruzat. In 1856 the United States Surveyor General approved all those grants and confirmed them. Later the " Cruzat Grants " were disputed, but as prior royal ordinances were accepted, the effect on the Indians was the same. They owned their lands, and to the silver-tipped cane given by the Spanish to every village governor, President Lincoln added another. The two now hang in the governor's house and will be proudly displayed to visitors on request.

The United States had recognized the Pueblo's right to his land, but the federal government, legally responsible for Indians as its wards, was so lax in guarding their interests that the pueblos had steadily lost lands and the even more vital right to water. This situation had gone unnoticed until 1922, when the Bursum Bill was introduced in Congress. Its stated purpose was " to settle the claims of persons not Indians within Pueblo Indian lands."

Somebody in Santa Fe read the bill, and the " art colony " fired up at once. It was easy to see that " settling the claims of persons not Indians " might well result in settling the Indians with no land at all. The magical pueblo life, so precious a repository of primitive culture, was seriously threatened. Rallying to the slogan " Let's save the Indians! " Santa Fe left its paint and its poetry and flooded the press of the country with the woes of the Pueblos and the beauties of their old life. They still needed weight on a national scale to put behind their literary spear-point. So they enlisted the women's clubs, and the General Federation employed John Collier as their representative. They all moved in on Washington, attended hearings, and faced committees with delegations of Indians who sat, blanketed and inscrutable, while nervous Congressmen tried to understand what it was all about.

The situation, as finally made clear, was this: There were thousands of claimants to lands originally granted to the pueblos, and they fell into three classes: towns like Taos settled early in the eighteenth century on invitation of the Indians who wanted protection; squatters, some of whom held deeds from the Pueblos and some of whom did not, and many who had bought their land in good faith from white owners; and less scrupulous whites who had moved fences or otherwise possessed themselves of Indian land. The Bursum Bill proposed to turn all such conflicts over to the state courts. It also provided that a survey, previously made to show what the contested lands were, should serve as proof that all land under dispute belonged to the white claimant, and gave the Indian no chance for defense. This would have meant for the Pueblos the loss of more than ninety thousand acres of land — their principal source of income. San Juan, for instance, supposed to own four thousand acres of irrigable land, would have been reduced to five hundred and eighty — a poor living for four hundred and thirty people. In all cases the supply of water had been lessened to the danger-point.

The only chance of saving his land for the Indian seemed to be to kill the bill and substitute another, which would set up a federal agency to deal with each case on its merits. By means of such vociferous, amusing, dramatic, and picturesque lobbying as Washington had never seen, this was accomplished. The Federal Lands Board was set up to consider and to settle all adverse claims to Indian lands. It is generally conceded to have achieved a fair measure of justice. The most arrant intruders were put off the pueblo lands; but most intruders, who had been innocently so, were permitted to stay. In such cases the Pueblos were given cash compensation. Cash for land! This is an interesting example of how people who are the most tolerant of the Indian and most eager to see his old ways persist manage to force him to accept the white man's standard of values.

Other enforced breaks in the Pueblo pattern resulted from the furor over the Bursum Bill. An All-Pueblo Council, organized to give the Indians a chance to share in that fight, was the first intervillage organization since Popé. During the land emergency its leaders were probably the men most powerful in the villages. Since then a new type of leader has emerged — often a young man who might not stand high in inner Pueblo councils, but who is needed as interpreter of the white man's ways as well as of his language. The All-Hopi Council, more recently organized, has also developed a new class of important men: generally Christian Hopis who live outside the old towns, at the foot of the mesas.

Associations organized to fight the Bursum Bill became permanent and continued to play an active role in Indian affairs. The Santa Fe Indian Association put a traveling secretary in the field, and her reports disclosed a tragic state of affairs. In the Indian schools she found children caged in ugly, airless buildings with smelly toilets, underfed, overworked, forced into the rigid mold of an outmoded educational system, forbidden their own language and customs, allowed to droop from homesickness and to die of disease. Conditions in the pueblos were bad, too: polluted drinking-water, infant mortality beyond all belief, a medical service inefficient at best. Missionaries of opposing faiths fought, almost hand to hand, for converts. Indian ceremonies were discouraged. Indian craft, vital for centuries, was dying of attrition.

Here was reason for battle, and a cause calculated to inflame any artist. The enemy, the Indian Service, embodied everything the artist most loathes: discipline, formalized education, religious intolerance; and especially a menace to the extraordinary primitive culture which it was their great office to vitalize in American life. So it was remarkable that the policy adopted was one not of violence but of co-operation — to work in harmony with the Indian office, pointing out deficiencies in politer terms than those here used, and offering to finance demonstrations of what might be done.

Several pueblos were supplied with public health nurses who had to combat distrust of white man's magic, indifference of government doctors, distance, and inadequate equipment. The tales those nurses told! And the things they did! Laundries and bath-houses appeared. Goats were supplied and babies and mothers taught the uses of a bottle. Windmills came to groan in places where the water was particularly bad. Certain stiff-necked employees were advised to seek other zones of influence. One or two schools, where tuberculosis was stronger than youth, were transformed into hospitals. Dr. F. I. Proctor, famous eye man, offered his services for a study of trachoma, took an Indian Service doctor to Europe to study it, even brought the great Noguchi to New Mexico, and interested the Rockefeller Foundation. Trachoma still flourishes, but at least the schools are no longer its best breeding-places.

Edgar L. Hewett in his *Indians of the Rio Grande Valley* says: " Twenty-five years ago in fifty per cent of the villages the making of pottery had ceased, and in only four or five was a high standard maintained. Basketry had disappeared from all but two or three and could be said to flourish in only one. Weaving, with decorative embroidery, was kept up mostly for ceremonial purposes in three or four villages. Work in turquoise was practiced in but two pueblos, and other villages still made a few shell ornaments. Painting, except as pottery decorations, had entirely disappeared. Dramatic ceremonies with musical accompaniment survived in all the villages but were steadily declining under the disapproval of government, church, and philanthropic organizations. Especially noticeable was the deterioration in costuming which was losing its symbolic character, its beauty, and its meaning to the dancers themselves."

The white man had managed to make almost a clean sweep of the Pueblo's arts. But the white man with a different point of view has brought many of them back again. The Museum of New Mexico took the lead at first. Through lectures, student groups, and two publications — *El Palacio* and *Art and Archæology* — it gradually trained a public taste which saw beauty in Indian crafts. The artists later carried the crusade far afield.

Indian dances are recognized as a form of art which nobody must miss. Indian potters have been given their own ancient designs, encouraged to make finer and finer ware, and helped to find a market. Indian weaving and embroidery have been used on smart clothes. An entirely new Indian art has been developed by giving paint and paper to Indians and urging them to make pictures of what they know. And here, as everywhere, the white man is putting his ways, his taste, his standards over on the Indian.

Under President Hoover these private demonstrations began to have an effect on the Indian Service. Abuses were corrected, reforms undertaken. The whole program has been carried along faster and farther under John Collier as Indian Commissioner. The schools now consciously try to teach the Indian child what he needs of the white man's culture without making it impossible for him to return to his people as a " good Indian." Those who do not wish to go back they try to help bridge the chasm between their native life and our urban life. Indian languages are no longer forbidden. Indian children are no longer forced to attend Christian churches; they are even excused to go home for the dances and for kiva training. And Indian craftsmen teach them Indian crafts.

Nevertheless the young Pueblo finds himself in a tragic dilemma. If he returns to his pueblo he finds there is little or no land for him and only occasional wage work. He is dependent upon his family for land, and often he must wait for ten years or until he is married before fields are assigned to him for his own use. He must wait even longer before he has a voice in the government of his community. And association with the white man is not conducive to patience. A few make a good living as potters or painters. Many have evaluated the tourist's tastes and produce gaudy and useless knick-knacks for a dime each, which brings in a few extra dollars. Some have opened shops in the villages, others dance for pay, though always insisting that they perform only the " pleasure dances."

If he goes to town the young Pueblo may find work as helper

in various trades, as laborer or domestic servant, or in shops that sell Indian crafts. These are the most pitiful. They work for low pay, humiliated to be shown off to tourists, and denied the Indian's great need for making beautiful things slowly, lovingly. In any case the Pueblo in town occupies a sadly anomalous position, accepted neither as fully white nor as fully Indian.

The sadness of the young Indian lost between two worlds must seem to the old Indians justification enough for all their efforts to fend off the onslaught of the white man, whether he comes as enemy or as friend. For the older Indians do fight in every way they can to maintain the integrity of the Pueblo life. They insist that their boys " enter the kiva." They summon their people for important festivals. Once when Laguna much needed rain, Albuquerque saw clerks leave stores, mechanics garages, maids kitchens, and bellboys hotels, in response to the shaman's call. The old men make young Indians feel themselves a part of the village life as long as they can. The really recalcitrant Indian they have been able, until now, to penalize. One who marries out of the pueblo is denied office, obliged to live outside the walls. One " who puts himself forward," forgets that his primary duty is to the group, may be ostracized, even exiled. Edwin R. Embree, in *Indians of the Americas*, tells the story of a Carlisle graduate who has lived a sad and broken life in his native Taos, separated from his people, unable to share their life. Everyone who knows Pueblos knows many stories that hurt as much.

But the old men, being wise, must know that it is only a matter of time before many insidious cracks in the surface of their hidden life will let in so much alien thought that the whole fabric will crack and crumble. They have had to yield in many ways that are funny, as well as pitiful. The old law that forbade a cropped Pueblo to dance is a dead letter, for every boy's hair is cut at school. In Santo Domingo, where a man should wear moccasins, they have compromised on taking the heels off store shoes. In Taos, where tradition demands leggings with breech-clout and blanket, men take the seats out of ordinary trousers and wrap sheets around their hips.

Modern inventions, which make for ease and comfort, win everywhere. Automobiles and stoves, window glass and tables and chairs, tractors in the fields, and sewing-machines in the house have all been first forbidden and then accepted.

A Taos girl, asked what she wanted for a wedding present, answered: " A bucket."

Nothing has more captivated painters and photographers than the Pueblo woman fetching water in a painted jar on her head. Grace of line and beauty of color; and a symbol, too, of a primitive life away from the world's hurlyburly. For the woman dipping a *tinaja* into Pueblo Creek is taking water that comes sparkling from the sacred Blue Lake. Yet the Taos bride wanted a bucket with a handle for greater ease in doing the work she had to do. I wondered if she could use her bright tin pail without losing something important that went with the hand-made jar — a sense of god-given water from a sacred place. She will surely lose the god and with him much hocus-pocus and superstitious fear. But can she, while taking on new ways and new concepts, keep the old reverence for life-giving natural things, the ability to use them without abuse, to share them without degrading herself or another? For this is what the ancient pueblo life had; this is what modern life threatens; this is the problem that faces every young Pueblo Indian.

An intelligent Pueblo man of forty has tried to help me answer these questions by telling me his own experience. When he was very small, he said, the medicine man used to come often. He talked to the mother; my friend thinks now that he talked for the children, who sat big-eyed to listen. If the medicine man asked for water, a child brought it and stood with folded arms until the cup was returned.

" He told us stories about gifted people with powers. Not gods, but people who know. They were the Real Ones.

" We used to watch the dances. It meant more than you see. You feel the rain, the sun, power. We understood the songs, but I think we felt it more, even when we were little and didn't know much.

" Yes, we learned about evil power, witches. He told us that we could avoid evil by keeping happy and good. ' Our fathers,' he used to say, ' won't let them harm you.'

" Good was building up; bad was tearing down. ' If you tear down or go the wrong way,' he used to tell my mother, ' you will suffer, or your children will suffer. You must live well to have a happy feeling.'

" He used to talk about honestness in doing. Truth is a reflection of inner honestness. Some people can't reflect truth. We have people who steal; we call a man ' John Steal,' for instance. He can't help it, and if he steals from you it is your fault.

" We were taught to be observant of everything, even little things. Walking with my father, he used to ask me questions to see if I understood what I looked at. You were supposed to learn all the time. They used to say: ' I can't do it for you, you have to learn for yourself.'

" ' If you do anything,' he used to say, ' do it as though you wanted to do that more than anything in the world. If you run, if you hunt rabbits, if you fetch firewood, even if you sit still and listen.' "

So this Pueblo child was fortified before he was six. When he was taken away to boarding-school at that age, he was very unhappy and uncomfortable. Shoes hurt his feet, sleeves were stiff, and a hat an unnecessary nuisance. He could not understand anybody except his cousin and they were punished for speaking their own language. He said he was a Baptist first because he heard another boy say that. But going to that church made him miss his dinner, so then he professed to be a Presbyterian and got back in time to eat.

" Some of the teachers were cruel, but I think just because they were ignorant. Some even tried to understand, but they could not. . . . The greatest happiness was getting home. . . . No, I never saw anything in the school I thought was better than our ways. . . . I think the schools made us pretty good Indians. . . . Except when they got us all mixed up. Some boys did. They went to Santa Fe to live, they changed their ways. I don't think they are very happy now. I dunno. I'm glad I came back here."

How much unknowing whites must help the old men in their effort to keep the Pueblo's inner life sacred and secure! In contrast with his own certainties, based upon tradition, bound up with every phase of his life, how weak our dissensions and divisions must seem! So many gods, so many creeds. Surely their missionaries, pointing to each other, can only point the Indian's way back to his kiva.

My friend, in spite of his mistaken professions at school, is a Catholic — as Pueblos are. They attend mass occasionally, confession rarely; offer their babies for baptism, their children for confirmation, themselves for marriage, and their dead for the burial service. But they also present the babies to the sun, induct their children into the clans or societies, solemnize weddings by the ancient rites, and carry their dead away from the church for final services before they are buried. It happened once that an Indian policeman was killed in the performance of duty, an act of singular bravery in defense of a white policeman. The city council of Albuquerque, wishing to do him honor, bought a casket. The Indians were distressed. Politeness required the acceptance of the gift; they appreciated fully the spirit behind it. But they could not let one of their own be enclosed in a board box. Happily one of the white men knew them well, and he managed to save the feelings of the white town and still make it possible for the Indian to go back to earth wrapped in a blanket.

Asked how the wise men helped children to make these necessary adjustments, my friend thought quite a while. Then he said: " I don't remember that much was said at one time, but I guess a lot must have been said all the time because I know we all believed the Catholic Church was all right; another way, maybe a right way; anyhow, we could go there and still be good Indians. . . . Everybody always said to be good Indians."

In answer to a question summing up, he said: " I think the old conception of religion is true. I think the whites are more irreligious than we are. Our beliefs keep the Indian calm, we live like in a calm lake."

The northernmost

pueblo is Taos. Alvarado found it there in 1540 and described its five-storied block of dwellings looking much as they do today. Taos appears on the earliest maps. An outpost on the Spaniards' northern frontier, it was a junction point for Indians of the plains, soon so mobilized by the horses the Spaniards gave them, and the Pueblos, whose runners beat narrow trails over the stiffest mountain grades. When white men came from the East, Taos gathered together the threads of commerce, and men shouldering their packs back on the Missouri agreed to meet next year and swap yarns in Taos.

Now Taos is known wherever men know paint: Taos, the Art Colony. Again the remote mountain town is gathering together the threads of many interests and weaving for itself a reputation out of all proportion to its size. Everybody wants to go to Taos. For Taos, more than any of the other Southwestern towns where artists forgather and work, stands for the living force of art. Within this generation the Rio Grande watershed, so recently the frontier of rough, unlettered men, has begun to appear on maps of the United States as a center of creative expression. No picture of the artistic awakening of the United States is complete without Taos.

XVII

TAOS AND THE ARTISTS

OWEVER APPROACHED, TAOS ALWAYS SEEMS TO BE A destination, the end of a journey. Even casually, one does not speak of going through Taos on the way to somewhere else. One goes " to Taos, and on to . . ." This enhances, or perhaps it is the reason for, the feeling of remoteness Taos gives. Even in these days of quickened travel the little town seems far away. The seventy-five miles from Santa Fe do not consume the hours as they used to do. But those long, uninhabitable stretches of marl, those twisting gorges cut through lava by the Rio Grande, so energetic up there in a tip-tilted landscape, prepare one for a different world. And so it looks. The old theatrical bounce-out from between straight cliffs, where trees cling to precarious root-holes, has been left aside for an easily graded ascent. But even after that gentle approach the emergence onto the sage-grown plateau of Taos catches the breath with surprise, like arrival at another planet. Coming in across the mountains is equally dramatic. From Raton by way of Cimarron, or from Las Vegas through Mora, one follows the clarity of a narrow stream, safe among sheltering pines and sycamores, until the trees suddenly fall back and leave one facing the vast plain, spreading smoothly off to disappear against the western sky.

North and south it sweeps grandly up to blue peaks in Colorado, dark-blue peaks near Santa Fe. And always its quiet gray and sand tones move gently like a sea not yet quite petrified. All day, and on bright starlit or moonlight nights, every tint and tone of green and blue plays across the surface of Pueblo Peak, which no Indian need tell one is a sacred pinnacle. And with sun warmth or moisture in the air, the sage emits its keen and healthy scent. Brightly colored bloom runs across that plateau and changes at every season. Blue and violet, magnolia white and deep purple, yellow and orange-red, but no daintiness of detail can ever weaken the plain's power, which booms like an organ.

The world of Taos is a different world. Backed by Pueblo Peak, the tripartite town spreads along from stream to stream, queening it over the plateau's still, impersonal beauty. The Indians' two communal houses face each other across Pueblo Creek. Don Fernando de Taos, the old Mexican plaza where the artists live, waters its fields and gardens from Taos Creek, and the *Río Chiquito*, the little river, has cut itself so deeply down at Ranchos de Taos that most people live half a mile above it on two steep cliffs. These streams and others water little valleys so fertile that Taos used to be New Mexico's granary. But they soon yield to the earth's inclination, leave the surface of the breezy plateau, with its patterns of clouds, and cut deep gorges across its face as they rush off to the Great River.

Remote as it is, Taos has always managed to be a center, generally a center of disturbance. Even the winds, draining down the canyons, hit the town with a force that whirls snowy or dusty eddies around the plazas or stiffens summer rains into huge watery brooms that sweep the fields and pour muddy torrents over adobe roofs and walls. One inclined to endow physical geography with human attributes might see Taos as a center of psychic confusion, too, so often have its upsets shown sinister undercurrents. But no mystical explanation is needed. There is no gainsaying the effect of altitude on nerves. Some people find the deeper pull of air into the lungs, the quickened heart-beat, only stimulating to the mind, lightening to the lift of the foot. Others, especially some women, grow shrill, excitable, and hectic. Trivial mouse-nibblings are magnified into momentous matters, and Taos appears again in press dispatches with a tragedy or tragicomedy.

Another explanation, if another is needed, is that Taos, through all its history, has attracted people of backgrounds so incomprehensible to each other, of points of view so irreconcilable, and of characters so strong that their coming together has never been a soft amalgamation; it has been a clash which struck off fire and confusion.

From the beginning, Taos' story has been turbulent. The pueblo had fought for its life before Spain knew it, and its peaceful pueblo stock had taken infusions of plains Indian blood. Its people are taller, sharper-featured, readier to fight openly than most Pueblos. There Popé, fleeing from his trial as a witch, found men who would plot with him in the kiva, and supply runners to carry his message of revolt throughout the province. From then until now Taos has played an important role in every Indian revolt New Mexico has known. And time, as it rolled along, only added newer sources of discord.

Against the threats of wild Comanches, Utes, and Arapahoes, Taos invited the Spaniards in, and soon found that its protectors were the enemies who took its lands. Then the mountain men made Taos their capital, the end of their every road. They came to sell their furs to merchants setting off for Chihuahua or the States, and to stock up on ammunition, flour, and bacon. But, above all, Taos was the town of the flesh-pots for men starved by months of loneliness, deprivation, and danger. Every first-hand account of the trails, of trapping and exploring, describes Taos and the delights of its low, smoky dance and gambling halls, and of the submissive Mexican girl. Mountain men have told their own tale, and told it well. In fiction it has been best done by Harvey Fergusson in *Wolf Song*, a poetic presentation of the pull in a man's heart between the masculine world he revels in and the love of a woman that binds him.

In 1837 Taos figured in another revolt. Egged on by certain ricos, who were disgruntled by Mexico's tax-gathering methods, a rabble of Indians and whites set out from Taos for Santa Fe. They defeated the Governor and chopped off his head, and chose a Taos Indian for their Governor. He was José Gonzales, whom Josiah Gregg described as " a good honest hunter, but a very ignorant man." His time was short. General Armijo, one of the original conspirators, felt a shift in the wind and was quick to turn his coat. Appearing as the Mexican government's loyal man, he defeated Gonzales at La Cañada.

When the Indian came before him, the general said: " How do you do, Compañero? Confess yourself, Compañero! " And then, to his men: " Now shoot my compañero! "

The white men who had elevated an ignorant Indian to the dignity of Governor were well advised.

A figure in that revolt was Father José Antonio Martínez, the parish priest in Taos. Born in Abiqui, educated in Durango, a vigorous and independent thinker, Padre Martínez probably still ranks as the outstanding New Mexican. Little is said of this priest's spiritual qualities, which were entirely overshadowed by his energy and his versatility in practical affairs. He owned ranches, a flour mill, and a press on which he printed *El Crepusculo* (*The Dawn*). Gregg described that newspaper as " a little foolscap sheet issued weekly for about a month to the tune of fifty subscribers, and then abandoned, partially for want of patronage and partially because the editor had accomplished his object of procuring his election to Congress." This forward-looking priest also printed textbooks, for he was so far ahead of his times that he had established schools, not only for boys, but for girls. His interest in children was truly paternal. He acknowledged the offspring of two women; rumors of others run into dozens.

Students cannot agree as to Padre Martínez's part in the revolt of 1846, when a mob assassinated Charles Bent, the United States' first civil Governor of New Mexico. There is no documentary evidence either to incriminate or to absolve the priest. It is hard to believe that so well informed a man did not know what was afoot. If he connived, he must have seemed a patriot to Mexico as well as a traitor to the United States. But a man as liberal, independent, and aggressive as he was should have recognized the newcomers as of his own sort. Padre Martínez, in spite of his name and heritage, was the first New Mexico gringo. One version of his story has been told by Willa Cather in *Death Comes for the Archbishop*. Archbishop Lamy, the reforming Frenchman, undertook to discipline the priest whose sins were so many and so unconcealed. His adherents say that Padre Martínez had lent the Archbishop money which was never repaid, and that he refused to deny the sacraments to people too poor to pay the fees. He even charged, in *El Crepusculo*, that the church collected more money than it cost to run the whole territory. Before the Archbishop could unfrock him, Padre Martínez " resigned " from the church, but continued to hold services in his private chapel, where most of his congregation followed him. Whatever his derelictions, Padre Martínez was a strong character, a fascinating man, a true liberal; and many Taos valley people are justly proud to be his descendants.

During Padre Martínez's pastorate a little girl was born in Taos: Teresina Bent, daughter of Governor Bent and his pretty wife, Josefa Jaramillo. Charles Bent knew the West from his brother's fort on the Arkansas all across the plains and mountains to Taos, where he and his *compadre*, Kit Carson, had married sisters and settled down.

In 1846 little Teresina was six years old. I knew her when she was seventy. A short woman, with wide hips which swayed under full, black skirts, she held her delicate head aristocratically high under black lace when she walked slowly to daily mass. After that, she sat all the long summer days in the open zaguan, from where she could see the work-patio at the rear and a corner of the plaza across the front patio, where the mulberry tree dropped purple fruit on flowerbeds and a little lawn. All the household duties were Miss Lena's, who had from her mother only big brown eyes and a Spanish accent. Otherwise she showed the driving yen for work of her German father, Aloysius Scheurich, who had seen that Kit Carson got his last wish — a dish of chile before he died. All day Miss Lena bossed the maids' scrubbing, cooked, canned, or dried fruit, sped in and out about her doings in the town, or settled visitors with her mother in the zaguan. Doña Teresina rocked in her curve-backed chair, with her tiny feet on a stool and her deft white fingers shuttling at her tatting.

She loved to talk and was always ready to retell her childish recollections of that tragic night when she saw her father killed.

As she grew older, little Teresina learned that her father had known there was trouble brewing when he came home from Santa Fe for that Christmas. But all she remembered was of being awakened by shaking and pounding on the big, locked door, and her mother's insistence that he must not open.

The child, startled, but warm in her bed, heard him say: " No, there is no danger; these are my friends."

She remembered the terrifying confusion: shouts, groans, her mother's screams, and somebody grabbing her out of bed. Her father had been struck down, shot full of arrows, and scalped, but was still alive when the mob went off. The women, alone in the darkened rooms, afraid to make a light, bound him up as well as they could. Then they dug a hole through the adobe wall into the next house. Teresina could remember that — how they worked hard with heavy iron spoons, and how the children were all hustled through, and how cold it was, and how they were told not to cry or they'd be killed.

For days they huddled there. An Indian woman sneaked in a little food. The Governor died, but they were afraid to take him out for burial. Teresina remembered his long, blanket-covered body lying there, and how her mother prayed. No priest came. The children were cold, and too frightened even to pray.

What went on outside was witnessed by young Lewis Garrard, a goggle-eyed youngster who had reached Taos in time for all the excitement. In *Wah-to-Yah* he writes of how the whole valley was aflame with horror. Word kept coming in that men on ranches had been killed, of the massacre at Arroyo Hondo. Two young men had set out to run the seventy miles straight across the hills to Santa Fe. But until help came, the town could only wait in terror. A peon who called himself " General " Montoya swaggered around, shouting drunken threats. Padre Martínez opened his house to dozens of women and children. And over in the pueblo the band of revolutionaries barricaded themselves in the church to await the inexorable coming of the United States troops.

They say that when Colonel Price arrived, his men were too drunk to be very discriminating. They pounded the old church to pieces with cannon, and they hanged seventeen men, including Indians. After that, there was no doubt about accepting the sovereignty of the United States.

Teresina remembered nothing of the hangings in the plaza, though many others could tell how women and children hid on the roofs to peer and see. Mrs. Scheurich only remembered how friends came and she was warmly bathed and could eat again. Her mother was never happy after that, nor did she recover from a blow given her as she struggled to drag her husband away from his assailants. Teresina spent most of her girlhood with her aunt and uncle " Car-són."

Kit Carson was the town's idol, who was becoming a legend in spite of his modest annoyance with it. My grandfather described him as " a small, thin, bow-legged man of about forty or more years. I enquired who he was, and when I was told that it was Kit Carson, I was much surprised. While on the road, I got hold of a book entitled ' The Life and Exploits of Kit Carson, the famous Hunter, Indian fighter, Guide and Scout of the Rocky Mountains.' When the road was good and the oxen did not need any attention, I used to sit on the wagon-tongue in the shade of the wheelers and read this book. It was profusely illustrated, representing all sorts of horrible situations, imaginary and impossible fights and c. In one picture an encounter was represented between a great big man with flowing beard, clad all over in ornamental buckskin, mounted on a powerful charger. He was in the act of killing two Indians, one on each side of him, also on horseback; while he shot the one with a pistol, he stabbed the other with a large Bowie Knife. Several dead Indians lay scattered around.

" When I saw this man ' in optima forma ' a clean-shaven man about 5 feet 6 or 7 inches high, with good nature all over his face and a thin voice, at the gaming table in Santa Fe, bucking at Monte or Faro, of course I was surprised. In later years in the '60's, when he was a Colonel in the Volunteer Service and was stationed with his Regiment at Albuquerque, I still had that book, and one day I showed him the pictures, and particularly the one referred to. ' Why,' he exclaimed with his thin voice, ' is that me? ' "

During the decades that followed, mining was the big news in Taos. Rich strikes in the hills above the Merino Valley made Elizabethtown boom with hundreds of people, saloons, stamp-mills, offices, hotels, even churches. Five millions of dollars were taken out, and then the town collapsed into a ghost town, which has today almost faded out of sight as its wood rots down into loam. Its heyday and the undying hopes it lit up introduced a new type into the pageant of Taos plaza — the long-haired prospector, bearded, booted, driving his burro. He is still there, making short buying trips, uneasy until he can get off into the hills again.

Such men always used to visit Doc Martin, until his death removed the one thoroughly competent interpreter of everything that Taos was. " The old Doc " told many people his tales; nobody will ever re-create the way he told them, parting his coat-tails before a snapping piñon fire, chuckling because he saw how funny human nature was, never blaming because he knew it to be frail. His stories used to start with queer callers in the middle of the night, bringing news of a fever, a knifing, a birthing forty miles or so away. Then the doctor and the padre, wrapped into the buckboard with plenty of whisky, were off to save a life or ease a soul — miles of swinging trot up a canyon, across streams, flashing up the eyes of sleepy animals, and finally to the stricken house. If the doctor could still be of service, the priest waited with the whisky. If it was too late for the doctor, he cherished the bottle while the priest performed his comforting offices. And every episode, detailing every actor's past, let in new light on the complicated human pattern of Taos. If Dr. Martin had written his book, we might even be able to understand its crimes and to laugh at its contradictions as he seemed to do.

In Taos everything that makes the Southwest dramatic is heightened and intensified. And almost every happening has an inexplicable element that puts it near improbability. When " old man Manby " was found beheaded in his house in 1929, it was said that that killing was only one of three ghoulish crimes — that Wilkinson, an E-town miner, had been mysteriously beheaded after death, and that his partner, Ferguson, had died insane with remorse and fear. Nobody was ever tried for Manby's death, the coroner's jury having found no evidence of " other than natural causes." The town was more amused by the romantic and fantastic side-lights of that crime than impressed by its horror. For Taos is used to crimes of horror. The county is too poor to indulge in more than one good murder trial a year, and perhaps the gaudiest one is chosen. Certainly when the town attends its June session of court as other centers the opera, it never lacks raw drama. A woman who charged her rival's kitchen stove with dynamite pleaded witchcraft in extenuation. A half-witted young sheep-herder who killed a young husband whose lunch he had shared said in his own defense that he had desired the wife. This one's weak-mindedness got him off. It is said that only one man has ever been hanged for murder in Taos County, and that was a gringo who killed a Penitente. Among unproved crimes are the mysterious night fires which, one after another, burned out the buildings around the plaza. Folk who like the mystical blame forces set in motion against whites who would profane the Indians' sacred Blue Lake. Men — staggering, half-blinded with sleep — passed buckets on those cold nights, but nothing could be saved.

Gaunt walls and chimneys still occupy one corner of the plaza, and the rest of it has been rebuilt in ways that give no hint of the distinction old Taos used to have. Merchants who have moved in as the town's growing fame brought business cannot understand that visitors admired some of the town's oddities as they never could the new dime store. Nobody bothered to save the old Columbian Hotel, with its long, pillared portal, its low windows opening out from pink-walled rooms with fireplaces, its paneled dining-room, and patios where Ruth Lucero kept her parrots. So it has been replaced with a new hotel as much as possible like Santa Fe. And many artists are moving off to Ranchos de Taos, which has not yet been struck by self-conscious New Mexico architecture.

But wherever they live, artists and their wives appear daily in the plaza of Don Fernando. Only there do Indians and whites meet in such close intimacy. Taos men in dusty sheets are in town every day — buying, working in gardens, or posing. Their women work as maids in homes and hotels, wearing huge white-buckskin boots, and calico shawls and dresses of soft, harmonious colors. And the whites who market on the plaza are of a diversity such as seldom comes together, except in great cities where thousands of innocuous and unnoticeable citizens cushion them against one another. In Taos they clash as brittle-edged individuals. Spanish is spoken on the plaza as much as English, and English varies from Southwestern lingo, so full of new, home-made words, to the Eastern seaboard's chirp, heavy with broad *a's*. As they all carry paper sacks out to their wagons, ancient Fords, or streamlined motor cars and stop in amiable chat, the atmosphere of sunny peace belies the hidden cross-currents which might roil it at any moment. In Taos one may, within a few hours, move through a dozen circles and gather evidence of how little living together makes for tolerance. Long-suffering forbearance seems to be the prevailing virtue. A lady of the most æsthetic circle, fully aware of her impeccable social condition, poured out tea and advice to a newcomer. " Whatever you do," she warned, " don't have anything to do with the village people."

The old doctor, comfortably of the village, said: " Well, she's crazy, but letting it run off as she does probably saves us a lot of other kinds of trouble."

An Indian, explaining a trivial theft near the pueblo, said: " I wish those Mexicans would stay away from here! "

Mrs. Scheurich, when an artist introduced a Navajo blanket to give a needed pattern in her portrait, said: " No, I will not have that! I am no Indian! "

And one old lady from Dubuque, tired of trying to follow what they were talking about, summed it up for herself and many others: " Crazy town, crazy people! "

No wonder Taos has attracted artists who find its human

scene as stimulating as the almost repellent beauty of the landscape, which defies every effort to trap it in words or in paint. Artists discovered Taos as long ago as 1881, when Montgomery Roosevelt made a few sketches there. Frederic Remington painted in Taos. But its first resident painter was Henry Sharp, who, in the nineties, began to add Taos Indians to his repertoire of Montana tribes. He was soon followed by others; Paris was palling on American artists, strong brown faces under white drapery were as romantic as Delacroix's Algerians, and Taos was a good place to live, as well as to paint.

Taos has never been the Southwest's only art center. Santa Fe drew many painters, and to this day artists debate the advantages of the two towns. Other places, from San Antonio in Texas to certain rocky, sea-washed villages on the Pacific, make much of their art colonies, support art societies and galleries, and offer frequent shows. But "Taos" is the name that most connotes "art colony." This is because artists flock. With the whole Southwest to choose from — vivid in color, striking in form, and full of paintable types — they cluster in a few places where they can watch each other's work, share each other's responses. And, sooner or later, Taos lures them all. The University of New Mexico maintains a summer school of paint there. Teachers from other, hotter states take their broods of pupils to summer in Taos. Unattached aspirants are discovered sketching at every corner. Boardinghouses, hotels, and rentable houses are filled with them, and with the poseurs and hangers-on who linger round, trying to catch some of the fine, free joy that creative workers seem to know.

Many first-rate men have painted in Taos. No Eastern show is complete without its quota of Taos Indians, Taos scenes, and one or two Taos men on the jury. They have brought back fat prizes, and Taos is a place that no artist can afford to miss. But it took a literary flurry to put Taos in all the public prints, whether they inclined toward art or not. About the time the war ended, Mabel Dodge Stern discovered New Mexico with such fresh enthusiasm that she could write: "Nobody had ever heard of New Mexico until I went there." She not only went, but she decided to stay. She married Antonio Luján, a Taos Indian, and she attracted front-page people of many kinds. A whole book-shelf has come out of the visit of D. H. Lawrence and his richly human wife, Frieda von Richthofen. Lawrence wrote of Indians, women wrote of Lawrence, and of each other. Mabel herself, in *Winter in Taos*, and *Edge of Taos Desert*, has written beautifully about the wide, pale valley with its deepening color tones, and the strange human scene with its dark depths. Better than almost any other books, they show why a remote New Mexico valley attracts and holds people who have known beauty in many parts of the world.

Taos has never developed a school of painting, though it has reflected every style the art world has known in forty years, and passed through certain phases of its own which seem inevitable, looking back. The first painters naturally saw the obvious. Taos Indians were posed in fire and sunlight; they shot arrows in wavering aspen shade; their women dipped water from iridescent streams, and men posed in the nude. Women were shy; getting a nude female model is a triumph. And children may be painted only in slumber, as no way has been found to keep them awake. In time, keen-eyed younger men saw the humor in the Taos scene and began to vary the standard poses with pictures of people about their regular affairs — plastering houses, winnowing wheat in baskets, shucking corn, even playing baseball. Time was when the whole colony moved up to Twining to paint aspens in autumn; now only the tyro or the old habitué paints yellow aspens. Modern men have followed modern methods, and nowadays one hears of dynamic symmetry and transcendental painting.

Every group has a laughing scorn of every other. They form associations and fall apart again. But always the Harwood Foundation holds the town together. As long as she lived, Elizabeth Harwood's home was a focus for the town's life — a sort of storm center of calm. Long years abroad had given her a sure judgment of beautiful things. Her own natural tolerance made it possible for her to move easily from faction to faction, always friendly, disregarding the wrangles. Her monument is the house where she lived for twenty years, which is now a permanent gallery where all may show.

The most arresting fact about painters, in Taos and elsewhere, is that the men who rank as Southwestern painters grew to maturity and learned their craft elsewhere. No matter how long they stay, they never quite forget their first impression of the country as foreign, and its people as odd, or at least unknown. For many years Southwesterners did not try to paint. Lately young native sons and daughters are aware of paint. Most of them still follow a teacher's guidance; only a few have struck out, with the promise of individual development. So far, only one has made himself known to Eastern critics, who have no kindly need to say that the boy paints well because he is a neighbor's son.

Peter Hurd of Roswell has never painted in Taos, and he comes into this chapter only because he is a New Mexican in very truth. Born on the rim of the great plains, speaking Spanish with a lilt that makes Mexicans call him " Chihuahueño," he knows his horse and his neighbors, and he feels his country as part of himself — interesting, but never strange. And so he paints — naturally, with a realism that is as free from cant as it is from any consciousness of his models as picturesque. Perhaps this one swallow makes an artistic summer for New Mexico.

But other painting promises development right out of the soil. Fra Angelico Chávez adorns his little chapel at Santo Domingo with frescoes, as his predecessors used to do. Young Pedro Castañeda of Texaco has suddenly won startled interest with his simple, primitive pictures of his own home. And Indians, by one of those unforeseeable developments which are so obvious once they have occurred, have won acclaim wherever their work has gone, in this country and abroad.

Fortunately the first Indian painters — Awa Tsireh, Fred Kabotie, Velino Shijé — were discovered by people of enough wisdom to give them paint and tell them to go ahead. The Indian's hand has inherited cunning from a long line of artists stretching back beyond all human ken. He is unexcelled in clarity and purity of line, in exquisite handling of mass, in the delicate direction of the observer's eye through the pattern. Indian painters paint what they know — cloud and earth forms, plants and animals, themselves and their own daily doings — hunting, fishing, planting, playing. The Indian is realistic, in that his deer and antelope are immediately recognizable. The buffalo-hunter hurling a lance, the dancer's lifted foot, are correct in every detail. But the Indian is untrammeled by any old-fashioned need for complete veracity. If it suits his mood, the antelope leaps across a fringed sash, the skunk parades along a rainbow, the dancer steps airily in empty space. Humor abounds; there is never a hint of sentimentalism.

What may come of these really native developments, nobody knows. In painting, as in so many other lines of endeavor, the foreigner has had to show the native what his country really has. Perhaps this office has been so well performed that we are at the beginning of the native's own expression in the arts.

Dropping from

any mountain town onto the level plain is like riding the descending swoops of a roller-coaster. The great Rockies loom behind, the road snakes through hills gashed with red sandstone canyons, or among ancient lava beds. Known all over the Southwest as mal pais, badland, the word has become, in Gringoese, malpie. As the hills subside, the warm rose and violet tints fade into gray and white, with only bits of yellow. Only at sunset the glow from the west lays long bars of red gold across the plains, makes every cactus and yucca plant shine with silver or copper tones, and tips a blue shadow up against every ridge in a dust-white roadway.

Years ago these plains were alive with bouncing antelope flashing their white rumps and fleeing in bronze and white droves like leaves. Beyond antelope, the buffalo, and always the promise of grazing for domestic stock. Like all the fenceless range, this has been squared off by barbed wire. Roads are posted with the warning: " Look out for Cattle," and white-faced Herefords peer through the wires, or stroll erratically along the highway. Driving across the plains, one senses — along with the swooping drops of the motor — endlessness and sameness. The skyline never changes; one never catches up with it. The great plains, wider than a man can ever see, seem falsely close and regularly bounded.

XVIII

THE HIGH PLAINS ARE THE
FORTY-NINTH STATE

N 1879, LAND-POOR TEXAS SWAPPED THREE MILLION ACRES
of its Panhandle for a state capitol. The Capitol Syndicate
erected an imposing edifice at Austin second in size only to
the one at Washington, and built of Texas granite. The ranch
they got in exchange covered ten of the thirty counties in the
Panhandle, and they registered the X I T brand, " ten in
Texas." Many citizens of those counties claim today that
Texas forgot them as soon as the deal was closed. It is even
proposed, perhaps in fun, but often, to invoke a provision in
the act creating Texas which would permit its division into
five states. Its inordinate size was due only to Northern determination to limit the number of Southern senators. After-
dinner speakers find secession a popular theme; newspapers
editorialize about the " high plains empire " and its right to
independence. Judge Hamlin of Farwell has been suggested
as the right man for first governor, and Carl Hinton, the
vigorous secretary of Amarillo's Chamber of Commerce, com-

plains: " The rest of the country thinks we belong to Texas, but our senators never heard of us." Amarillo, metropolis of the Panhandle, with fifty-five thousand inhabitants, is also the center of a trade area that might suggest the limits of a forty-ninth state. Those limits approximate a state of mind as well as a geographical and economic division. Oklahoma's Panhandle would certainly be included; its folk are similarly disgruntled, remote from the center, bound to Texas' Panhandle by every social and economic interest. The name Texlahoma has even been proposed, but that hardly seems inclusive enough, as it leaves out New Mexico's high plains country.

New Mexico's eastern counties turn toward Texas rather than toward New Mexico. Cattle country, their business leads them eastward; they read Texas newspapers, send their children to Texas schools and the University of Texas; they even root for Texas football teams against the University of New Mexico. They complain as bitterly of neglect on the part of " those Mexicans at Santa Fe " as the Panhandle Texans ever did about politicians " down in the skillet."

I do not know Oklahoma or where the forty-ninth state's eastern boundary should run. But its western line is readily perceptible to one motoring east. On Highway 60, Fort Sumner is plainly a New Mexico town. On the banks of the Pecos, many of its citizens have Spanish blood, many of its houses are of adobe. There Billy the Kid was visiting his sweetheart in the home of Pete Maxwell, son of Lucien B. and Luz Beaubien Maxwell, when Sheriff Pat Garrett shot him dead. There his grave shares tourist honors with the ruins of old Fort Sumner and the Bosque Redondo, where the Navajos were held captives. All this is New Mexico.

The towns beyond bear the marks of the high plains.

Clovis, made by the railroad, is now an important cattle-shipping center. Portales, south of it, was first a nooning place on the old Goodnight-Loving Trail, and then a station on the Pecos Valley Railroad (called the Peavine from its look of dangling down to Carlsbad and Pecos), now a branch of the Santa Fe. Portales now has a junior college, where a student can pay his board by adding a milch cow to the dairy herd, a hundred chickens to the poultry yard, or a side of beef to the commissary. Both Clovis and Portales are strong Baptist towns with a tinge of Methodism, almost none of the formal Episcopalian or Presbyterian influence, and very small Catholic congregations. Both towns show a preponderance of men at Sunday service, and stores, offices, and schools close for revivals. Teachers' contracts include an agreement not to dance, drink, or play cards, but luckily somebody has figured out a way to play card games with dominoes. This type of Christianity does not preclude scorn of Catholics or snobbish discrimination against people of Spanish blood. It was cited as an evidence of growing tolerance that Spanish and Anglo students now dance together at the college parties in Portales.

How this state line should run north of where the Pecos bends west is a question. Perhaps the county names sufficiently indicate the proper division — Guadalupe, San Miguel, and Mora can only belong to New Mexico; Harding, Quay, and Union speak of another tradition. Like the whole high plains country, their Spanish history is only of a passing.

Beyond the Pecos the mountains are left behind; one even forgets them. The horizon is as level as water in a bowl between pale grass and a pale sky. Even in summer the grass is light; in winter it has cured into straw-colored fodder, and signs on the fences warn one to be careful of grass fires. The

Comanche's old weapon, the prairie fire, is still a danger. Between the towns, twenty or thirty miles apart, are isolated ranch houses, each with a tall windmill whirling its shining blades so fast they make a misty daisy on top. Now and then a road-runner races the car, or a hawk wheels its shadow across fences and white-faced cows. Castañeda, who rode there with Coronado in 1541, wrote that nothing was to be seen but cows and sky: " Such great numbers of cows that it already seemed something incredible." Buffaloes, of course. He told how easily men lost their bearings in that trackless sea of grass. " The country there is so level that at midday after one has wandered about in one direction and another in pursuit of game, the only thing to do is to stay near the game quietly."

But level as it is, the plain is cut across by jagged arroyos, often unseen until too late. Castañeda again, writing of stampeding buffalo: " As these fled, they trampled one another in their haste until they came to a ravine. So many of the animals fell into this that they filled it up and the rest went across on top of them. . . . Three of the horses that fell in among the cows all saddled and bridled were lost sight of completely."

That might have been any one of hundreds of splits in the land, but only Palo Duro Canyon, where the Red River rises, seems large enough to fit his description of a ravine " like those of Colima." Twelve hundred feet deep and thirty miles long, Palo Duro Canyon shows the stratification of many-hued rocks, which is best known in the Grand Canyon of the Colorado. Here plains history began in every sense, for its rocks go back to the Permian Age; dinosaur, saber-toothed tiger, and the prehistoric elephant roamed here; prehistoric Indians left their arrowheads and bone-scrapers; their descendants were settled there when Coronado's army came along. Driving into it now, along an easy road blasted out of impregnable escarpments, one senses even from a cushioned motor how refreshing those leafy groves must have looked to eyes light-weary from weeks on the treeless plain. Junipers and piñon trees on the slopes give way to cottonwood and hackberry noisy with birds along the creek, and to the *palo duro*, hard wood, which Indians took for arrows.

The Indians told Castañeda they were Teyas or Texias. The word meant " friend," and Texas has adopted it for a motto. These Indians spoke of other white men. Perhaps they had seen Cabeza de Vaca with Dorantes and Estevan. Castañeda remarked an Indian girl " as white as a Castilian lady " whom a romancer might credit to Dorantes. Another Indian girl whom one of Coronado's men took along said that she had belonged before to other white men far to the east. Surely De Soto on the Mississippi! By 1541 Spanish explorers had crossed the continent from Florida to the Gulf of California.

Somewhere beyond the Palo Duro, Coronado's suspicions of the Turk grew to certainty, and he killed him and took another guide, still hoping to reach the Grand Quivira of so many false promises. But all the Indians he found were half-naked nomads, the only jewels a copper bell around a chief's neck. Coronado gave up at last and returned to the Rio Grande. Castañeda wrote: " It was impossible to find tracks in this country because the grass straightened up again as soon as it was trodden down." So the white men passed, and their route is still in dispute. Perhaps they went as far as northeast Kansas or even into Nebraska. The gold they sought was not there; black gold in vast, underground lakes would have done that age no good if they had found it. Coronado went back to face a Spanish viceroy with a tale of failure.

Other Spanish expeditions — because young men were inquisitive and venturesome — crossed the land of cows and sky where grass held no trace of their passing. It was country the Spanish had no use for, except as a field for adventure and sport. One of Oñate's captains, Zaldivar, hunted buffalo there and carried jerked meat back to Oñate's capital on the Rio Grande. For a couple of centuries thereafter *ciboleros,* buffalo-hunters, went annually from the settlements to the plains. From Las Cruces to Taos, young hidalgos with their peons and friendly Indians rode out for from six weeks to three months in the sparkling autumn weather, astride fine horses, to share with other men the atavistic joy of killing with high artistry and some personal risk. For buffalo-hunting, as they practiced it, would make polo look fit for an old lady sit-by-the-fire. Ponies were bred for it, often of the creamy stock Queen Isabella sent to Mexico, *palomillos;* or pintos, which later Texans called " paint horses." Corn-fed and highly trained, the horse was as expert as the man, as intelligent and quick as a polo pony. Ciboleros in leather jackets and breeches and flat straw hats wore quiverfuls of bows and arrows and carried steel-tipped lances fluttering with silken tassels. As the pony ran alongside the buffalo, the hunter hurled his lance at the right split second to hit the one vital spot. A man might kill a dozen beasts in a few moments. A wounded beast might turn on him, horn and throw his mount, even thrust a man's lance into his own abdomen. But New Mexicans liked the sport and never took to the plainsman's method of slaughtering buffalo with guns. As late as the eighties, they hunted with lances. Hunters were followed by creaking *carretas* driven by men who could butcher almost as fast as the killing, strip the meat, and hang it to dry: *charqui* to them, " jerky " on the English tongue. It was shipped, tons of it, to Mexico along with the tanned hides and an occasional likely Indian wench or sturdy boy to sell as a slave.

Another sport that took these men to the plains was walking down wild horses. *Mesteñeros,* the takers of mustangs, using many mounts and never pushing them beyond a walk, could keep a stallion and his band of mares moving until they wearied utterly, and could be roped and thrown. Many a fine stallion was taken back to the settlements to breed racers or buffalo ponies. Often horses and cattle were got from the Indians. Cheyennes, Kiowas, and Comanches met the Mexicans in Palo Duro Canyon or at other watered places, set up their tents and wickiups, ran races, held powwows, and traded. Gregg, in his *Commerce of the Prairies,* wrote that the Mexicans " launch upon the plains with a few trinkets and trumperies of all kinds, and perhaps a bag of bread and another of *pinole.* Later they brought ammunition, lead, paint, beads, knives, and manta." They got from the Indians buffalo robes and horses, which had often come from barbarous raids against Texas homes. Mexican traders thus furnished Indian depredators with ammunition and a market for their stolen stock — a practice which did not improve relations between those natural enemies, New Mexicans and Texans.

These hunters and traders to the plains generally followed a trail from Las Vegas to the Canadian, down that stream and across to where the modern town of Canyon is now. A favorite meeting-place was called *Las Lenguas,* the Tongues, because so many languages were used there. The way back led to La Laguna near Fort Sumner, and so to Santa Fe. Upspringing grass covered those trails as soon as the men were gone, so they marked them with buffalo skulls, or with stakes which could be followed like blazes from one to the next. So it was called *El Llano Estacado,* and is to this day. Gregg, whose journey in 1839 was the beginning of the southern branch of the Santa Fe Trail, called the plains " only fitted for the haunts of the mustang, the buffalo, the antelope, and the migratory prairie Indian." And Captain Randolph B. Marcy, who found the source of the Red River in Palo Duro Canyon, thought the plains " inhospitable, possessing few attractions to civilized man." So for years the westbound man from the States knew the plains only as an alternate route to Santa Fe. When the Indians were not too dangerous, it was easier on men, animals, and wheels to cross from Dodge City to the Canadian, near where Tucumcari now stands, and so on to Santa Fe. " Even there," says Gregg, " some of the watering places are at intervals of fifty or eighty miles and hard to find."

Every account of the Santa Fe trade refers to the horrors of these dry crossings. Franz Huning, who crossed the trail some forty times, wrote: " The last water on the Cimarron is in Sand Creek. Here the road enters on the level, dry plateau called the Jornada, fifty miles to the Arkansas River without any water, but lots of grass in most places . . . probably the best natural road to be found anywhere for so long a distance, and when there was water at the Battle Ground about half-way there was no suffering." In another place he explains *jornada* as " a day's journey, generally without water," and adds: " Our boys called it Horn Alley."

The Santa Fe Trail, even this southern route, did not touch Texas, and it comes into our Forty-ninth State only if we include Oklahoma's Panhandle.

Settlement of the Panhandle began in '76, when Charles Goodnight, caught in a bank failure in Colorado, thought of the plains with their fine buffalo and mesquite grass. It was magnificent country, teeming with every sort of game, from grouse and ducks to elk and bear, and almost cleared of buffalo. He drove sixteen hundred head of cattle into Palo Duro Canyon, and became unquestioned lord of an empire. His nearest neighbors were at Bent's Fort, where the Santa Fe Trail crossed the Arkansas. Later Colonel Goodnight went into partnership with Mr. and Mrs. Adair, English people who introduced evening dinner, afternoon tea, and such clothes as the hands had never dreamed of. But they liked Mrs. Adair's skill with horses, and the unfailing sportsmanship of both.

The excellent Panhandle-Plains Historical Society Museum at Canyon shows the skeleton of a prehistoric horse, Indian artifacts, a Spanish coat of mail, and a rusty pair of handcuffs that might have manacled the discredited Turk. But its most interesting collections come from the great ranches. Cattle brands decorate its portal; it displays boots and saddles, spurs and ropes, branding irons, clothes and household goods, and priceless files of papers and interviews with old-timers. Surely this museum is unique in that the ancestors it commemorates drop in to bring their horse-gear, their photographs or cash books, to admire themselves in the murals, and to approve or criticize the arrangements.

Panhandle history has all happened within a generation. It is our nearest frontier, our newest land. And its people show the characteristics of our pioneers all the way west from the Alleghenies. Frederick Jackson Turner in *The Frontier in American History* describes the frontiersman as resentful of the easier and more conservative people he had left behind. Buoyantly self-confident and self-assertive; too busy conquering, building, subduing, to care for art, literature, or the refinements of life; impatient of restraint, even of law; full of dreams of mighty things, generally material; above all he was democratic. One man might be richer than another and honored for it; no man was better than another.

High plains people still show these characteristics. The very conception of the Forty-ninth State speaks of resentment of what was left behind; every town, flaunting a ten- or twelve-story building among vacant lots, asserts a buoyant belief in future greatness; and the right of a man to kill his enemy is still an arguable matter. Twenty years ago a jealous husband was acquitted of murder in Amarillo, though it was proved conclusively that he had killed the wrong man. The " unwritten law " was popularly held to justify the killing of somebody; the wrong man was just out of luck. And the practice of the arts, condoned in women, is viewed with suspicion for men who should be concerned with the making of money.

Above all, the people who might make a Forty-ninth State are homogeneous, Nordic and Protestant, democratic, and untrammeled by a past. Separated from the rest of Texas, the Panhandle is cut off from the tradition of the Lone Star Republic, rooted in the Alamo, and of the Confederacy. Many of the citizens came from the Middle West; it is whispered there are Republicans among them; Amarillo, naming its streets for the presidents, did not skip Lincoln and Grant. Unlike New Mexico, West Texas has no background of Spanish-Catholic culture. Tascosa, the first town in the Panhandle, was a Mexican placita; a few families named Trujillo and Tafoya still live along the Canadian. But most of the adobe towns have been long abandoned.

New Mexico sheepmen used to drive their flocks into the Llano Estacado, leaving the mountains in January, drifting down the Canadian and out onto the plains for the lambing and back again for the fall shearing. The wealthy Armijo family often sent their flocks on two hundred and forty miles farther to the Dodge City market. There was no serious trouble between cattle and sheep man, largely because Colonel Goodnight had persuaded the New Mexicans to keep off the cattle range. The agreement was broken now and then, once by one of Goodnight's men. Hating the very smell of mutton, he stampeded a whole band of woollies into the river, where four hundred were drowned. It was good cowboy stuff, but by a mischance those sheep belonged to a governor of New Mexico; and they turned out to be costly.

On another occasion Goodnight, trailing cattle-thieves, located six hundred animals of his own brand on the Gallinas near Las Vegas, which was considered a good mart for stolen stock. Sure of his proof, the Texan brought suit, but a Mexican jury managed to fine him seventy-five dollars. The expressed cause I have forgotten; the reason was clear — he was a Tejano. On the whole, though, Goodnight's line between cattle and sheep country held; few flocks entered the Panhandle after the early eighties, and the Llano Estacado was the country of the gringo.

In spite of its late start, the Panhandle knew most of the West's wildness. It fought Indians and then rustlers. But its most bitter feuds were between the big cattlemen and the homesteaders who had taken up government land. The stockmen fought them vigorously by every fair means and foul. They found it easy to make charges of rustling, and to judge and execute very quickly. A tale impossible to authenticate, but that might well be true, is that Mrs. Goodnight, shaken by these lawless hangings, was utterly outraged by the lynching of a young boy.

" Charley Goodnight," was her ultimatum, " if one more man is lynched by the Vigilantes, I'll leave you."

That, according to the tale, ended Vigilante executions in the Panhandle.

Colonel Goodnight, even according to his perhaps too admiring biographer, J. Evetts Haley, was typical of his time and kind. Fair with people who saw his way, scrupulous in keeping his word, he could be ruthless with those who opposed him. One who knew him well, said: " The old colonel was all right, but if he thought a thing was so, it almost had to be that-a-way."

In the nester the cattle king met his match. Of the same breed, these settlers were not so easily discouraged as Mexican sheepherders, and time was with them. The stockmen fought change as long as they could; finally they fenced their lands, put up windmills, bred up their stock, even took to farming here and there. But they did not really understand the land they knew so well. They were empire-builders who saw everything in the large, figured on the most grandiose scale.

Our national era of expansion was nowhere more expansive than in the Southwest. Men counted property in hundreds of square miles and cows by hundreds of thousands; borrowed money in millions, incorporated banks for millions, and went broke for millions. Any book on the period is largely composed of superlatives. Everything was the biggest in the world, the state, or at least the county. They even got around in time to the best. In the Panhandle the big owners introduced Hereford cattle and boast of the best herds " in the world." They are, too, the biggest.

It was an age of giants. In spite of democratic talk and the prevailing simplicity of manners, men made empires for themselves and ruled as unquestioned despots. Over on the Cimarron in New Mexico, Lucien B. Maxwell, through his marriage with Luz Beaubien, became lord of a Mexican grant which crossed the New Mexico and Colorado line. He ran sheep and cattle, mined, and cut timber, lit his cigar with the twenty-dollar bill someone offered him in payment for his hospitality, founded a bank in Santa Fe, invested in railroads, and died poor. His grant, bought by one syndicate and then another, grew by methods that have been questioned, until it was worth millions and included millions of acres.

Down in the lower Pecos Valley men of vision undertook great irrigation projects. One stream, stopped by a costly dam, disobligingly went underground. But in the nineties artesian wells were tapped, and huge pipes poured clear, never failing streams over old Uncle John Chisum's cattle range. Orchards replaced grass, cotton was introduced, and capital brought from far and wide to make more millionaires.

James J. Hagerman, who had made a fortune in Colorado mines, built a stately brick home filled with imported treasures, surrounded by gardens, and provided with a station for his private car. It was the old " Chisum place," but now the cowboys' bunk-house was away out back; the setting was perfect for an ancestral estate. But as so often happens in the Southwest, one generation outlived the dream. The place has been taken over on a mortgage by Cornell University, the house has been dismantled, and sheep browse on what was the lawn.

Even the glorious promise of artesian water almost failed. Wasteful use lowered the water level until a serious shortage threatened. Within this decade the federal government has intervened to plug wells running wantonly to waste, and so has probably saved the chief value of the valley. It is as though the country were forcing the people into a way more suited to their democratic tradition. For the empire-builders' vision of

a land greatly productive is about to be realized, but by, and
for, small owners.

Many of these empire-builders, who remembered when dew
from the grass would wet a man's boot as he rode through it,
lived to see the range deteriorate into stubby herbage. And
they saw the extensive planting of wheat, beginning in 1917,
and watched mechanical plows powder the plain into hideous
dust that blew away. They had the forlorn satisfaction of
seeing that they were right about the farmers all the time. The
high plains are grass country, and meant for stock. The government is now trying to bring them back to that, but with
a difference: instead of the haughty lord of endless acres, the
small stock rancher; instead of all cattle and no farming, a
little of both in careful adjustment.

The high plains, with fifteen or sixteen inches of annual
rainfall, offer the perfect mean between too heavy rains and
the too dry lands farther west. The ideal is small ranches of
a couple of thousand acres, running from fifty to a hundred
and fifty head of stock, and a small farm to winter-feed the
stock and supply seventy per cent of what the family needs.
With proper methods, there should be a surplus to sell, and to
fill granaries and silos with food for at least a year of crop
failure or drought. This is a system the pueblo Indians have
always understood; white men are just learning it. The great,
expansive plains folk are going to have to learn the cautious,
far-sighted ways of the European farmer.

Opposition has naturally been vigorous and picturesque.
But evidences of success are all around. Stiff-necked individualists are now buying good bulls and expensive farm machinery, and even owning silos co-operatively. They are beginning to try to save their crops and gardens by planting hedges
and close-set trees. Nobody who has not seen it can visualize

a Panhandle blow. Strong enough to lay sturdy young trees flat, to plaster a burro up against a barbed-wire fence, to lift roofs off houses, and roll the soil into a stiff, hard blanket of sand, wind on the plains cuts plants off short and buries gardens under tons of dust. Only many windbreaks can cope with such a force; and windbreaks are proving it. In 1934 the government began to plant shelter belts of trees, and to encourage farmers to do so. Nothing roused more raucous mirth, more scornful caricature and witty burlesque. But the sturdiest cowmen are beginning to weaken.

Two rode jogging along, and one pointed to a line of trees along a fence. " More New Deal nonsense," said he.

And the other: " Well, I dunno's I think they stop the wind, or the dust either. . . . But them leaves is kinda purty."

Even banks, burdened by too many farms, are asking the government's advice. So the dispossessed, instead of moving on to California, are being put back on their own land and taught its proper use. Hundreds of farmers now conserve moisture by proper plowing, keep land fertile by rotation of crops with fodder, and raise a family's food in gardens, poultry yards, and dairy herds. Within ten years such methods should bring land back to its best and breed up an original fifty head of cattle to a hundred and fifty better animals. It involves educating the farmer as well as improving the land. And Uncle Sam, like all lenders, can specify methods he approves.

I talked all this over with a native-born Panhandler. He thought it sounded fine; he thought it might work. As he talked, he persuaded himself that two sections of land — twelve hundred and eighty acres — might be enough. He thinks the fifty-six counties of northwest Texas, which showed a population of half a million in 1930, ought to support a

million. He agreed with the government man that these stock farmers, raising most of what they need, could in time have a car and a radio and send their children to college or to an agricultural school. True to his training, this gentleman was probably too optimistic, but he appreciates the need for new ways anyhow.

Life is changing on the high plains; the Forty-ninth State promises to be more like the rest of the United States — less picturesque perhaps, more metropolitan. The towns were built by the railroad's coming at the beginning of this century. But it was oil that began the great changes. People leased their land for fabulous sums and moved into Amarillo, Dalhart, and El Paso to learn how to spend money. Oil towns doubled and trebled in size in a few weeks or months. Windmills were dwarfed by derricks standing like forests of gaunt, burned trees over towns that spread like pools of black oil onto the golden plain. Monsters of machinery cut tracks and wallows deeper than the buffalo ever made, and oil talk brought a more vicious riffraff than Tascosa ever knew. It brought also technicians, engineers, and managers who had lived all over the world, and who gave the Panhandle a new sophistication. Children of the first oil barons went in for social distinctions, and snobbery appeared on the frontier where the richest and most powerful old cattle baron got no toadying from the twenty-five-dollar-a-month cowhand — such a short time ago!

The latest oil development is at Hobbs, where two thousand wells spume flame and smell up the sky. Texas' richest oilfield is in New Mexico — or in the Forty-ninth State! Driving into it at night is a choking experience. Roads are rutty and corrugated by mammoth trucks, whch have pulverized their surfaces into smothering dust, cut by the acrid smell of burn-

ing oil. Huge balls of murky fire hang low in a heavy sky. The town's one street runs like a neon streak of red, green, and white lights. Chain stores, with familiar fronts and window displays, alternate with bars and movie houses advertising double features of " horse operas " and their popular stars. Every place, on a Saturday night, poured out a violent blare of radio noise. Through that came a sound truck, followed by a procession of cars, and emitting a din too deafening to catch the words. As it passed, it clarified into coherence: " Where are you going tonight? " Ah, a movie ad. But it went on: " Are you laying up treasures in heaven? " A revival, then, trying to publicize salvation loudly enough to outshout picture shows and radio programs.

Next day, driving westward toward the Pecos Valley, that high-pitched, vociferous religion seemed somehow expressive of the Forty-ninth State. The high plains is a country no human life ever grew out of. Indians went there to hunt buffalo, and went away again, their travois and their women loaded with skins and jerked meat. The Spaniards garroted the man who led them there, and returned to the valleys. When the Nordic took them, it was rape. He denuded the prairies of their grass, and violated them with steel. His towns are not rooted in the soil, but stand on top of it. The land dares a man to defiance; even its religion is defiant. If God exists behind that bland, unhearing sky, its very immensity forbids any quiet, intimate approach, as with a palpable saint in an adobe chapel. So the typical religious expression of the high plains is the revival. Every town has summer-long orgies of emotion in frame tabernacles or sun-heated tents, where professional revivalists assail God with voices trained in speech and song. Skillfully they work their hearers up until they shriek and roll, confess and know salvation, and return refreshed to their

knitting or their gossip, their love-making or their trading. Those who do not gain release through religion go in more smartly for drink and dance. Whatever his mode, the impersonality of that round plain and round sky seem to inspire puny man to violent expression.

For miles beyond Hobbs the country is flat and arid. Then it begins to swell up toward the mountains and to break down into draws. Comfortable trees soften the windmill's defiance and make the houses seem less starkly alone. Finally, far away, the sky shows the faint blue shadow of El Capitan peak. A mountain is something sky can make contact with; the empty vastness of its arch deepens into richer color where it meets the solider blue of earth. Heading for the peak, the road runs through a cut like a slice in a chocolate cake with layers of nuts, and the Pecos Valley lies below.

Carlsbad's caverns have brought the lower valley world-wide fame and a steady income, but its character is made by its climate and its trees. Every little town has shaded streets; houses stand in gardens, and even fields in the country are divided by poplar rows. Their social bent, perhaps, was given half a century ago by such lyric dreamers as James J. Hagerman and by Colonel de Bremond, a Swiss who laid out vineyards and imported Italians to till them and to make wine. In Roswell the New Mexico Military Institute, whose first commandants brought many traditions from V.M.I., adds a uniformed sophistication to the town's easy life, and a balmy climate makes tennis and polo possible all winter. No, the Pecos Valley, even with the same people as the high plains, is not the same. With its gentle ways and Southern clime, it is more like San Antonio than Amarillo or Albuquerque. Here ends the Forty-ninth State.

There is

no surer way to get at the real nature of a people than to observe them on their feast days and bonfire nights. Every folk has its times for fun and release, for commemoration and renewal, for prayer and thanksgiving; then its best and its worst come out; its truest character is revealed.

Do they feast or fast? Do they illumine their celebration with bonfires or with neon lights? Do they watch trained men battle against arbitrary rules about a ball? Do they perform traditional ritual of unalterable form, or do they work themselves up into an emotional lather that violates their own everyday concepts of decent behavior?

Does everybody take part, or only a selected few? Do they pray, or pay for tickets? Do they invite their friends and set out food for all comers, or do they advertise and calculate profits?

The Southwest has all these kinds of holidays in their purity and in malassimilated combinations. But their yeasty fermentation is already settling into a standard form as truly of the Southwest as is the lingo which expresses its complicated interrelationships.

In Texas you go to a rodee-o; in New Mexico to a ro-da-o; in Arizona the pronunciation is a moot point.

In any case, the talk goes something like this: " Well, time to vamoose. Le's figure on a junta for nooning at the chile joint. Then while you wrangle your dudes, I'll see what I can round up for the baile at night. Got enough dinero? Hasta luego! "

XIX

DANCES, FIESTAS, FAIRS, AND RODEOS

HE SOUTHWEST HAS SO MANY FEAST DAYS THAT ITS notable dates are days when nothing in particular is going on. In planning the Coronado Cuarto Centennial, it was necessary only to make a few adjustments in the regular sequence of gala events; to encourage every town to go on as it had been doing; to publish a calendar of festivities, and to declare the state " in fiesta." And there was such a world's fair as had never before been known; no particular place — because New Mexico has no town big enough to accommodate a crowd of unusual proportions; and because neighboring states, in the friendly, Southwestern way, decided to come in and join the fun. No particular date — because the easy-going way of the Southwest got El Paso started months before the time everybody thought was set; Mexico was dilatory, though interested in participating; and several towns, getting into the swing of the thing rather late, carried it on beyond the closing date without any formality of announcement.

Two dicta mark this celebration as they mark fun-making in the Southwest generally. " You can't start until you're ready, can you? " and " Why quit, if we're still having fun? "

In making its plans, the Coronado Cuarto Centennial Commission faced a dilemma. How to advertise, attract the people who would like to see our fiesta, without attracting so many that there would be no place for them to sleep? The best suggestion finally prevailed: not to advertise much; just let people come if they wished; give them a chance to spread out all over a state, the very sight of which is enough fiesta for most people; extend the traditional Southwestern hospitality which offers one's best without apology. And, to forfend any possible contretemps, advise everybody to bring his own bedroll.

The Southwest has three kinds of holiday. The Indian's we call a dance, though to its performers and its Indian audience it is an intense religious expression, on which even life itself may depend. The dance we see is only the last act of a long and complicated preparation by fasting, continence, and spiritual exaltation. All of it, including the dance, is prepared with knowledge and care, performed with accuracy and meaning, requiring for its success the meticulous correctness of every detail. The onlookers are thoroughly informed and critical; they understand its purpose and recognize its skill. They are also quick to note any lapse or error which may defeat the purpose of the prayer. For in its uncorrupted state the Indian dance is pure prayer.

The Indian dance, in even approximate purity, is not often seen any more. Twenty years ago, when Taos and Santa Fe were filling up with people who recognized the Pueblo ceremonies for finished works of art, it became the thing to see them all. Not to sit all day on a roof, in sun or storm, vibrating to the drumming and hypnotized by the shifting colors of

341

the brilliant ballet, was to brand oneself as unappreciative indeed. That resulted in the swamping of the near-by pueblos with hundreds of visitors. Even as deeply significant a ceremony as the great Santo Domingo dance on the fourth of August has been so cheapened that a painting of it shows underdressed women, painfully shocking to the Indian, massed hot-dog and soft-drink stands, and only an inset of a dancing Indian to suggest the past, as medieval painters used to do.

The second type of holiday we still call by its Spanish name, fiesta. It came from Spain, and its reason for being is still the Catholic patron saint. Every Spanish-speaking town, like many larger centers, honors its holy patron or patroness, as does every Catholic town in the world. The day begins with mass in the village church, though festivities may well have begun the night before with vespers, and arriving guests. Morning mass ends with a procession to carry the venerated statue of the saint around the town. Many householders prepare private altars, where the bearers may rest and the priest pronounce a benediction; often it is a day for baptisms, first communions, or weddings.

These religious duties properly attended to, the rest of the day is for diversion. Maskers may have appeared in the saint's procession, stepping comically to the scrapings of a violin or the deeper notes of an accordion. They are a preview of a play to come later. Drama in New Mexico begins in 1598, when Los Moros (The Moors) was presented by Oñate's men at San Juan. Mary Austin said not only that it was the first play on the soil of the United States, but that it had had the longest run; for it is still on the boards. Los Moros was designed to teach the glories of Spain. Others set forth the glories of religion. Adan y Eva appears now and then. El

Niño Perdido (*The Lost Child*) is a favorite for Lent; and *Los Pastores* (*The Shepherds*) is an unfailing feature of a village Christmas. *Los Matachines,* more dance than play, has a long history, taking it back to Morocco through Mexico and Spain. Its cousin, according to Rodney Gallop in *Mexican Maze,* is the morris dances of Old England.

All these mummeries, whatever their history, are pure folk festival by now. For they are done by people whose ancestors have performed them, and modified them, for centuries. Directors are old men, who learned the parts when they were young, and who teach the lines by rote. Costumes are home-made — gaudy and malapropos, but often eloquent of ancient prototypes, as the Matachines, with tall miters and fluttering ribbons, suggest the Moors and the morris dancers.

A truly New Mexican folk drama is *Los Comanches,* which appears in three versions, as Arthur Campa has shown in a University of New Mexico bulletin, *New Mexican Secular Drama.* The first is purely religious. Comanches carry off a child in a village raid. Not knowing that they have the Holy Child, they offer to trade Him for a blanket. But His Holiness being proved, the savages are converted, and the dance drama ends with them on their knees, offering gifts. The second represents an actual battle of 1774, when the Comanche chief, *Cuerno Verde,* Green Horn, was pursued over onto the Staked Plains and defeated. This is dashing, virile sword-play, and all done on horseback. The third has to do with a legend of Tomé, which had been so harried by the Comanches that it offered battle of equal forces; but fight as they would, the Indians could never win, because one of the Mexicans fighting them was Santiago on his horse. The conversion of the savages is the denouement here, too.

A fiesta day is marked also by more spontaneous forms of

fun. Guests throng every house, wine and stronger drink add their glow to the proceedings, which may run on for days and nights, and end only when the cash is all spent or brawls have broken out. Horse- and foot-races and " chicken pulls " are nearly inevitable. To pull a live chicken out of soft dirt, where it has been buried and its head dodges helplessly, may look savage, but it's fun for the boys.

Somebody will have rented a hall, greased its floor, and engaged an orchestra to play all day and all night. Impromptu singers, almost professional troubadours, no longer go from fiesta to fiesta to make up satirical verse about the dancers. But ballads still appear with the regularity of published reviews. When Senator Cutting was killed in an airplane crash in 1935, it was being sung about within the week. The young Mexican aviator Román Zarabia, who had been a student in a New Mexico college, figures in a heroic ballad recounting his tragic death in the Potomac.

Not gay, but very Spanish, of the period which produced tortured saints and gory crucifixes, are the observances of *Los Hermanos de Luz,* better known as Penitentes. Alice Corbin Henderson has written of them under the name they prefer: *Brothers of Light,* and with sound historical knowledge and sympathetic appreciation of the strong, stern faith which keeps alive a medieval expression in a modern world.

Not all the Southwest religious folk festivals are Catholic. Protestants of certain faiths gather in huge tents to hear " preachings," sway to their singing of the rousing old hymn tunes, and let themselves go through the long, hot day until mounting fervor breaks through their stiffly starched correctness, in rolling, sobbing, " getting religion." Such a day is marked, too, by great quantities of food, and if neither liquor

nor the dance is an open and above-board part of the ceremonies, the end is often marked by similar results.

All these festivals, religious in inception, are for the people
who make them. Indians dance whether there is an outside
audience or not. The most sacred dances are still guarded
from the profanation of white man's eyes; and the most sacred
part of every dance is performed in the ceremonial chamber,
and no white man may approach within hearing distance of it.
Those in the know prefer to see an Indian dance which has,
so far, by some grace escaped publicizing: to be the only white
person in a pueblo while a hundred brilliantly costumed dancers go slowly, reverently through the evolutions of an ancient
ceremony. No Indian can pay a white a greater or a more
appreciated courtesy than to drop a hint as to when and where
such a dance may be seen. Nothing is more important than
the dance; nothing of less moment than the onlooker.

So with the village fiesta. The saint is honored. The people
express their faith at the altar; and they entertain themselves.
Visitors are treated with courtesy, though they are often only
a nuisance, often distressingly rude in church, or regardless
of the feelings of performers. The best fiesta, like the best
Indian dance, is one the outlander has not heard about and
does not attend.

The third type of festival, and the one which promises soon
to engulf the others, is the money-making show. The country
over, the Fourth of July oration and the prayer of Thanksgiving have been almost drowned out in the din of the commercialized sports that mark those days. Christmas and Easter
have developed into merchants' benefits. So in the Southwest.
But a genial climate, millions of tourists to be amused, and a
wide choice of merry-making customs have brought every

crossroads town out with its special stunt day: Fair, Fat Stock
Show, Pioneer's Day, Cotton Carnival, Old Timers Week,
Rodeo, Fiesta. Every such affair is boosted by the Chamber
of Commerce, " sold " to merchants, who hope to take in more
eventually than their public spirit puts up, and widely advertised. Lately every town has cannily flavored its offering with
something designed to catch the traveling public as well as the
country cousins.

This highjacking of one people's practice by another has
speeded up the interfusion which was going on anyway.
Doubtless it will hasten the coming of something that may, in
time, become a true Southwestern culture; except that by then
it will be on the way to transforming itself into something else.
Nothing is surer than change, nothing more futile than to
mourn it; nothing more instructive, really, than to watch it.
And, in this case, we may watch the lumps of various widely
different types and stages of culture bobbing, still undigested,
in a sort of sunny stew.

The white man has modified the Indian's ceremonies, first
by stern prohibitions and requirements, later in more subtle
ways, which have been both good and bad. The Spanish
priests erected the church, and the Indian convert was obliged
to make obeisance there, though he was still permitted his own
ceremony afterward. So we have the oft-noted anachronism
that a pagan dance begins with mass in the church, and goes on
in the presence of the statue of the patron saint. The Indian
scored a point in that he does dance. What he believes is his
own secret.

In the Rio Grande pueblos, Catholic missionaries, by their
disapproval and charges of witchcraft, forced into hiding
many ceremonies like those which the more recalcitrant Zuñi
and Hopi villages perform quite openly.

The Protestant missionary has shown himself even more intolerant than the Catholic, and his weapon has been scorn. Any Indian expression was laughed at as ludicrous, something to be ashamed of, if not actually sinful; and the Indian school clumsily interfered with many important traditions.

More disquieting because more obvious to the visitor eager to see Indian ceremonies at their best, are the white man's more blatant manifestations. Approach any dance that has been publicized, and you will hear, see, and smell the commercial world long before you penetrate to the performance you came to see. Automobiles line the roads and are banked in open fields. Many are commercial cars, hauling the curious for pay. Walking from the end of that line to the center of the feast, one passes every kind of carnival attraction. Even the Hopis, eighty miles from the railroad, and Santo Domingo with its stern opposition to change, have let themselves be surrounded by merry-go-rounds, temporary dance-halls with canned swing music, peanut and popcorn carts with shrill steam whistles, eating-booths, and popcorn stands. The nose is affronted by the rancid reek of sputtering grease, and the sensibilities by half-drunken youths decked out in advertisers' hat-bands or sweat-shirts. Having or selling liquor on an Indian reservation is a penitentiary offense.

Happily, in most places the dance is insulated by a wall of attentive observers, and the rhythmic thump of the drum and men's deep chanting is heavy enough to drown out the whine of music bought in tins. There one understands the good that has been done by white men who felt no need to judge the Indian's rites, but knew them to be beautiful in themselves, and important as authentic expressions of belief and culture. Such people have given the Indian renewed self-esteem; and, by insisting that the Indian perform his dances properly and in correct costume — even when he dances for pay — they have helped to perpetuate them as an art form, even if they are doomed to lose their religious meaning.

The Indian is likewise steadily modifying the ways of the white. Carl Jung, the Swiss psychiatrist who has visited the Pueblo Indians, and whose essays contain many references to their culture, speaks of " the mysterious Indianization of the American people." But even one untrained as a student of the mind sees evidence on every hand that the white conqueror has not been unconquered. The Catholic church has yielded, sometimes gracefully, sometimes not; but it has been affected. Spanish, and through it English, are heavily inter-larded with Indian words. Many are Aztec, brought up from Mexico by priests and colonists. " Tamale," " metate," " ocote," and " chile " have gone as far as *Webster's Diction-ary*. " Kiva " in the Rio Grande valley, and " hogan " on the reservation, are in daily use. Most neighbors of the Pueblos invoke the Shiwanni, even if Mr. Webster has not yet heard of those helpful spirits; and travelers across the deserts know a chindi hogan for a haunted one, where somebody has died.

Indian influence appears in clothes, as well as in words. Navajo jewelry, Navajo blouses of velveteen, and moccasins are taken straight. Smart clothes are being modeled on In-dian styles, and embroidered Indian designs are well received in New York.

The few white men who have been initiated into Indian clans or societies speak of them with great respect, keep their secrets, and permit no derision. Even some who came to scoff have remained to pray. In 1921 a group of business men in Prescott put on a burlesque of the Hopi Snake Dance as a fea-ture of their summer fair. Hopis had once been known as Moquis, or Mokis — a Navajo word meaning " dead," and

348

offensive to the Hopis. The Prescott crowd named their act the *Smoki Snake Dance*. But the force of the real was too strong for their mummery. In time they grew interested, even without understanding the inner significance of what they did. Every year they improved on their costumes, bettered their dancing; they even took to handling live snakes. At last their imitation was good enough to impose upon the *Encyclopædia Britannica*. That esteemed authority, in Volume 14 of its Fourteenth Edition, actually publishes the photograph of a Prescott citizen as an example of savage " Make-up." Plate I, opposite page 700, shows a Chuncho Indian of Peru, a Fiji Islander, Australians with bodies gashed and puffs of cotton in the gashes, and a *" Snake priest of Smoki Indians, face and body painted."*

This is unique. Generally the white man has not masqueraded as an Indian; he has instead snapped up his dances as money-makers. Few fairs, in New Mexico and Arizona, fail to feature Indian dances as top-line attractions. Tucson makes much of its Yaqui Indian Easter. Phoenix brings Apache dancers to its Citrus Show. Flagstaff brings many tribes in to its annual Pow-wow. But the outstanding Indian show is the Gallup Inter-Tribal Ceremonial. Since 1922, when a few Indian traders devised the scheme to point up and intensify the growing interest in Indians, the Ceremonial has grown from the gathering of a few neighboring tribes to a concourse of seven thousand Indians from six states, and nineteen tribes. Cheyennes from Wyoming, Cherokees and Kiowas from Oklahoma, Utes from Colorado, and Piutes from Nevada compete with Hopis from Arizona, Pueblos from New Mexico, and Apaches and Navajos from both those states.

For days they come by train, truck, or passenger car, in covered wagons, on horseback or afoot. No dance-team has yet chartered a plane, but that will surely follow soon. Mornings they parade, decked out in their tallest feathered warbonnets, their richest and softest buckskin and furs, their most massive silver and turquoise jewelry. They so fill the town that thousands of visiting whites are scarcely noticed among them. They camp on the bare hills in tepees or fresh-cut juniper shelters, practice chants with rattle and drum, and encircle the town with a living panorama of primitive life.

The daytime shows include races and tugs of war, and certain concessions to the less cultivated taste in vaudevillian imitations and sentimentalized Indian songs. But the night programs are staged with skilled and calculated effectiveness. The white audience, in a grand-stand, faces the Indian audience — tiers of dark-skinned people in bright colors, such as might watch an Indian ceremonial in its native setting. The clarity of floodlights is mitigated and filled with flickering mystery by enormous bonfires between whites and Indians. Through their glow, dance groups may be seen moving along in front of the living background, getting ready for their entrances. Cautious direction has, without regimenting the Indian's natural ease, controlled the timing enough to move the acts along without delay. Dance follows dance, interspersed with song or, now and then, the heavy accents of a Navajo announcing the distribution of the sacred parts of a butchered buffalo, or the loss of a three-year-old Navajo girl; or a call in English for a Navajo policeman.

When the last night's show ends with the wildly leaping, softly yodeling wonder of the Navajo Fire Dance, even the most captious must admit that here, at least, the white man has turned the Indian's art to commercial uses without spoiling it.

The Indian has influenced the money-making Nordic more

than he has his closer neighbor of Spanish descent. The Spanish village is, as a rule, snobbish toward the Indian. And the Spanish-American's scorn is equaled only by the Indian's scorn of him. The Indian seldom appears at a fiesta, even if he has wares to sell. Spanish-speaking young people are beginning to show up at Indian dances, a bit supercilious, and dressed like dudes from Santa Fe. This gift for looking smartly modern has led some village maidens around a historical circle, most amusingly. In a northern New Mexico plaza I saw little Mexican girls all unwittingly wearing their ancestral dress. Long ago New Mexican women wore short, full skirts, low-necked blouses, bright sashes, and sandals on bare feet. Such costumes are still worn in Mexico, where many " North American " women have admired them and bought them to wear at home. And the little Mexican miss, copying the Gringa, has come round to her grandmother's dress of a century ago!

This dress, and its many variations and masculine counterparts, mark the Santa Fe Fiesta. Decreed by De Vargas in honor of the Virgin, to whose gracious intercession he credited his reconquest, the Santa Fe Fiesta had struggled on for generations, trying to keep up with the new. Then the artists took it in hand and prescribed more of the old, especially Indian dances and Mexican folk plays. Later the Indian features passed over to Gallup, and Santa Fe centered on its Spanish flavor. Nothing in the Southwestern calendar is more beautiful than the candlelit procession to the Cross of the Martyrs, erected in honor of the Franciscan missionaries who died for their faith. And nothing gayer than Santa Fe in gala dress.

The seductive Spanish costumes, from the peasant woman's simple skirt and blouse, to the spangled silken elaborations of the China Poblana, and the stately court dress with lace mantilla, tall comb, and Chinese embroidered shawl, add glamour to fiestas that have long lost their primary religious meaning. San Antonio, celebrating Texas' defeat of Santa Anna at San Jacinto, makes a truly Spanish fiesta of it; but pronounces the melodious name in a way that can only be spelled *Sanjy Cinta.*

Santa Barbara, at the other tip of the Spanish Southwest, dedicates every August full moon to the romance of old California. Time was when life on the great California ranches was so lazily luxurious that a hidalgo's only concerns were horsemanship, friends, love and honor, games and gaiety. His short jacket and tight trousers of buckskin were elaborated with embroideries in gold and silver thread, and his saddle was heavy with precious metals. His horsemanship has never been excelled; only he cared to ride down and rope a grizzly just for fun. Even his lady rode, closely veiled against the sun. Nights were filled with softly thrummed music, languorous love-songs, and stately dancing. Many of the descendants of those storied families still own the saddles and the costumes; many of them have gone over to new Californians with Irish, Scotch, or Scandinavian names. For here, as everywhere, the Southwest is in flux.

No interchange is livelier, or perhaps more pregnant of the future, than is the Southwest's rapidly evolving language. Cowboy lingo is nearly all mispronounced Spanish. Geography and flora and fauna are generally known by Spanish names, or some corruption of them. The English, or American, language has been enriched by several hundred words, most of which are given in our dictionaries. But the dictionaries do not know the half of it: for they know not the Spanish we speak, and how far it has grown from pure Castilian.

Its base was sixteenth- or seventeenth-century Spanish, for Spain had little communication with her remote colonists, and they could only keep on using the speech of their ancestors. Later, when English came in and new customs demanded new names, the New Mexican made up words as he needed them, basing them on English, but softening the pronunciation and inflecting them according to the rules of Spanish grammar.

I asked a professor of Spanish how many English words are now in common use in our daily Spanish. His answer was: " Three or four hundred certainly — I could not tell you exactly without knowing how many have been invented to-day." Then he quoted this speech: " No parquea su carro allí, porque se escratchea." " Don't park your car there, because it will get scratched." " Park " is not Spanish, and " carro " does not mean automobile, but wagon. And the corruption of *scratch* is probably the most barbarous hybridization yet recorded!

Ask a direction in Arizona, or western New Mexico, and the answer may be like this: " Well, you go on up this wash until you get to the second tank. Then follow the caprock till you pass a couple of Texas gates and one cattle-guard. There's a doby there. Then bear right, pass a chindi hogan, and keep on up the potrero and you'll drop right over that saddle onto Horse Thief Mesa. You can't miss it."

Oh, can't you? To translate: a wash has nothing to do with laundry, but is a stream-bed temporarily unoccupied by a stream. A tank is a dip in the ground which, in good seasons, holds a little water, where stock may drink. Etymologically, it is a descendant of the Spanish *tanque*, pond. A Texas gate is a section of barbed-wire fence swinging loose on a pole, which fits into loops of wire at top and bottom of the gatepost. Open, it lies on the ground, looking innocent enough, but it is capable of going into a hideous snarl of tangled wires and vicious barbs; and even after you get the butt of the pole into the bottom loop, its top will enter the upper loop only under such strain as may spring the whole contraption back into your face. Still, all gates, even Texas gates, must be closed, if you do not wish to rate as the worst sort of dude. A doby is an adobe house. A potrero is a narrow ridge between canyons, and a saddle is a sag between peaks.

This sort of talk goes with the folksiest folk show in English, and the one that is probably the crucible wherein the final Southwestern festival is taking shape. It is a neighborhood jamboree, where everyone has a chance to shine. Originally, the fun-making roundup came at a slack season to give the boys a chance to show what they could do. Prizes were offered, and often a big, barnlike hall housed cattle and patchwork quilts, farm produce and school work. But the roping and bulldogging were the thing. Top men showed up with English, German, Spanish, or French names; many an Indian in off the reservation could out-throw and out-tie the field.

Stamford, Texas, boasts that its rodeo is the only one still entirely non-commercial. It pays nobody, charges nothing, and conducts the whole affair as it has done since 1897. Its invitation reads:

" Hollywood cowboys are barred from all contests. Contestants are cowboys from the ranches of Texas, Oklahoma, New Mexico, Arizona, Colorado, and Kansas. A civic enterprise, there are no salaries and no dividends. In 1930 a few old bow-legged waddies tossed money into a hat to start this show and agreed never to take any out of it."

The chairman of the board, who signs the invitation, is Walt Cousins, probably the original drugstore cowboy. Walt, when a very young but thoroughly competent " hand," " threw his

YOUNG MEN HAVE SHORT HAIR, BUT EVEN A
LONG-HAIRED INDIAN CAN USE A FOUNTAIN-PEN

[*photo, Ruth Frank*]

INDIANS TRAVEL FOR MILES TO SEE THE DANCES

[*photo, Ruth Frank*]

saddle over the fence," and went to town to take a job as a soda-jerker. He jerked so well that now he owns a big store in Dallas, edits a pharmacists' magazine, and goes back to the range only to renew his soul on the Fourth.

The Coronado Cuarto Centennial was designed to re-create such spirit for the whole Southwest, and to honor the first white men who brought Christianity and European culture to our present United States. Until 1940 the actual footfall had not been determined. What curious contrast with New England's proud cherishing of Plymouth Rock, marked by a bronze tablet and set off by a fence! Perhaps it was not dilatoriness; those villagers from England had made a momentous journey. But Spain, receiving reports from hundreds of explorers, covering a continent and a half, was so little impressed by one young man who added a few thousand square miles of territory that his name is little known, even now. Only his four-hundredth anniversary lifted professors from their swivel chairs to saddles, and they located the exact spot where first Marcos de Niza, and then Coronado, stepped onto the soil of the United States. There one can look for fifty miles up and down the San Pedro Valley. From there one might visualize five or six states, making festival for many months in many ways, to honor not one man, nor one people; but to recognize that people of three lines of descent have managed, somehow, to get along together for so many centuries, and to hope their first four hundred years may prove to have been the hardest.

No place

or period really lives in the general consciousness until it has been written about. Most people, seeing a place for the first time, hasten to provide themselves with books about it. They want not their own personal reaction but information as to how it has seemed to others. Consequently places have no true individuality to the general run of travelers; they are a composite of what many travelers, more perceptive, more daring, or more expressive, have said about them.

Our Southwest has perhaps suffered unduly from this mental habit. People who have never heard of a Spanish missionary's memorial think what they think about the Southwest because monks wrote fully and later writers helped themselves freely to what the monks had said. So the observations of four hundred years ago, spreading as quietly and as widely as oil in sand, have permeated today's conceptions. But they have been modified too by the changing moral and political climate, until at last the Southwest we think we know is a variegated pattern composed of many literary interpretations.

XX

THE INTERPRETERS

VERY SORT OF PERSON HAS WRITTEN ABOUT THE Southwest. The country is so strong in all its aspects that impressionable individuals, including some who could scarcely write and many who could not spell, have felt impelled to express their experience with it. There have been almost as many reasons as writers: to inform the King of Spain what one found and why one did not find more; to recount one's trials as a missionary among a people for whom the writer knew no prototype; to report on the resources of a new land; or only to reflect one's own courage in such places and among such people as nobody back home knew anything about. And always, from the most casual letter or diary to the most scientific study or mystical exposition, an effort to interpret unprecedented experiences in a country which still remains strange after four hundred years. A roster of writers about the Southwest would run up into thousands, and there are excellent bibliographies. *Books of the Southwest* by Mary Tucker is intelligently compiled and covers the field. But to set forth the types of people who have tried to explain or

357

express it may contribute to a general picture of the Southwest. And to mention the books I have found most entertaining may offer suggestions to those who would like to read more than any one book can contain.

The first to see and to write about our Southwest was Alvar Nuñez Cabeza de Vaca. Morris Bishop has written the life of this strange man, in *The Odyssey of Cabeza de Vaca;* and Mrs. Bandelier, and others, have put into English his *Relación* of the Journey from Florida to the Pacific, 1528–36. Alvar Nuñez wrote to his King of his distress, with some notes on the people and the country he saw. But his eyes, like those of many Spanish chroniclers, saw little of the country's magnificence. To him a river was hard to cross, or trees gave welcome shade; he mentions no joy in the beauty of leaves reflected in water. Perhaps the sixteenth century had not discovered our romantic response to scenery. Nor did Alvar Nuñez reveal much of his travail among savages, and of how he, naked, often starving or enslaved, found the power to heal them and himself. This inner spiritual experience has been most sensitively imagined by Haniel Long in *Interlinear to Cabeza de Vaca.*

Hundreds of Spaniards followed Cabeza de Vaca — men who explored, conquered, converted, or colonized, always as personal representatives of the King, and generally " at their own expense." Open to constant attack from men close to the royal ear, it behooved them to make the most of the dangers they encountered, the numbers of savages they subdued, and their own worthiness. That certain of the most important and revealing of these chronicles have not as yet been translated into English deprives us of some of the greatest adventure stories of all time. Fortunately the Quivira Society, founded in 1929, is slowly making Spanish chronicles available in

English, and the Coronado Cuarto Centennial Commission contributes its monument to the first white conqueror in the United States in a series of reprints and translations.

It is a pity that nobody in Mexico City reported the boastings of the black slave Estevanico, when he inflamed that capital with what must have been magniloquent promises of wealth away up north. But nobody bothered to write down what he said; they acted upon it. Francisco Vásquez de Coronado, who set forth in grandeur to prove the truth of what the slave and the monk had told, was fortunate in his chronicler. Pedro Castañeda de Nagera, in his *Relación de la Jornada de Cíbola*, tells an adventure story seldom surpassed; and while he never dwelt on scenic wonders, he described what he saw in phrases one does not forget: " A country so flat one sees the sky under the belly of a horse." Contemporary with Coronado's *entrada*, Castañeda's book was, by some mischance, not published until 1840. The best translation is *The Coronado Expedition*, by George Parker Winship.

The several sixteenth-century expeditions left accounts, some of them full of suggestions for drama or romance. But the first formal piece of writing came at its end: *La Historia de la Nueva Mexico*, by Gaspar Pérez de Villagrá. Gaspar Pérez, who is forever marked as a better soldier than poet, wrote in resounding cantos, celebrating the prowess of warriors and the religious fervor of missionaries and martyrs. His hero and leader, Don Juan de Oñate, fought the most dramatic and exciting battle in our whole history when he took the impregnable rock of Acoma, and Villagrá's account of it, even four hundred years later, is exciting. It has been excellently translated by Gilberto Espinosa for the Quivira Society. Perhaps it is most accessible in Paul Horgan's *The Habit of Empire*.

The seventeenth century, which left only light marks on Southwestern history, fortunately started off with Fray Alonzo de Benavides as custodian of New Mexico. When he left the twenty-year-old capital of Santa Fe in 1629, Fray Alonzo wrote his *Memorial* to the King. Mrs. Edward E. Ayer has put it into English which retains the original trenchancy of expression. Fray Alonzo was so keen and intelligent an observer that his account very adequately covers the century. He had a tendency to magnify numbers; modern scholars make a practice of dividing his estimates by five or ten. But to know what New Mexico was like when the Pilgrims were landing on their rock-bound shores, and the cavaliers exploring the streams in tidewater Virginia, and all of them experimenting with government, read Benavides. His picture of the royal colony of New Spain, rigidly administered from distant capitals, and held sternly to one faith, best explains why the descendants of the Pilgrim fathers and the descendants of the Spanish colonizers had such difficulty in understanding each other when they met two hundred years later.

An equally telling contrast with the small, close-knit colonies on the eastern seaboard is presented in Father Eusebio Francisco Kino's *Historical Memoir of Pimería Alta, a Contemporary Account of the Beginnings of California, Sonora, and Arizona, 1683–1711.* A fine, modern telling of the tale is Herbert E. Bolton's *A Padre on Horseback.*

Priests, always literate, had much to say. Fray Gerónimo Sarinte Salmirón gave himself plenty of room under the title: *Account of Everything in New Mexico which has Been Seen and Known by Sea as well as by Land from 1538 to 1625.*

The seventeenth century, so lamblike at its opening, ended with the hideous turbulence of the Pueblo Revolt, and the Reconquest. Of that period we have *The Flying Mercury,* translated from the original of Don Carlos de Sigüenza y Góngora, by Irving Albert Leonard for the Quivira Society. It tells the story of Don Diego de Vargas's capture of the capital at Santa Fe, and of the wily and pacific measures by which he won over the Indian rebels without resort to warfare.

Following de Vargas's reconquest in 1692, Spain went back to maintaining her colonial pattern in New Mexico. Little changed until the coming of the Nordic along two routes — into Texas, and over what was to be known as the Santa Fe Trail. How this newcomer wrote would show what he was, if we had no other means of judging. Here are no efforts to propitiate king or superior, he acknowledging none. Even Army officers and officials reporting to the government wrote with freedom, complaining of one another, or of official feckless-ness.

First, both as Army man and as personal raconteur, was Zebulon Montgomery Pike, whose *Expedition* covered so much of our Southwest that it serves as a first-rate introduction.

He was closely followed in Texas by Bigfoot Wallace, whose book was written for him by John C. Duval, as *The Adventures of Bigfoot Wallace*. Frank Dobie calls Duval " Texas' first man of letters," and writes of his book: " there is in all American literature, so far as I know, no other book like [it]. . . . Duval lets Bigfoot tell his own story in his own way . . . and the narrative rollicks along as naturally and as sprightly as a colt when grass greens and ponies shed their hair." Wallace went to Texas from Virginia just after it had won its independence, and was a part of all its life until he died, in 1899.

Texas' epic conflict with Mexico produced libraries of formal writing; and a few poignant first-hand accounts of its incidents. Thomas J. Green's *The Mier Expedition*, which ended in the decimation of the captive group, and *The Prisoners of Perote*, by William P. Stapp, account sufficiently for a hundred years of bad feeling against Mexico in Texas. Another intensely interesting sidelight on that war and that state of mind is George W. Kendall's *Texas Santa Fe Expedition*. Mr. Kendall, editor of the New Orleans *Times Picayune*, wrote a thrilling account of the tragedies of battle, capture, and imprisonment in Mexico City, where the Texans finally wound up. Mr. Kendall, the first newspaper man to report on the Southwest, set a high standard of vivid writing.

While Texas was fighting Indians and border battles and settling her manifold internal disputes, the mountain men were laying out a new way that was to become the Santa Fe Trail. Many of them wrote or dictated recollections of those days on horseback watching for Indians, and nights in blankets listening for Indians. Always they are readable, because their tales are so utterly without fake. Facing daily hazards, these men wrote with even calm, mentioning their dangers and their dead along with what they had for dinner, and how many miles they had covered. Fortunately, among the illiterates and the tellers of tales too tall for belief were a few who wrote well. I mention Lewis H. Garrard's *Wah-to-Yah and the Taos Trail* because of its subtitle: *Prairie Travel and Scalp Dances with a Look at Los Rancheros from Mule Back and the Rocky Mountain Camp Fire*, and because it is such a boyish account of a boy's thrilling adventure. Just as engaging, and with the added charm of the woman's point of view, is Susan Magoffin's *Down the Santa Fe Trail and into Mexico*. George Frederick Ruxton, a British sportsman, knew the Southwest just as Mexico was yielding it to the United States. His *Life in the Far West*, serialized in *Blackwood's Magazine* in the forties, is full of character and incident. A bit condescending, in the British manner, nothing is better for description of dress and manners. But the classic of the Santa Fe Trail is Josiah Gregg's unequaled *Commerce of the Prairies*. Not far behind him, in time and type, rode Randolph B. Marcy, who, in *Thirty Years of My Life on the Border*, and *Prairie Travelers*, drew some enlightening pictures of people and country.

W. W. H. Davis, the first United States attorney in New Mexico, exhausted his stock of humor in naming his book *El Gringo*; for he was a righteous gentleman, who guessed wickedness even when there was none to see, and saw plenty on the surface of things. This makes his book as delightful for its unconscious humor as for its detailed information on everything that would strike a lawyer who was easy to shock.

With the American Occupation began the long series of official reports. Far from being dry, they are the finest books yet written on the Southwest. Few such volumes are made now. In printing, binding, and illustrating — with fine lithographs, some in color — they are exceptional. These books were the result of fully equipped expeditions, headed by the military, but including geographers and cartographers, astronomers, geologists, botanists, and artists. Their task was to render as exact and as full a report as possible, that the bigwigs in Washington might decide what to do with the newly acquired realm. If only Washington had heeded their suggestions! Their maps are marvels of accuracy; their drawings not only exquisitely done, but with surprisingly modern feeling. No trick cameraman excels these Army artists at taking a slanting view up against an overpowering cliff, of setting a . lonely *pitahaya* against a wide desert, of dwarfing a man against a waterfall. Intelligent and trained men, they were also keen, eager, young, brave, and full of fun. And how the best of them could write! With clarity, precision, and a humor which still bring alive the Mexican guide, the Indian chief dickering for calico, the muleteer, even the mule.

First, in point of time, was John Russell Bartlett, whose *Personal Narrative of Exploration and Incidents in Texas, New Mexico, California, Sonora, and Chihuahua* was a commentary on his work as the first United States Boundary Commissioner. Starting at Indianola, Texas, Mr. Bartlett was entertained at every important house from there to San Diego. He was accused of being a political appointee, whose work as Commissioner was negligible, but his ever open eye, his gift for characterization, and his readiness to leave the dull surveying of a boundary for a romantic episode — he once dashed off into Sonora to rescue the maid Iñez from Indians — make one grateful he was not a more dutiful officer.

Following Commissioner Bartlett came Lieutenant James Henry Simpson. He covers so much in his *Journal of a Military Reconnaissance from Santa Fe, New Mexico, to the Navajo Country*, and *The Search for the Seven Cities of Cibola*, and so excellently, that most later books seem quite unnecessary. He crossed from Santa Fe by way of Jémez to Chaco Canyon, and on to the Canyon de Chelly, and he wrote sharp sketches of everything he saw; of Navajos: "What was our astonishment when they commenced tripping down the almost vertical wall before them as nimbly and as dexterously as minuet dancers!" Lieutenant Simpson's books were illustrated by R. R. Kern, whose paintings, reproduced in color by P. S. Duval of Philadelphia, are as freshly vigorous, as true to the reality of what he saw, as the lieutenant's words. Both these young men carved their names on *El Morro*, Inscription Rock, which itself should come into an account of Southwestern literature. Surely that flat-sided mesa is unique, with its prehistoric pictographs, its *Pasó por Aquí* (" there passed by here ") of every important Spanish explorer, and autographs of United States Army officers, pioneers, and teamsters.

Another officer whose account should be read was William Hensley Emory, whose *Notes of a Military Reconnaissance from Fort Leavenworth in Missouri to San Diego, California,* includes reports of Lieutenant J. W. Abert and Philip St. George Cooke. Lieutenant Emory is especially entertaining on everything non-military that he noticed — food, dress, household decorations, and fandangos.

Of the Army on active campaign rather than on reconnaissance, there is no end of books: Philip St. George Cooke's *Conquest of New Mexico and California;* Paul I. Wellman's *Death in the Desert, the Fifty Years War for the Great Southwest.* As nothing was more important to the Army than its scouts, a book as formal as Allan Nevins's *Frémont* really must be supplemented by various books on Kit Carson. *Kit Carson's Own Story, as Dictated to Col. and Mrs. D. C. Peters about 1856,* and edited by Blanche Grant, is a marvel of understatement — as though the old fighter, who could not spell at all, had cramped his gnarled fingers down to the pen and scratched. The best of the Carson books is Stanley Vestal's *Kit Carson.*

Most of our generals who have distinguished themselves in Cuba, in the Philippines, even as late as the World War, started in chasing Apaches. At least one of them has left a readable record. General Nelson A. Miles's *Personal Recollections* covers a long career beginning in the Civil War, but its most interesting chapters deal with life in remote Southwestern posts.

Of that period is J. Ross Browne's *Adventures in the Apache Country,* which seems to me unequaled for spicy humor and a peculiarly fresh and impudent slant on what he saw, to say nothing of his ability to illustrate — or cartoon — his own writings. It is a pity this book has been so long out of print.

As the Army made the country safe, it was followed by students of all kinds. There is a literature, constantly growing, on Southwestern flora and fauna as they might menace or aid man; of its exploitable resources in waters to be impounded, in mines needing capital, and in buried treasures requiring faith or a divining rod. Most of these are for specialists who will know where to find them. Students of man in every stage of his development have found a particularly fertile field.

Beginning with Bancroft and Bandelier, archæologist as well as historian, serious historians and anthropologists have steadily pushed our horizons back. Herbert E. Bolton in *Spanish Borderlands* and *Explorations in the Southwest* conveys the richness of the Spanish archives still so largely locked away in vaults in Seville, in churches in Mexico, or in sixteenth-century Spanish. George P. Hammond and Agapito Rey of the University of New Mexico, editing the Quivira Society Publications, continue to do sound research and to put old Spanish into readable English. Carlos E. Castañeda of the University of Texas has had the temerity from that institution to write of the *Texas Revolution from the Mexican Point of View*.

None of our three states has produced its definitive history, though Eugene C. Barker's *History of Texas* is an excellent textbook. The reigning history of the parent state is still *Leading Facts of New Mexico History* by Ralph Emerson Twitchell. Mr. Twitchell prepared his material like a lawyer's brief; fortunately for those more interested in how things were than in dated facts, Mr. Twitchell's copious footnotes contain everything one really needs to read.

An entertaining venture in sampling outstanding sources and presenting them for students is *New Mexico's Own Chronicle*, adapted and edited by Maurice Garland Fulton and Paul Horgan.

Indians have always been a lure, but interest has circled round from the old wish to fight Indians to sentimentalizing, which may be an even more ignominious way of killing them off. Each approach produced its books; from dime thrillers of savages biting the dust, to works of scientific observation, or rhapsodical conceptions of the Indian soul. Here again the best writers were the sober students reporting to government bureaus: Jesse Walter Fewkes's studies of the Hopis, their arts and ceremonies; Frank Hamilton Cushing's *Zuñi Folk Tales*, and Matilda Cox Stevenson's *The Zuñi Indians*, John Gregory Bourke's *The Medicine Men of the Apaches*, and Washington Matthews's several scholarly volumes on Navajo medicine men, ceremonies, and crafts. Among these men was Adolph Bandelier, one of the great tradition which produced Baron von Humboldt — archæologist, anthropologist, historian, naturalist. For the casual reader, Bandelier's obvious book is the *Delight Makers*. A novel of sluggish Victorian flow, it is so full of the truth of Indian life and lore that it is still readable over a quiet week-end or when recovering from a broken leg.

Trudging along in Bandelier's train went sturdy little Charles F. Lummis, a college-bred New Yorker. Impressionable and emotional, Mr. Lummis was forever an advocate. When he wrote of Indians he found Spaniards cruel and despicable. When he wrote of Mexicans he transferred that hate to the Gringos. He lived with the Isleta Indians, married one, gave his children Indian names and brought them up in the Indian way. Queer and quaint, he was always lovable. The first of that endless procession of seekers after the picturesque which still snakes across the Southwest, Charles Lummis made phrases that do not fade: " See America First," " Catch your archæology alive," " The Land of Poco Tiempo," " Sunshine, silence, and adobe."

Lummis was one of a host of Eastern writing men who deliberately came west to share the life of camp, mine, and range and to write about it.

The best of these books are classics. Andy Adams's *The Log of a Cowboy* is fictionized, but it is authentic in every word. And Emerson Hough's *The Story of the Cowboy* will never have to bow to better writing or truer stuff. A later writer in the same vein is Dane Coolidge, who writes what he knows in *Arizona Cowboys* and *Texas Cowboys*. And Alpheus H. Favour, who first wrote a complete study of *Old Bill Williams, Mountain Man*.

Fiction-writers are legion. They vary from very bad to very good, but even the best of them are bound to the standardized cowboy. Men like Eugene Manlove Rhodes, a writing cowboy, O. Henry, Owen Wister, Stewart Edward White, Will Levington Comfort, have all written excellent, workmanlike, readable tales. In every detail of ranch life, of cowboy gear, or Southwestern lingo, of flora and fauna, their novels and short stories are technically perfect. But they have, among them, presented us with a world so fully realized, and so populated with such inviolable types that nobody has yet bothered to debunk the cowboy. His humor is the same; his women are good, though bad, or straight out of the Elsie Books; even villainy is of a wholesale outdoor variety. Far from fading, this world of the last century persists in the *horse opera*, though it is hard to find in actuality.

Perhaps inspired by these writers, the men who had done

their own shooting began to write, and to write well. The leader was Charles A. Siringo, whose several opera were finally revised and reissued as *Riata and Spurs*. I know no title more expressive of the frontier's attitude toward life and killings than *The Authentic Life of Billy the Kid by Pat Garrett who killed him*, which was actually written by M. A. Upson. William French in *Some Recollections of a Western Ranchman in New Mexico* pictures Socorro County, where Gringo and Greaser met with extreme bitterness. Another figure of that life who told his own tale, though Kyle Crichton wrote it down for him as *Law and Order Limited*, was Elfego Baca. That all sorts of men could shoot when need arose is nicely set forth by Henry F. Hoyt in *Frontier Doctor*. And by Miguel A. Otero, for nine years Governor of New Mexico; *My Life on the Frontier* names names. " Governor Gilly " continues to write, as diffuse and charming a raconteur on paper as he is in his study, and as spunky at eighty as he ever was as a youth on the trail.

The Texas Rangers, who rate and have produced a literature all their own, have done some writing too. *Six Years with the Texas Rangers*, by James B. Gillett is good reading, not only for its straight telling but for its oblique revelations of how free Rangers were of the stupider requirements of the law. Noah Smithwick, also a Ranger, did not write his *The Evolution of a State* until he was an old man sitting out the century on a California porch. But it covers Texas history and is absorbing reading.

These men, though they wrote more, wrote no better than the women who peered over their shoulders as they fought. Mary Maverick's *Memoirs* of Texas, Sophie A. Poe's *Buckboard Days* of New Mexico, and Martha Summerhayes's *Vanished Arizona*, of Arizona, were written of different periods in places far apart, but they picture the same kind of woman: devoted to her man, but seeing him clearly too; courageous, but making no point of it; and realistic always. Two women still living who come into this category are May D. Rhodes, whose *The Hired Man on Horseback* about her husband lets in a warm and laughing side-light on Eugene as he was around the house. And Mary Kidder Rak, a cultivated Eastern woman who married an Arizonan and wrote *A Cowman's Wife*, a lively book about ranching and him.

With the new century came a new type of discoverer. Perceptive people, finding the Southwest excitingly their own, felt impelled to record their unique responses to it. The cult of the Indian came first. Based on the sound anthropology of older writers, it often steamed off into a mysticism which is best exemplified by Mary Austin. Studying the Amerindian, she discovered *The American Rhythm, The Land of Journey's Ending,* and grew loftily esoteric in her understanding of primitive religion. Embittered by personal tragedies, hurt because the paying world did not appreciate her peculiar gifts, Mrs. Austin wrote, as Fra Angelico painted, on her knees; and her work suffers from lack of blue-penciling. Her best is full of vibrant pictures and real feeling for primitive and simple people. This is especially true of such books as *The Flock, One Smoke Stories,* and *The Basket Woman.*

This last is a book for children. Many of the best books about Indians are for children, as though the Indian's world were so inaccessible that whites can only present it in baby talk. Aileen Nusbaum's *Zuñi Indian Tales,* Elizabeth De Huff's *Tay-Tay's Tales* and *Tay-Tay's Memories* are good reading at any age. These stories are told by women who knew their Indians at first hand; as are *Hopi Girl* by Dama

THE CROSS THE SPANIARDS BROUGHT
STILL DOMINATES

[*photo, Ruth Frank*]

Margaret Smith, *Turquoise Boy and White Shell Girl* by Eda Lou Walton.

Not for children but full of good tales is Frances Gillmor's *Traders to the Navajos*, which she wrote with Louisa Wade Wetherill. Next to having Mrs. Wetherill write her own vast treasure of Indian lore and knowledge of Indians, this is best. Franc Newcomb, one of the rare women who never feel defrauded however lonely the post, improved her years on the Navajo reservation by copying sand-paintings. Her *Sand Painting of the Navajo Shooting Chant*, with text by Gladys Reichard, is a volume of great beauty.

Several recent books on Indians promise a valuable new approach. Anthropologists, besides writing their scientific studies, are taking time to write simply and companionably of the Indians they have known and learned from. Gladys Reichard's *Spider Woman* and her *Dezbah* give quiet homy pictures of Navajo life, with the added advantage of photographs so closely expressive of the text that they supplement rather than illustrate it. For Papagoes and Pueblos, Ruth Murray Underhill has done as sympathetic a job in *The Autobiography of a Papago Woman* and *The First Penthouse Dwellers*.

Many creative writers, best known for other work in other parts of the world, have found sustenance or reassurance in the Southwestern country or its primitive folk. D. H. Lawrence includes our Indian dances in his *Mornings in Mexico*, struck as a foreigner would be with how they belong there. In *The Woman Who Rode Away* he describes a Pueblo dance as an ancient Aztec rite.

Much of the best poetry too has been written by newcomers to the Southwest. Alice Corbin Henderson's *Red Earth* is surely the best book of Southwestern poetry so far. Witter Bynner's *Indian Earth* is in some ways deeper. Like D. H. Lawrence he commingles Mexican and New Mexican backgrounds, yet puts them both through a Chinese sieve; a sensitive and poetic recognition of the Asiatic heritage of the American Indian. William H. Simpson, a traffic manager of the Santa Fe, though he never published a book, wrote Arizona and New Mexico poems of great brevity and pith.

It is astonishing that a country as excitingly impressive as the Southwest has not stirred poets to new forms of expression. But far from striking new cadences to express alien peoples, or inventing new forms to present novel landscapes, our poets keep on singing tunes composed in England or New England; they ever revive old images. A West Texas poet, living on the greatest piece of flat territory in all the continents, purls smoothly along of Attic days, Capri nights, enchanted woods. Even when Southwestern poets try to " write Western " they are apt to stick to the easy rhythm of cowboy songs and to rework the swing of range riding. But even when sights and sounds are Western, the locutions are old.

Only Lynn Riggs, in *Cherokee Night,* invented a form as part of his stirring drama of Indians lost in today. Though that play is of Oklahoma, Lynn Riggs wrote it in Santa Fe, and he is of the Southwest in spirit.

The Southwest, it seems to me, has not yet matured to the point of writing its own literature. Most of its writers have not had roots that go deep enough to feed really creative genius. Those who are most rooted in the life and soil are the Indians and the Spanish. And they are not ready to write.

Good books have been written about Indians, notably Oliver La Farge's *Laughing Boy,* and *Enemy Gods,* which rings truer to the difficult Navajo character and his dilemma in the modern world. But the real book about Indians will not be written until an Indian writes it. That is not yet, because Indians are not yet sufficiently at home in English and in the stranger idiom of the white man's way of thinking. Nor has any Indian shown that objectivity and perspective which are essential to great literature even if the inner heat is great.

The same is true of the Southwesterner of Spanish heritage. Though he may know the language adequately, his thinking is different. Like the Indian he lacks the cool and distant view and the humorous freedom from personal resentment which might produce a great novel of the impact of the Gringo on his own people. The first Mexican who can draw the Gringo as he really looks to the man of Spanish and Catholic heritage will add a great figure to literature. The nearest approach was made by a young man from the East who failed to get well in sunny Santa Fe, Ray Otis. His *Miguel of the Bright Mountain* is written with such deep and strange sympathy that it has peopled the Santa Cruz Valley as only a vital characterization can do.

Curiously enough, even Southwesterners whose language is English have not yet produced real literature — with a few possible exceptions. Until very recently they have been too absorbed in living to write more than the personal chronicles we have noted. Or they have been, as Frank Dobie complains, too influenced by professors who followed Eastern or European traditions as dependencies ape the mother country. Only recently have native writers begun to delve into their own backgrounds for material. So far their best work has been in collecting, collating, and interpreting. They see clearly and appreciatively; scores of their books are up to a high standard of writing, with frequent flashes of insight.

Frank Dobie, prime mover in the Texas Folklore Society

and ardent advocate of a literature rooted in its own cultural background, shows in everything he writes that he loves Texas, " as no eagle ever loved its rock." The best of his books — *The Flavor of Texas, A Vaquero of the Brush Country,* and *Apache Gold and Yaqui Silver* — are so vibrant, so full of knowledge and love of his own country, that, for all I know, they may be real literature. And everything he does is increasing the rich treasure trove from which later writers will profit. Walter Webb, in *The Great Plains* and *Texas Rangers,* has done as much in his field. Ruth Laughlin Barker in her summing up of New Mexico's Spanish background, *Caballeros,* writes with the deep and humorous appreciation that could come only out of a lifetime lived in it. Similarly close and true is Nina Otero Warren's *Old Spain in Our Southwest.*

Ross Santee, though he was not born there, must rank as an Arizonan; *The Cowboy* and *Men and Horses,* which seem to have been written to illustrate his drawings, are too true not to be native. A few true natives speak in poetry. Texas has chosen Lexie Dean Robertson as its poet laureate. To the outsider Mrs. Robertson's well-finished verse suggests that she has lived more truly in great poetry than in Texas. When she remembers her office and writes of neighborhood things, her homespun verse is pleasing. But she has not yet found expression for the real problems of our generation and culture in her country and her people. That has been more nearly done by Peggy Pond Church, of the third generation of a New Mexico family. Her *Foretaste* and *Family Journey* are rich with her feeling for her background and watermarked too with the poignant psychic problems of a modern woman. Fray Angelico Chavez, a Franciscan trained in Ohio but living in his native state again, sings out his joy and reverence in lovely

374

lyrics. His only published volume, *Clothed with the Sun,* has been hailed by critics as the voice of a true poet.

These poets stem from roots that go very deep. So also do the most vital of the novelists. Jack O'Connor's *Conquest* and *Boom Town* are far from the traditional performance. They present such real Arizona men as he has known. Harvey Fergusson, also, writes of country as it can be known only to one who has absorbed it through every experience of his life. His *Rio Grande* is the river he has swum in, hunted along, jumped when it was low, fought when it was high. He grew out of it as truly as did the cattails along its margin; he comes back to it as surely as a migrating duck. He knows its people that way too. When he writes of Ramón Delcasar, he writes of a playmate, a schoolmate with whom he vied for his first girl. When *Blood of the Conquerors* was published, many people were indignant, but they could all identify Ramón, though with many different youths, and that could be only if the book were very true. Such a picture of sixty years earlier is *In Those Days.*

Paul Horgan is another. Born in New York State, the boy was very young when his family moved to New Mexico. But his young mind took the imprint of life in a health-seeking town, he went to school with ranch boys, his most significant work is about New Mexico. A prolific writer, he turns out a good deal that probably will not endure, but his best work is excellent. *The Return of the Weed* pictures failures with real feeling for how the passing of the old makes way for the new. *Far from Cibola* is also only regional in its setting. Its theme is tragically universal — for everywhere the failure of people to be responsible for each other results in the defeat of all. Cibola can only truly be found by decent humanities.

Only a few Southwestern writers have so far dared to place such truths in this strong and tragic scene, and they are the ones who know it best. The era of strangers recounting their amazing adventures in a foreign land is about to yield to the age of serious writers, expressing truth as they see it, and laying their scenes in the Southwest, not because they find it picturesque, but because it is what they know best.

INDEX

Abert, J. W., 365
Adams, Andy, 368
Alamo, The, 42, 46 ff., 52
Albuquerque, 15, 18, 194, 196, 199, 227 ff.
Alvarado, Hernando de, 266, 302; Hotel, 194 ff., 200
Alvar Nuñez Cabeza de Vaca, 41–2, 75, 96, 325, 358
Amarillo, 322, 330, 336
Amsden, Charles, 201
Anglo-American Occupation of the El Paso District, The, 84
Anza, Juan Bautista de, 99
Apaches, 102–3
Arizona Historical Review, 178
Arizona State Teachers College, 124
Armijo, Governor, 267, 270, 306
Art and Archœology, 295
Austin, Mary, 280, 370, 457
Austin, Moses, 44–5
Austin, Stephen, 45
Austin, Texas, 5, 39

Ayer, Mrs. Edward E., 360
Aztec ruins, 127

Baca, Elfego, 369
Bancroft, H. H., 366
Bandelier, Adolph F., 114, 124, 129, 366–7
Bandelier, Fanny, 358
Barker, Eugene C., 366
Barker, Ruth Laughlin, 374
Barnes, Will C., 24, 33
Bartlett, John Russell, 63, 100, 102, 364
Basket Makers, 114–15, 119 ff.
Baumann, Gustave, 129, 275
Benavides, Fray Alonzo de, 212, 266, 290, 360
Bent, Governor Charles, 253, 307
Bent, Teresa, 253, 308 ff.
Bernalillo, 192, 258
Big Bend National Park, 144
Billy the Kid, 30, 253, 273, 322
Bisbee, 93
Bishop, Morris, 358

i

Bolton, Herbert E., 360, 366
Books of the Southwest, 357
Bourke, John Gregory, 367
Breakenridge, W. M., 101
Browne, J. Ross, 101, 105, 155, 365
Bursum Bill, 291 ff.
Bynner, Witter, 216, 372

Cabeza de Vaca, Alvar Nuñez, 41–2, 75, 96, 325, 358
Campa, Arthur, 343
Canyon de Chelly, 122
Cárdenas, 202
Carleton, General, 64, 85, 174, 213
Carlsbad Caverns, 10, 338
Carson, Kit, 81, 213, 253, 308, 310
Casa Grande, 113, 118
Castañeda, Carlos de, 366
Castañeda, Pedro de Nagera de, 324, 325, 359
Cather, Willa, 307
Chaco Canyon, 128–9
Chama, 9, 145
Chávez, Fray Angelico, 374
Chihuahua, 43, 66, 80–1, 83, 88, 92, 173, 253, 306
Chisolm Jesse, 32, 36
Chisum, John, 29, 34, 104, 333
Church, Peggy Pond, 374
Cíbola, 24, 123, 172
Clum, John P., 103, 105
Clum, Woodworth, 103
Collier, John (Indian Commissioner), 220, 292, 296
Colorado River, 10, 11, 65
Colton, Dr. Harold S. and Mrs., 123 ff.

Comfort, Will Levington, 368
Cooke, Philip St. George, 365
Coolidge, Dane, 368
Coronado, Francisco Vasquez de, 24, 66, 76, 96 ff., 130, 226, 289, 324–5, 355, 359; Cuarto Centennial, 340, 355; Cuarto Centennial Commission, 131, 359; International Monument, 66; State Museum, 131
Court of Private Land Claims, 259
Crepusculo, El, 307–8
Crichton, Kyle, 369
Crook, General George, 103–4
Cummings, Byron, 126
Cushing, Frank, 114, 125, 367

Davis, W. W. H., 82, 271, 363
De Huff, Elizabeth, 370
Díaz, Bernal, 24
Díaz, President Porfirio, 88–9
Dobie, Frank, 39, 84, 107, 280, 361, 373
Doniphan, Colonel Alexander W., 83
Douglass, Dr. A. E., 119
Drama in Mexico, 342–3
Duval, John C., 361

Earpp, Wyatt, 105
El Palacio, 295
El Paso, 75 ff., 100
El Tovar Hotel, 195, 202–3
Embree, Edwin R., 297
Emory, William H., 114, 365
Epitaph, The, 105
Espéjo, Antonio de, 76, 98, 172–3, 226, 289

ii

Espinosa, Gilberto, 359
Estevan, 96

Favour, Alpheus H., 368
Federal Writers' Project, 41
Fergusson, Harvey, 266, 306, 375
Fewkes, J. Walter, 114, 125, 367
Fiesta, 342 ff.
Flagstaff, 123–4
Folsom Man, 10, 11
Forest Service, 140 ff., 146
Fort Bliss, 85–6
Fort Defiance, 208
Fort Whipple, 158, 174
Fort Wingate, 208, 221
Fort Worth, 21 ff.
Forty-ninth State, 321 ff.
Franklin, 82–3
Frémont, John C., 179
French, William, 369
Fulton, Maurice G., 367

Gadsden Purchase, 64, 100
Gallop, Rodney, 343
Gallup, 208 ff.; Intertribal Indian Ceremonial, 208, 349
Garcés, Francisco Tomás Hermengildo, 99, 113
Garrard, Lewis, 309, 362
Garrett, Pat, 20, 322
Gerónimo, 103–4, 253
Gilfilian, Archer B., 176
Gillett, James B., 369
Gillmor, Frances, 371
Gladwin, Mr. and Mrs. Harold, 115
Glorieta Pass, 272
Goad, Edgar F., 97
Goodnight, Charles, 34, 36–7, 328, 331
Gran Quivira, 24

Grand Canyon, 10, 189, 202
Grant, Blanche, 365
Green, Thomas J., 362
Greene, Bill, 106–7
Gregg, Josiah, 81, 232, 306, 327–8, 362
Guadalupe Hidalgo, Treaty of, 62, 64, 84

Haley, J. Evetts, 34, 332
Hall, Sharlot, 184 ff.
Hallenbeck, Cleve, 42
Halseth, Odd S., 115, 118
Hammond, George P., 97, 366
Harvey, Fred, 189 ff., 217, 279; Harvey House, 189 ff., 275
Harwood, Elizabeth, 317; Foundation, 317
Haskett, Bert, 178
Haury, Dr. Emil, 115
Hayden, Charles T., 156 ff.
Henderson, Alice Corbin, 279, 344, 371
Henry, O., 368
Hewett, Edgar L., 125, 295
Hobbs, 336, 338
Hohokam, 115–17
Hopi Indians, 122; Hopiland, 286, 288
Horgan, Paul, 266, 359, 367, 375
Hough, Emerson, 27, 368
House of Navajo Religion, 126
Houston, Sam, 32–3, 45–6, 54, 61
Hoyt, Henry F., 369
Hubbell, Lorenzo, 216–17
Hurd, Peter, 317

Indian dances, 341 ff.
Indian Service, 220, 294, 296
Inscription Rock, 78, 364

James, George Wharton, 179
James, Marquis, 45
James, W. S., 29
Johnson, Dana, 276
Joralemon, Ira, 106, 180
Juárez, 78, 81, 89, 92
Jung, Carl, 348

Kearny, General, 82, 267, 269
Kendall, George W., 267, 362
Kidder, Dr. Alfred V., 115, 129
Kino, Eusebio Francisco, 98, 113, 360

Laboratory of Anthropology, 126
La Farge, Oliver, 372
Lake, Stuart, 105
Lamy, Archbishop, 271, 307
Las Vegas, 31
Lawrence, D. H., 288, 316, 371–2
Lawrence, Frieda, 316
Lee, Robert E., 51, 61
Leonard, Irving A., 361
Lockwood, Frank C., 105, 175
Long, Haniel, 358
Luhán, Mabel Dodge Stern, 316
Lummis, Charles, 176, 188, 367

Magoffin, James W., 82, 85, 267
Magoffin, Susan Shelby, 267 ff., 362
Manning, Reg, 167
Marcy, Captain Randolph B., 328, 363
Martin, Dr., 311–12
Martínez, Father José Antonio, 306 ff.
Matthews, Washington, 367
Maverick, Mary A., 49, 50, 369
Maverick, Maury, 8, 53

Maverick, Samuel, 29
Maxwell, Lucien B., 322, 332–3; Land Grant, 259
McCormick, Cyrus, 262
McCormick, Florence, 262
Mesa Verde, 120 ff.
Mesilla, 63–4
Mexico, Republic of, 44, 68, 267
Middle Rio Grande Conservancy, 261
Miles, General Nelson A., 365
Mitchell, David D., 270–1
Mormons, 159
Morris, Ann Axtel, 127
Morris, Earl, 120, 127
Museum of New Mexico, 125, 275, 295
Museum of Northern Arizona, 123 ff.

Nambé, 262
National Park Service, 67, 118, 121, 142 ff.
Navajos, 207 ff.
Nelson, Dr. N. C., 114
Nevins, Allan, 365
New Braunfels, 50–1
Newcomb, Franc, 217, 371
New Mexico, occupation of, 68
New Mexico Historical Review, 290
New Mexico Normal School, 125
New Mexico Stockman, 177
New Orleans Times Picayune, 362
Niños Heroes, 49
Niza, Fray Marcos de, 59, 66, 96, 355
Nusbaum, Aileen, 370
Nusbaum, Deric, 120

O'Connor, Jack, 375
Old Trails Drivers Association, 36
Oñate, Don Juan de, 76, 98, 250, 326, 359
O'Neill, Bucky, 181, 183–4, 188
Otermín, Governor, 79
Otero, Miguel Antonio, 275, 369
Otis, Ray, 373
Out West, 188

Pajarito Plateau, 129
Palo Duro Canyon, 324, 327–8
Panhandle-Plains Historical Society Museum, 329
Parsons, Elsie Clews, 287, 290
Pattie, James O., 100, 189, 211
Penitentes, 254, 344
Phoenix, 116–17, 153 ff., 179–80, 228
Pike, Zebulon Montgomery, 43, 81, 232, 361
Pimas, 63, 116
Pimería Alta, 63, 98
Poe, Sophie A., 369
Popé, 285, 305
Powell, Major J. W., 135–6
Prescott, 172 ff., 348
Prince, L. Bradford, 274
Pueblos, 129, 135, 283 ff.; people, 121; Grande, 115, 117

Quivira Society, 358–9, 361, 366

Raine, William McLeod, 24
Rak, Mary Kidder, 370
Rangers, Texas, 61–2, 86
Reclamation Service, 145
Reichard, Gladys, 214, 371
Rey, Agapito, 97, 366

Rhodes, Eugene Manlove, 26, 368
Rhodes, Mary D., 370
Richthofen, Frieda von (Frieda Lawrence), 316
Riggs, Lynn, 372
Rito de los Frijoles, 125, 129
Robertson, Lexie D., 374
Roswell, 34, 338
Rudo Ensayo, El, 113, 118
Ruxton, George F., 362

Salado, 117, 118
Salmirón, Fray Gerónimo Sarinte, 360
San Antonio, Texas, 12, 24, 32, 39 ff., 315, 352; Conservation Society, 43
San Jacinto, 48, 54, 61
Santa Anna, 46 ff.
Santa Barbara, 352
Santa Fe, 83, 197, 235, 241, 264 ff.; Fiesta, 351; Indian Association, 293; Railroad, 136, 191, 192, 198, 227–8
Santa Fe New Mexican, 276
Santee, Ross, 374
Scholes, France, 290
Segale, Sister Blandina, 235
Sigüenza y Góngora, Don Carlos de, 361
Simpson, Lieutenant James H., 364
Simpson, William H., 372
Siringo, Charles A., 369
Smith, Dama Margaret, 371
Smithwick, Noah, 61, 369
Smoki Snake Dance, 349
Soil Conservation Service, 147–9, 220
Sosa, Castaño de, 76

Southwest Review, 22
Southwestern Historical Quarterly, 84
Staked Plains, 252
Stapp, William P., 362
Star Telegram, Fort Worth, 22
Steinbeck, John, 148
Stephenson, Matilda Cox, 367
Stern, Mabel Dodge (Mabel Luhán), 316
Stevens, James, 139
Summerhayes, Martha, 369
Sweet and Knox, 27

Taos, 302 ff.
Texas Folklore Society, 373
Thorp, N. Howard (Jack), 28
Trails: Butterfield, 87, 100; Chihuahua, 87; Chisolm, 32–3; Dodge, 33; Goodnight-Loving, 34, 323; Santa Fe, 60, 232, 241; Turquoise, 81, 253; Western, 33
Travis, William, 46–7
Tubac, 63, 99, 105
Tucker, Mary, 357
Tucson, 63–4, 94 ff., 179
Turner, Frederick Jackson, 329
Twitchell, Ralph E., 366

Underhill, Dr. Ruth Murray, 117, 212, 371
University of Arizona, 180
University of New Mexico, 128, 262, 275, 315, 322, 366

University of Texas, 37, 39, 322, 366
Upson, M. A., 369

Vargas, Don Diego de, 79, 266, 286, 361
Vasconcelos, José, 57
Vestal, Stanley, 365
Villa, Pancho, 66, 89
Villagrá, Gaspar Pérez de, 76 ff., 130, 359

Wallace, Bigfoot, 280, 361
Wallace, Lew, 273
Wallace, Susan E., 273–4
Walton, Eda Lou, 371
Warren, Nina Otero, 374
Webb, Walter P., 9, 60, 374
Wellman, Paul I., 104, 365
Wentworth, Colonel Edward N., 177
Wetherill, John, 216
Wetherill, Louisa Wade, 216, 371
Wheelwright, Mary, 126
White, Owen P., 57
White, Stewart Edward, 368
Wickenburg, 171, 182
Wickenburg, Henry, 154
Winship, George Parker, 359
Wister, Owen, 34, 368
Wootton, Uncle Dick, 34

Yuma, 63, 99

Zuñi, 96, 123, 137, 285–6, 290